# ARIS Design Platform

Rob Davis and Eric Brabänder

# ARIS
# Design
# Platform

## Getting Started with BPM

 Springer

Rob Davis
BT OneIT,
British Telecommunications plc, UK

Eric Brabänder
IDS Scheer AG, Germany

British Library Cataloguing in Publication Data
A catalogue record for this book is available from the British Library

Library of Congress Control Number: 2007923594
ISBN-10: 1-84628-612-3          e-ISBN-10: 1-84628-613-1
ISBN-13: 978-1-84628-612-4      e-ISBN-13: 978-1-84628-613-1

Printed on acid-free paper

9 8 7 6 5 4 3 2 1

Springer Science+Business Media
springer.com

# DEDICATION

**For Sally and Serena**

# Contents

# Acknowledgements

It is thanks to a great many people that we have been able to write this book.

Rob would like to thank all his colleagues at BT, many of whose ideas have contributed to the store of knowledge he has built up and which has enabled him to write this book. Also thanks to the staff at IDS Scheer in Germany and the UK who have provided much help and assistance.

Eric would like to thank his colleagues at IDS Scheer who supported him with their knowledge of ARIS best practice and ideas about what should be included in a book about the ARIS Design Platform. He also thanks Karl Wagner who gave him the freedom to spend some time in writing this book and to Sinje Seidler and the ARIS product marketing team for their feedback and reviews. A very special thank you goes to Eric's wife Serena and his children Noah and Simon for their understanding and tolerance while he worked on the book.

We would like thank Springer-Verlag for the opportunity to publish the book. In particular Beverley Ford for her enthusiasm for another ARIS book; to Catherine Brett for all her help and support, and to Frank Ganz for his assistance on the book layout.

We would also like to thank IDS Sheer AG for permission to reproduce screen shots of the ARIS Platform and to use figures and text from ARIS promotional and technical documentation.

Rob Davis
Eric Bräbender

# Foreword

At the end of the 1980s, Professor August-Wilhelm Scheer developed ARIS as a meta-model for organisational modelling and to provide a procedural model for recording, analysis and optimisation of business processes and their implementation in software systems. In 1993, IDS Scheer released ARIS Toolset; the first version of the ARIS modelling software based upon the ARIS methodology.

Today, the ARIS Platform is confirmed by the Gartner Group (2001) and Forrester Research (2006) as the worldwide market leader in business process modelling and BPM software. The Platform consists of more than 20 different products covering the whole BPM lifecycle from business process strategy, to process design and through process implementation to process controlling. The ARIS products and the ARIS method are also delivered through strong partnerships with companies such as SAP or Oracle. This success shows that IDS Scheer is always aligned to the wishes and requirements of our customers and partners.

While ARIS Toolset still exists, and the ARIS methodology remains one of the pillars of successful Business Process Management, IDS Scheer offers two new version 7 products: ARIS Business Architect and ARIS Business Designer. These new products strengthen the product portfolio by providing platform independent web-enabled modelling clients based on new, but proven, technologies (e.g. Java) and which offer many new features to help customers to implement more efficient BPM. By working closely with our customers, and with well-known usability labs all over the world, our new products were completely re-designed to be more user friendly and easier to use.

Following on the success of Rob Davis' first book about ARIS Toolset, it was a must for Rob Davis and Eric Brabänder to produce this new book on ARIS Business Designer and ARIS Business Architect. Rob's expertise in ARIS is of great help in introducing the new products to both new and existing customers.

This book focuses on helping people beginning BPM with ARIS Business Designer, but also offers ARIS experts insight into the new features of ARIS Business Architect. With their practical examples, and step-by-step description of the new ARIS products, the authors enable users to get the best from the products by explaining new features in a clear and simple way. They also show how use of ARIS fits into a BPM project and the BPM organisation.

This book is a must-have guide and reference for new and existing users of ARIS Business Designer and Business Architect. The book can be used as a companion for ARIS training and as a reference for experienced users.

I wish all readers the same pleasure I had reading this practical guide to the ARIS Design Platform.

Dr. Wolfram Jost
Member of the Executive Board of IDS Scheer AG, Saarbrücken

# Chapter 1    An Introduction to BPM

In this chapter we give a brief overview of the history of Business Process Management; we discuss what business processes are and why we have to manage them. We look at the lifecycle of BPM and its four phases.

## 1.1    Brief History of Business Process Management

### 1.1.1    The Need for Business Value

When people first started living together in social groups, a few entrepreneurial people found opportunities to trade goods and services to others in the group. In later times this grew into the formal business structures and monetary systems we are familiar with today. Businesses are formed to earn profit and grow the personal wealth of their owners. This means the main objective of the owners and employees of a business is the generation of a financial return in exchange for their input. This input is mostly in the form of time, resources, and money.

Every kind of business provides products or services to their customers with the objective to generate revenue and to add value to the customer at the end of the '*value-chain*'. This value can be created in different ways depending on the kind of business. For instance, the added value created by a retailer for outdoor equipment is the optimal delivery of quality products for their targeted customers, while the added value of a car manufacturer consists in producing different types and models of cars to meet the needs and wishes of their customers. With ever-increasing competition for different markets, resources, jobs and skills; only businesses that can deliver value to all their different stakeholders, in an efficient and cost-effective way, will survive.

### 1.1.2    The Production Line

In 1910, Henry Ford is reputed to have said the well-known words:

> **"A customer can have a car any colour he wants so long as it is black."**

This clearly shows the target market for which he was positioning his new and highly innovative product: 'the car'. The market was at an early stage and the competition between manufacturers was mainly driven by delivery and price. The customers were not given the opportunity to express their individual customer requirements; even the colour was fixed.

Ford concentrated on achieving the highest efficiency in terms of time and cost by the use of a 'production line' or 'assembly line' continually repeating the same, optimum, sequence of tasks. Using this procedure to decompose a large piece of work into small measurable and optimised tasks, Ford dramatically reduced the cost of manufacturing.

Similar ideas also came from Frederick Winslow Taylor, whose 'Taylorism', or 'Scientific Management', continues to influence us today. Taylor developed five principles of Scientific Management:

1. Scientifically study each part of a task and develop the "One best way" of performing it,
2. Select the best person to do the job,
3. Train, teach and develop the worker,
4. Provide financial incentives for workers who follow the methods,
5. Divide work and responsibility so managers are responsible for planning the work methods and workers are responsible for executing the work accordingly.

The sequencing of tasks and allocation of the right people and resources to produce the end result is what today we call a '*process*'.

### 1.1.3    The Process is Your Business

Almost everything we do in business is driven by processes. They may be the very rigid processes of high-volume production-lines or the more flexible office-processes for the definition and sale of insurance or credit. The idea of analysing and optimising processes was transferred from manufacturing industry to other sectors such as the finance and service industries. Processes may also be the ad-hoc processes we operate in our everyday lives. Everything that operates in a company or organisation, creating value by offering products or services, is controlled by the processes. Processes are the veins or the nerves of a company.

**"Processes are not just something your business does; processes are your business."**

Managing those processes means focusing on the important activities and resources of a company, such as: markets, strategy, people, financial aspects, material management, intellectual properties, data and information, legal and many other areas.

### 1.1.4    Business Process Re-engineering

In the late 1980s and early 1990s, many traditional businesses started to go through a period of dramatic change brought about by the opening of global markets and the removal of many legal and traditional barriers to trading. Many businesses had to change the way they operated and to think about their business processes. This situation led to the rise of '*Business Process Re-engineering*' (BPR) as a concept for optimising the efficiency and effectiveness of a business by documenting, analysing and changing the business processes. The common theme was to re-engineer a business and the underlying processes. Hence it was necessary to understand the existing '*as-is*' processes.

One of the well-known innovators of the BPR idea was Michael Hammer. In a discussion about the definition of a process he gave a good 'rule of thumb':

**"If it doesn't make three people angry, it isn't a process."**

Of course, this quote is provocative, but it underlines the basic idea of Business Process Management (BPM): not to focus on a department-oriented view, but on the most efficient way to bring all resources together in an end-to-end cross-departmental process that adds value to the customer.

Once a model of the 'as-is' business process is available, various analytical methods can be used to check if the process delivers the product or service in the most optimal and cost-effective way. In particular, each task can be analysed to ensure it 'adds value' to the business as opposed to being a bureaucratic operation wasting time and money.

As we have already seen, even before the 1990s, many businesses had realised that automating parts or even all of their business processes could save cost and time. In the manufacturing industry this meant the introduction of automated production lines and robots. In the service industry, or in the service areas of a manufacturing company, it means the use of computer systems and electronic data interchange.

By this time many businesses had been through BPR, 'down-sizing', 'right-sizing' and many other trendy techniques prevalent at that time. The lucky ones came out the other side 'leaner and fitter', but many had gone through drastic change for little benefit. The main reason for this was businesses were frequently being optimised against the wrong metrics and often only individual, isolated, aspects of the process were taken into account. For instance, drives to reduce call-handling times in customer call centres often neglected to take into account customer satisfaction measures or the increased rework costs due to failure to resolve customer complaints properly on the first call.

Many businesses realised it was necessary to take a much more holistic approach to quality and business metrics. This was the beginning of the development of integrated management systems like '*Total Quality Management*' and '*The Balanced Scorecard*'. These approaches offered more than just re-engineering a process based on efficiency metrics. They offered a holistic and organisation-wide view of '*Key Performance Indicators*' (KPIs) and their influence on process change. Furthermore these approaches delivered reference structures and reference models for organisation-wide process architectures.

The ARIS Method and ARIS Software Platform offers support for such a holistic approach to Business Process Management allowing every aspect of a process to be analysed and optimised.

## 1.1.5    The Growth of IT

The rapid growth in the use of computers and electronic data interchange not only transformed traditional manufacturing and services industries, but also gave rise to a completely new sector of information-based businesses. As a result, computer systems, and the data held within them, became central to the operation of most businesses. No longer was it sufficient to model and re-engineer business processes by considering systems and data just as a resource; the status of systems and data was now on a par with process. Thus BPR now encompassed process modelling, data modelling and systems analysis.

Aligning with this trend there was the rise of new and innovative IT technologies providing IT Systems support to all areas of the organisation. More and more the idea grew of integrating the IT applications tightly together and having all the business-relevant information of the company in one central *Enterprise Resource Planning*' (ERP) system. The key question was how to bring business-related functions (e.g. sales, material management, capacity management, procurement, production planning, etc.) together with technical functions (e.g. product design, construction, transportation, logistics, etc.). To answer this question, in the early 1990s, Professor August-Wilhelm Scheer developed the Y-CIM reference model for manufacturing industries (Fig. 1.1). This model was the basic idea for the later development of the '*ARIS Method*' and the ARIS Software Platform.

The necessity to describe a process and all its related data, systems and information was the starting point for developing a model-based language to describe and analyse all the information needed to describe the integrated business processes.

## 1.1.6    Today's Process Challenges

Today we face similar challenges. In the 1990s, integrated application systems like SAP R/3, Oracle, Baan etc. offered numerous already integrated, pre-defined and standardised business processes for all the important areas of a company (e.g. sales, management, financial accounting, etc.). But, by the end of the 1990s, there were new trends and topics focusing on cross-company business processes such as '*Supply-Chain Management*' (SCM) or '*Customer-Relationship Management*' (CRM). Customers or other partners in the supply-chain were now the focus of the business.

As a consequence of this trend, the software vendors developed new types of CRM and SCM applications. However, for these 'best-of-breed' solutions to work within the end-to-end business process, they needed access to the same company-wide, or cross-company, data and information. To integrate these different application systems, 'Enterprise Application Integration' (EAI) systems were used to avoid redundant data being input into the different systems. At the user-side, portal-systems were used to integrate the different back-end systems and to give a single access-point to the business user.

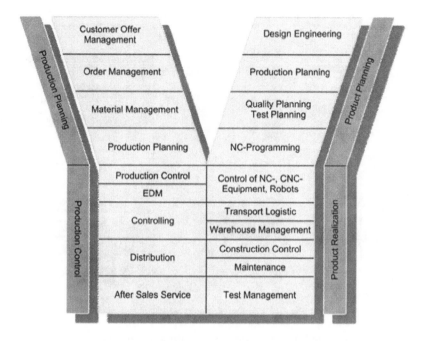

**Fig. 1.1** Y–CIM Model

Today, organisations face many challenges. Besides price and cost pressures, businesses are becoming global and new markets such as China are developing rapidly. Furthermore, there is rapid technological development and product life-cycles are shortening. It is no longer enough to define customers by market segment; there is increasing expectation that products will be configured for individual customer needs. On top of all these trends there are country-specific or industry-specific regulations and compliance issues to which companies must respond (e.g. Sarbanes-Oxley, FDA, Solvency II, etc.).

All these challenges are forcing companies to react to new requirements and changes using flexible business processes. The software vendors are aware of this and starting to offer new concepts and technologies to support business process flexibility. SAP is now offering a Business Process Platform based on new concepts such as '*Service-Oriented Architecture*' (SOA). Oracle, Microsoft, IBM and other vendors are also supporting their IT-offerings with SOA. At this point SOA is just a technology to support flexibility in business process implementation, but increasingly BPM and SOA are becoming inextricably linked.

So Business Process Management is being driven to closer and closer integration with IT (Fig. 1.2). In addition, organisations are changing their structure to be

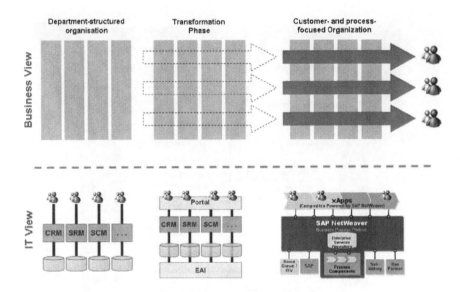

**Fig. 1.2** The Development of Business and IT

more process-oriented, more flexible and more agile and this is being supported by IT-technologies which themselves have more flexibility and better alignment with the business.

## 1.2    Realising Business Process Management

Today everybody talks about Business Process Management (BPM), but often they have different ideas in mind. We therefore need a common understanding of what Business Process Management means and we need to work out the ideal way to set up BPM in an organisation. First we need an easy, but workable definition of a business process:

> **Business Process** – the definition of the tasks, and the sequence of those tasks, necessary to deliver a business objective.

Based on our definition of a business process we see it is not easy to analyse business processes, to define them and to install them because a lot of business information is needed to understand the process. Furthermore, if businesses and business strategies are changing, the underlying business processes also have to be changed and adopted.

So let us have a look at the basic concepts of BPM and the key factors necessary to consider when implementing BPM within an organisation.

> **Business Process Management** – a systematic approach to managing and improving an organisation's business by the active, coordinated management of all aspects of the specification, design, implementation, operation, measurement, analysis and optimisation of business processes in order to effectively and efficiently deliver business objectives.

This is rather a mouthful, but in short BPM seeks to make business processes more effective and more efficient in a way that is more capable of adapting to an ever-changing business environment.

This means all activities performed by businesses to optimise and adapt their processes are a part of BPM. To fulfil this requirement of adapting business processes to an ever-changing environment, BPM itself is structured like a continuous improvement lifecycle. This is the basic difference between BPM as a holistic approach and the analysis of business processes as an isolated initiative or as part of an ERP-implementation or a BPR project. BPM is not done in a project. BPM itself is a process which has to be implemented and executed inside an organisation. It has to ensure its own processes support the flexibility and changes required in the organisation.

The BPM lifecycle consists of four major phases (Fig. 1.3):

- **Business Process Strategy**,
- **Business Process Design**,
- **Business Process Implementation**,
- **Business Process Controlling**.

## 1.2.1 Business Process Strategy Phase

Only those organisations that define and regularly modify targets can work towards them and be successful in the marketplace. The core business processes enable organisational solutions to optimally support the strategy, or as Alfred D. Chandler once put it: "*Structure follows strategy*". Therefore, the Business Process Strategy Phase forms the foundation for aligning business processes to the general corporate strategy.

Depending on the market environment, organisations adjust their strategies, often in very short time periods. These changes in strategy need to be reflected in the business processes. Thus, with every strategy change, a company must pay careful attention to the underlying business process strategy and the changes of business processes. There are various management approaches for establishing strategy management, for instance the Balanced Scorecard (BSC) approach.

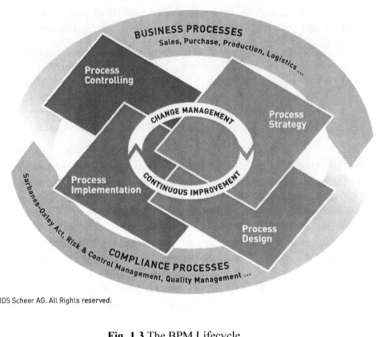

**Fig. 1.3** The BPM Lifecycle

Key success factors in introducing a strategic management tool are the commitment of top management and the involvement of employees through an appropriate communications strategy. Knowledge of the company's strategy and business objectives is essential to align this with the appropriate business processes.

So, if you are defining a business strategy you will implement this strategy by changing your business; for instance, by addressing new target groups, positioning new and innovative products or by changing sales channels. Every change in your business to realise a new strategy will also have an impact on your business processes.

For example, when a PC manufacturer decides to change their sales strategy from being a normal supplier in the value-chain to direct sales via the Internet, it is clear this will have a tremendous impact on the business processes in the sales area. Furthermore, if the manufacturer decides to offer customers the option to individually configure their own hardware during the Internet ordering process, it will have a significant impact on many processes from the sales order process through the whole production process and to the suppliers in the value-chain.

This example shows how corporate strategy and its realisation in the organisation is driven through changes to the business processes. So, every time a strategy is defined, there is normally a direct impact on the operational processes. The definition of corporate strategy and objectives is, in most cases, coupled with the re-engineering of existing legacy processes. The defined strategic objectives and goals are reviewed by weighting appropriate key performance indicators related to the business processes and comparing them with the desired objective.

## 1.2.2       Business Process Design Phase

The major goal of the Business Process Design Phase is the alignment of a company's processes to the needs and requirements of the market, including the design, analysis and optimisation of the processes as part of a continuous improvement loop. The function of the design phase is to provide transparency of the current as-is process-flow and to ensure the efficiency and quality of the processes. This requires a method-based approach and a unified, structured and understandable description language.

The design phase answers the questions: "Who does what, in what sequence, what services or products are produced and what software systems and data are used to support the process?" As part of the process analysis, organisational, structural, and technological weak points in the processes are revealed and improvement potential is identified. This can be done just by visualising a business process, but it is also possible to simulate processes to find out more detail about bottlenecks, costs and resource-problems. The results of the analysis, combined with corporate goals, are used to derive and to define target or '*to-be*' processes (i.e. processes that – when implemented in IT – will help the company to create better value in the future).

The first step into professional BPM involves the related areas of design, analysis, and optimisation. Design consists of recording the actual status of existing 'as-is' processes. Processes can only be visible and subject to detailed analysis after consolidation of all the knowledge about them. This knowledge exists primarily in the minds of the employees who are in charge of, or involved in the operation of, the processes.

The analysis phase provides detailed information about the structure and efficiency of business processes. Cost centre and resource utilisation levels as well as process bottlenecks caused by media breaks and breakdowns in the underlying IT systems become evident. Evaluation and reporting (i.e. process cost analysis, what-if analyses or process simulation), provide organisations with important process indicators.

The process design phase not only includes design, analysis and optimisation of business processes; it also comprises the analysis and optimisation of other views (e.g. IT landscape, organisational structures, etc.) and the publishing and communication of the designed processes and company information. Only if all relevant process information is published to all people involved in the process can the feedback-loop be closed. The feedback from these people about the quality of the modelled processes, and ideas on how to optimise these processes, is the first step in a continuous change and optimisation process centred on the process owners and process operators.

## 1.2.3       Business Process Implementation Phase

BPM does not end with the modelling and improvement of business processes on paper (or in ARIS software). The information technology to support, implement and improve company processes is assuming ever greater importance. More and more, IT departments are taking on the role of business process innovators through the implementation of evolving IT technology. IT must be flexible enough to cope with the rapid pace of change in the corporate environment, and powerful enough to meet the demands of changing business processes in the future.

The Business Process Implementation Phase focuses on the seamless mapping of business processes and business requirements into operating application software with minimum information loss. An organisation must first focus on the business processes to be implemented and, only then, on the actual implementation and IT systems. Because most process improvements cannot take place without IT support, the value IT brings to a company is the optimisation of corporate processes by providing transparency of execution times and costs.

Organisations today are struggling with numerous IT systems and technologies. Introducing new or modifying legacy IT solutions is very costly because, in many cases, there is no uniform description of the business processes to be supported by those systems or technologies. The implementation of business processes through underlying IT systems can be achieved in three basic ways:

- Implementation of standardised ERP-systems,
- Service-Oriented Architecture,
- Classical software engineering and individual software development.

### Implementation of Standardised ERP-Systems

The implementation, update, or harmonisation of business management application systems, such as SAP or ORACLE, provides an opportunity to optimise existing structures and processes within the company in the context of a business process optimisation project, thus reducing costs. Implementing ERP-systems also allows standardisation of processes throughout the organisation and the re-use of well-tried best-practice for dedicated industries.

Ultimately, IT systems must be adapted to the company's strategy and business logic – not vice versa. Current integrated process and application architectures make this procedure significantly easier. Nevertheless, the most important task in any implementation project is selecting the alternative business processes relevant to achieving corporate goals from those offered by the ERP-system and adapting them to the individual needs of the company.

### Setup of a Service-Oriented Architecture

A Service-Oriented Architecture (SOA) is a software architecture that defines the use of loosely coupled software services (software components for defined business functions) to support the needs of the business. In an SOA environment, services are made available as independent services that can technically be accessed without knowledge of their underlying platform implementation.

By setting up an SOA, business processes dictate the business requirements to be met by the services, not the other way round. Hence, an effective BPM must be the basis for a successful implementation of an SOA. This 'service focus' enables new, and above all more flexible, ways of implementing business processes at the IT level.

### Classical Software Engineering and Individual Software Development

Despite the broad range of ERP systems and integration software available today there is still an enormous demand for customised solutions because standard software is expensive or not perceived to be flexible enough.

In some cases, the software is not available at the right time or is unsuitable for particular industry sectors. While standardised application software is often used in manufacturing industries, banking and insurance industries have their own business processes supported by in-house developed legacy IT systems.

Business-driven software engineering enables the development of customised software which maps to the business logic for all business processes and supports their execution. It is always important to communicate requirements and technological solution approaches in a manner comprehensible to project participants, to organise development projects efficiently, and to ensure custom systems can be adapted to satisfy future requirements.

In this part of the Business Process Implementation Phase, the highest value is derived by a deep integration of business process design information and software development information. There is a lot of interest in '*Model-Driven Architecture*' (MDA) approaches where the IT-logic and source-code is generated directly from process models related to the implementation technology.

### 1.2.4 Business Process Controlling Phase

"If you can't measure it, you can't manage it." Almost everybody studying business or economics has heard this advice from Peter Drucker. Even if you have never heard it before, you can appreciate the logic of his statement. The Business Process Controlling Phase enables qualitative and quantitative measures to be compared against targets, thus revealing areas with potential for improvement and greater productivity.

The Business Process Controlling Phase involves measurement of the efficiency of the business processes implemented with help of the IT systems and the implementation of internal control systems to monitor compliance with a wide range of regulations. The basic target of process controlling is to ensure the implemented business processes are running as they were defined during the design phase and all process control steps are in place and working.

Furthermore, process efficiency is measured and analysed against targets defined for the Key Performance Indicators (KPIs) to identify opportunities to make changes to close the BPM optimisation loop. This improvement potential can be analysed on the basis of actual data, such as throughput times, return frequencies, and deadline reliability.

Complete control of operational processes allows companies to install proactive BPM. Strategic corporate goals are monitored by installing a process performance management system which continuously monitors each 'as-is' process instance against a set of 'to-be' targets. This can provide prompt warnings of deviations from planned figures and allow the implementation of appropriate countermeasures. Continuous monitoring of actual business processes bridges the gap between corporate strategy and its operational implementation.

# Chapter 2     Introduction to the ARIS Platform

In this chapter we give an overview over the ARIS Platform and the ARIS products. The structure of the book is described with advice for different reader groups.

## 2.1     Business Process Management with ARIS

In the first chapter we discussed the meaning and evolution of Business Process Management. We described the phases of the BPM lifecycle that represent a procedural model for real-life business process management and help to handle all BPM related tasks. The '*ARIS Platform for Business Process Excellence*' from IDS Scheer (Fig. 2.1) provides all the necessary tools to manage these BPM tasks and the related corporate information.

The ARIS products are aligned to the BPM lifecycle and offered in an integrated software solution grouped into four ARIS Platforms:

- **Strategy Platform**,
- **Design Platform**,
- **Implementation Platform**,
- **Controlling Platform**.

The system architecture of the ARIS Platform allows globally distributed organisations to set up common scenarios for designing, analysing, and optimising processes, IT, and software architectures.

Web-based products such as *ARIS Business Optimizer*, *ARIS Business Architect*, *ARIS Business Designer*, and *ARIS UML Designer* can access a centrally managed *ARIS Business Server* from anywhere in the world via a three-tier architecture. These products are designed for use beyond firewall limits utilising low bandwidth connections (e.g. dial-up, ISDN, etc.). Web-based clients can be started directly from within a Web browser or, alternatively, they can be installed as a desktop application manually or by automated software distribution. In both cases, any necessary client updates can be set up and controlled centrally to facilitate the rollout process.

A central database server (e.g. Oracle) is used for data management. All ARIS clients access the database server via the *ARIS Business Server* and thus work with a common database.

The ARIS Platform offers a high level of system scalability and availability. For instance, the majority of modellers can use *ARIS Business Designer*, while a smaller number of expert users can provide central administrative functions (e.g. management of access privileges, available reports, conventions/filters, etc.) using *ARIS Business Architect*.

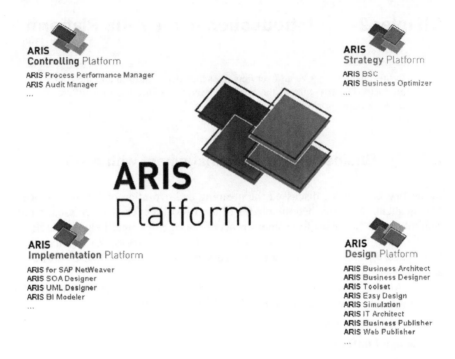

**ARIS Controlling** Platform
ARIS Process Performance Manager
ARIS Audit Manager
...

**ARIS Strategy** Platform
ARIS BSC
ARIS Business Optimizer
...

**ARIS Implementation** Platform
ARIS for SAP NetWeaver
ARIS SOA Designer
ARIS UML Designer
ARIS BI Modeler
...

**ARIS Design** Platform
ARIS Business Architect
ARIS Business Designer
ARIS Toolset
ARIS Easy Design
ARIS Simulation
ARIS IT Architect
ARIS Business Publisher
ARIS Web Publisher
...

**Fig. 2.1** ARIS Platform – Major Products

The Windows-based client products of the ARIS Platform, *ARIS Toolset* and *ARIS Easy Design,* can operate in parallel via the Local Area Network (LAN) on the central *ARIS Business Server*. As these products require higher bandwidth connections, a terminal server, such as Windows Terminal Server with Citrix MetaFrame, is necessary when the products are used in a Wide Area Network (WAN).

The integrated software solution of the ARIS Platform has two key characteristics:

• Central data repository,

• Common language and semantics.

ARIS is based on a database concept offering a central database for all modelling items (e.g. models, objects, symbols, connections, etc.) and all administration information. Everything described, designed and analysed within the different ARIS products is stored in this central data repository.

All ARIS products have been developed by IDS Scheer without the need to integrate any 'foreign' software not based on the central repository concept. This ensures every new product added to the ARIS Platform is built on the central repository.

Integration also means everything you model and describe using the ARIS Platform products is based on common language and semantics that can be understand

by all users. The semantics of describing process models and enterprise information is the underlying concept which gave ARIS its name "ARIS – *Architecture of
Integrated Information Systems*" and it will be described in more detail later in
this book.

## 2.2      The Strategy Platform

The *ARIS Strategy Platform* includes two major products that can be used during
the strategy phase:

- ARIS Balanced Scorecard (BSC),
- ARIS Business Optimizer.

### 2.2.1      ARIS Balanced Scorecard (BSC)

*ARIS Balanced Scorecard* (BSC) supports the organisation-wide design and definition of a strategy management system following the principles of '*The Balanced
Scorecard*' as proposed by Robert Kaplan and David Norton.

With ARIS BSC it is possible to define organisation-wide strategic objectives
and to identify key success factors. It is possible to model and analyse cause-
and-effect relationships and to assign '*Key Performance Indicators (KPIs)*' to the
strategic objectives. Special reports and analysis enables the calculation and comparison of actual and target values and evaluation of the achievement of the different objectives.

ARIS BSC is used to define and to analyse the structure of a Balanced Scorecard System. Because ARIS BSC is integrated with the common repository of the
ARIS Platform, all strategic corporate goals can be directly mapped to the business processes which are also described in the repository. This helps to align the
business strategy with the underlying business processes.

### 2.2.2      ARIS Business Optimizer

*ARIS Business Optimizer* can be used for calculating and analysing performance
indicators of various process management structures defined in the ARIS Platform. It is possible to run '*what-if*' scenarios to provide visibility of the '*as-is*'
process, to identify best practices and to evaluate future '*to-be*' process designs.

Because of its flexible calculation engine, *ARIS Business Optimizer* can be used
for different scenarios dealing with process-based KPI management:

- Setting up and analysing a BSC,
- Process cost accounting and activity-based costing,
- Product costing,

- Safeguarding strategic 'make-or-buy' decisions
  (target costing, outsourcing, etc.),

- Personnel requirement planning and resource planning.


## 2.3      The Design Platform

The *ARIS Design Platform* offers all the products needed to support the business process design phase when business processes are modelled, analysed, simulated and the results are published to all employees of the organisation. The ARIS Design Platform includes the well-known product, *ARIS Toolset*, and, in addition, new products such as *ARIS Business Architect* and *ARIS Business Designer* which we will describe in detail in the rest of this book.


### 2.3.1      ARIS Toolset

*ARIS Toolset* represents the flagship of the ARIS Platform. First released in 1992, it was a big success and has been continually innovated every year since. It is used for business process modelling in a range of organisations from small companies up to very large global organisations. The worldwide use of *ARIS Toolset* by professional customers has led to multi-language handling and multi-user support facilities being made available in more than twenty different languages. *ARIS Toolset* is recommended by leading tool evaluators and software analysts such as Gartner (www.gartner.com).

The *ARIS Toolset* Windows-based client is designed for anyone involved in projects managing organisational change in terms of BPM and its components enable organisation-wide and global design, analysis, and optimisation of business processes. Although focusing on the design of business processes, *ARIS Toolset* allows the modelling of all aspects of an '*Enterprise Architecture*', such as IT systems, IT landscapes, organisational views, data views, etc.

*ARIS Toolset* supports professional business process modelling and includes all the necessary project administration features. It has an integrated report engine with development environments for Visual Basic and Java. This report engine enables project managers to analyse all the information about business processes stored in the repository.


### 2.3.2      ARIS Easy Design

While the *ARIS Toolset* client focuses on the professional business process manager within an organisation, the target group for *ARIS Easy Design*, with its functions for modelling, presenting, and reporting, is the employees in operational departments. In addition, it is suitable for occasional business users who need to document their process knowledge in the form of graphical models. *ARIS Easy Design* can be used in many situations without prior expert knowledge.

In general, the methods offered in *ARIS Easy Design* are limited to modelling methods relevant for the target group. The objective is to ensure the operational departments possessing process knowledge can independently enter and document their knowledge. The repository-aided process design of *ARIS Easy Design* lets the user perform simple evaluations with the help of predefined reports.

### 2.3.3      ARIS Web Publisher

For an organisation-wide BPM approach it is necessary to document business processes and organisational structures within multiple project groups and carry out analysis across several locations. The results must be distributed quickly to all employees.

*ARIS Web Publisher* supports world-wide communication of business process via the Internet and Intranet. All information stored in the ARIS repository can be selected for the generation of a static HTML-based process Web site. To view these process models, users only need an Internet browser. The desired process information can be accessed quickly and easily from all locations, and access can be organised by technical topic or role.

### 2.3.4      ARIS Business Designer

The web-based *ARIS Business Designer* was launched together with *ARIS Business Architect* in 2005 based on Version 7 of ARIS. The development of *ARIS Business Designer* and *ARIS Business Architect* is the result of an ongoing web-strategy of IDS Scheer which will develop all new products based on the Java platform-independent programming language.

IDS Scheer has concentrated a great deal of effort in the user-friendly layout of the new, web-based interfaces for *Business Designer* and *Business Architect*. For instance, individual window sections can now be hidden to provide a maximised modelling area.

The user interface of *ARIS Business Designer* was developed to focus on the needs of employees in operational departments and occasional business users. Only the necessary functions are provided to align with these user roles. *ARIS Business Designer* for the process modeller comprises: the *Explorer Module* for accessing database contents (e.g. groups, objects and models), the *Designer Module* for actual modelling and the *Matrix Editor* for efficient relationship maintenance.

### 2.3.5      ARIS Business Architect

*ARIS Business Architect* (Fig. 2.2) offers a web-client with facilities for modelling, analysing, and optimising business processes similar to that which *ARIS Toolset* provides for the Windows-client users. *ARIS Business Architect* offers all the functions needed for the administration of databases, users, scripts, etc. thus providing project managers and BPM experts with an efficient configuration, evaluation, and management tool.

In addition to the *Designer Module*, *Explorer Module* and *Matrix Editor* available in *ARIS Business Designer*, *ARIS Business Architect* offers the *Administration Module* for database/user management via the Web and the *Script Editor* for creating scripts for reporting and analysis purposes. Operations such as *Model Generation*, *Merge*, or *Consolidation* of database contents are performed at server level allowing users to access these functions efficiently via the Internet.

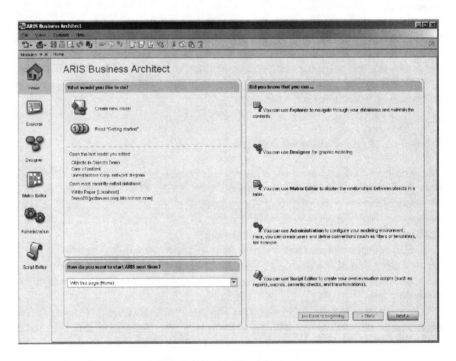

**Fig. 2.2** ARIS Business Architect

### 2.3.6      ARIS Business Publisher

*ARIS Business Publisher* is the publishing component of *ARIS Business Architect*. It is a new, web-based tool for sharing current process knowledge with all the organisation's employees.

In contrast to *ARIS Web Publisher*, with its static HTML models, *ARIS Business Publisher* transfers the contents of the ARIS repository directly to a Web server where HTML pages are generated dynamically in response to user requests.

The automatic, on-demand, generation of web pages allows flexible representation of the contents of the repository. The published business process can be accessed through role-based or target group-based interfaces.

### 2.3.7     ARIS Simulation

Simulating business processes delivers, through statistical methods, information about the performance of processes, their weaknesses, and resource bottlenecks.

It is not enough to simply describe business processes. Before you make costly process modifications, you can use the simulated process KPIs (i.e. process cycle times, process costs, etc.) to evaluate various alternatives and apply true-to-life benchmarking.

Windows-based *ARIS Simulation* provides analysis options to provide insight into the dynamic interaction of the various processes stored in the ARIS repository. Through instantiation of the processes, times and costs are calculated via statistical methods. Within the process models there are direct analysis options, such as object animation and attribute animation. In object animation, visual changes to individual objects during the simulation define whether process branches were actually run through. Attribute animation provides more detailed information about the state of individual objects, such as the number of times a function has been carried out at a certain point in time. Additionally, cumulative and detailed statistics provide precise information about a wide range of KPIs supported by graphical representation of the simulation results.

## 2.4       The Implementation Platform

The *ARIS Implementation Platform* supports the implementation of the designed and analysed business processes into different application systems, target platforms or technologies. With *ARIS Implementation Platform* products, the gap between business processes and IT is closed. The major products of ARIS Implementation Platform are:

- ARIS for SAP NetWeaver – helps design the process architecture for SAP solutions that have been optimally adapted to the organisation's business processes,

- ARIS SOA Designer – with special ARIS Interfaces supports the seamless implementation of business logic in executable applications,

- ARIS UML Designer – enables modelling with UML 1.4 standard diagrams and the creation of relationships to ARIS business models.

Most products of the *ARIS Implementation Platform* are additional products to the existing design tools such as *ARIS Toolset* or *ARIS Business Architect*. *ARIS Implementation Platform* supports industry standards such as XMI, XPDL, BPEL, BPMN and Web services-related standards.

### 2.4.1    ARIS for SAP NetWeaver

*ARIS for SAP NetWeaver* enhances *ARIS Toolset* or *ARIS Business Architect* to provide a rich BPM solution for SAP solutions. It provides ARIS reference models for SAP business processes including all SAP functions and transactions. Based on the reference models, which are synchronised with SAP Solution Manager (a tool for implementing and operating SAP Systems), it is possible to implement or upgrade SAP Systems such as SAP ERP or SAP CRM. The business processes representing the requirements from business departments can be used as a blueprint for further SAP configuration and customisation enabling process-oriented SAP application usage. The rollout of SAP can be supported by user training and help systems based on the modelled ARIS processes. With the BPEL export connectivity, *ARIS for SAP NetWeaver* also provides process orchestration using NetWeaver XI for processes spanning multiple applications.

### 2.4.2    ARIS SOA Designer

*ARIS SOA Designer* enables a *Service-Oriented Architecture* (SOA) to be designed based on the organisation's business processes. The business process designs determine the required performance of individual services and the associated orchestration of all the services making up a process.

Through a service browser integrated in *ARIS SOA Designer*, users can identify services for automating business activities. The connection between the technical service description and the business activity to be automated enables the generation of executable BPEL processes out of ARIS EPC models. BPEL processes can be exported for execution in platforms like IBM WebSphere, BEA WebLogic or SAP XI. By merging the business and technical SOA levels in ARIS, dependencies become apparent and can be controlled. At the click of a mouse, users can find out which service is used in which process.

### 2.4.3    ARIS UML Designer

Whether customising standard software or developing individual solutions, close cooperation between business and IT managers is key for success in all software projects. *ARIS UML Designer* is an add-on tool to *ARIS Business Architect* and combines business process modelling with software development methodologies.

Based on UML diagrams, it provides a consistent, integrated approach to developing business applications from process analysis to system design. *ARIS UML*

*Designer* is the tool for supporting both 'business process language' and 'software development language' supporting all the diagrams of UML 1.4 (e.g. class diagrams, use case diagrams, activity diagrams, state chart diagrams, collaboration diagrams and component diagrams).

## 2.5      The Controlling Platform

The *ARIS Controlling Platform* offers two major products to support the controlling phase of Business Process Management:

*   ARIS Process Performance Manager – for measuring and analysis of process performance,
*   ARIS Audit Manager – for control test and quality check of business processes.

### 2.5.1      ARIS Process Performance Manager

*ARIS Process Performance Manager* (PPM) offers the automatic analysis and visualisation of real '*as-is*' processes. A visualisation of the running process flow is generated based on time and resource information extracted from the underlying IT systems. ARIS PPM obtains time stamps from the systems by implementing specialised measuring points.

Based on this process information, process performance (quantity, time, cost, quality) for end-to-end processes is made visible and can be measured for every process. Process data can also be aggregated and offered in the form of a 'management cockpit' or 'dashboard'.

ARIS PPM enables continuous monitoring of planned values against actual status ('track and trace') and can be used as an early warning system for success-critical KPIs. Based on the analysis of the process data, the BPM lifecycle can be closed by identifying improvement potential.

### 2.5.2      ARIS Audit Manager

*ARIS Audit Manager* provides an audit workflow to ensure an organisation's processes meet the compliance requirements of a wide range of statutory and regulatory standards, such as Sarbanes-Oxley, Basel II, etc.

The *ARIS Audit Manager* workflow tests the process-critical control steps defined with *ARIS Business Designer*. The test workflow ensures the defined process controls are implemented and are working as expected. This helps organisations to identify process faults and potential risks.

## 2.6      What's in this Book

Our aim in writing this book is to provide a practical 'how-to' guide to using the *ARIS Design Platform* and an easy, but well-founded, start to Business Process Management based on ARIS modelling. Using the guidance in this book we want to enable you to use *ARIS Business Designer*, out of the box, for effective modelling of business processes.

This book is not a substitute for attending any of the ARIS training courses offered by IDS Scheer Academies worldwide (which we strongly recommend). It is a step-by-step introduction to the basic ARIS methods, functions and techniques we believe are most useful.

There are several target groups for this book:

- People having their first contact with the topic of Business Process Management who wish to learn more about *ARIS Business Designer* and *ARIS Business Architect*,

- People working in business departments who want to use *ARIS Business Designer* or *ARIS Business Architect* to describe their business requirements and business processes,

- People who wish to use the *ARIS Design Platform* for the development of organisation-wide BPM systems,

- People with experience and knowledge of *ARIS Toolset* or *ARIS Easy Design* who want to migrate to the new, reworked and optimised web-based ARIS products.

For all these groups we want to offer an easy to understand and practical 'how-to' guide which starts with the basic questions regarding BPM and ARIS modelling without discussing too much theoretical detail. In just the same way that, if you want to learn a programming language like Java or C#, you have to start by learning the basic syntax elements before you can develop your first business application.

We then address the basic modelling facilities of *ARIS Business Designer* or *ARIS Business Architect*. We will not explain the more powerful, but also more complex, features of *ARIS Business Architect*, such as variant handling, model merging, administration features, simulation or scripting. Those will be described in a future book. However, we have made sure there is enough space to provide you with lots of hints and tips regarding the practical use of *ARIS Business Designer*.

Rob has been using ARIS in British Telecommunications plc. for more than eight years and was responsible for implementing ARIS at BT. He had to introduce ARIS, both to process modellers familiar with other tools, and to people with little experience of tools or modelling. He and his colleagues had to work out what standards they needed to define, how to publish them, how to review them and how to overcome natural resistance to change. Although most users had been trained, what they needed above all was an easy to understand guide to how to apply the tool for modelling *their* business.

Eric has been working at IDS Scheer in ARIS product management since 1999 and has had contact with many customers during that time. He identified they had the same needs and questions as described by Rob at BT.

After the success of Rob's first book on ARIS Toolset, *Business Process Modelling with ARIS – A Practical Guide*, we jointly decided, during IDS Process World 2006, to work together on a new book describing BPM with *ARIS Business Designer* providing the following types of information:

* How to establish BPM with ARIS,

* Background to modelling and the ARIS Method,

* Basic instructions for using *ARIS Business Designer*,

* Selected information on using *ARIS Business Architect*,

* How to structure a business process architecture,

* How to set and use standards,

* Hints and tips on *ARIS Business Architect* and *ARIS Business Designer*.

We have tried to mix detailed advice about how to operate key aspects of *ARIS Business Designer* and *ARIS Business Architect*, along with guidance on how to go about process modelling and using ARIS in your organisation. Wherever possible we have stuck to the ARIS Method, but by no means did we use all of it. Our approach won't suite everyone, but if you use it as a starting point you can develop your own style and techniques as you progress.

Inevitably, this is *our* pragmatic approach to modelling *your* business in ARIS based on our experience and ARIS user feedback. It is not intended to replace the published information on the ARIS Method or the ARIS product range, the ARIS help files or any training you may receive from IDS Scheer. We have given our own viewpoint on many *ARIS Business Designer* and *ARIS Business Architect* features and, where possible, explained where we have departed from the ARIS Method.

We have described and illustrated *ARIS Business Designer* and *ARIS Business Architect* version 7.02 (as of December 2006). There may be small differences with later versions of ARIS, but nevertheless the basic principles of modelling with *ARIS Business Architect* and *ARIS Business Designer* should remain the same. We have prepared this book with due care and attention, but can take no responsibility for the consequences of any actions readers take as a result of reading this book. If in doubt, consult IDS Scheer AG.

## 2.7    How to Use this Book

We have written this book with the intention it should be read a chapter at a time. Rather than producing a reference manual of all the ARIS Business Architect facilities, we have tried to describe in a practical way all the important aspects of the tool in the context of the modelling work for which you will be using it.

Each chapter builds on the concepts introduced in preceding chapters, with the more complex material appearing in the second half of the book.

We would not recommend anyone to try to read the book in one go. Using ARIS successfully is based on practice and experience. It is best to read a few chapters and try out the techniques described, moving on to more complex material as you become more familiar and confident.

Of course you can use this book also as a kind of reference book and search for special topics of interest regarding business process modelling with *ARIS Business Designer* and *ARIS Business Architect*.

To draw your intention to hints and tips, and to make you aware of possible problems, we have used the following icons:

 **Warning** – this is a warning symbol. These warnings should not be ignored, otherwise dire effects will be experienced which will influence your work with ARIS. You have been warned so there is no excuse if you go ahead and do so. We take no responsibility for any subsequent loss or damage.

 **Hint** – hints will help you to work more efficiently with *ARIS Business Architect* or *ARIS Business Designer*. Following these hints will speed up your daily work or, at the very least, will allow you to impress your colleagues!

 **Expert Tip** – these tips will give you examples of more detailed, and sometimes more complex, facilities you may wish to try once you have mastered the basics.

 **FAQ** – we have often heard the same questions from different people working with ARIS. We have tried to identify the most common '*Frequently Asked Questions*' and provide you with some answers.

 **ARIS Business Architect** – our explanations aim at users of *ARIS Business Designer* because this is the tool you normally start working with. The same facilities are also available in *ARIS Business Architect*, the expert tool, but we will use this symbol to highlight features only available with *ARIS Business Architect*.

## 2.8     For New Users of ARIS Business Designer

We recommend readers new to *ARIS Business Designer* should initially concentrate on reading Chapter 2 through to Chapter 7. These chapters describe: the principles of business process modelling with ARIS, the main parts of the ARIS modules, the interface and introduce the *Event-driven process chain* concept.

A good understanding of the basic modelling methods of ARIS and the *Event-driven process chain* is essential for the correct use of ARIS.

Once you are comfortable with these concepts, read Chapters 8 and 9 to enhance your knowledge from 'drawing' a business process to 'modelling and design' of business processes, and to understand working with *ARIS Business Designer* more in detail.

Continue reading Chapters 10, through 15. At this point you should be ready to start using ARIS in earnest to model new process designs, or to capture and model the detail of existing processes.

Once you have been modelling for a while, return to the book and read Chapters 16 and 17. They offer a good overview of how to implement Business Process Management with ARIS in your organisation, how to standardise process modelling with ARIS and which roles will be necessary in your organisation for implementing a BPM approach.

## 2.9     For ARIS Toolset and ARIS Easy Design Users

Functionality is similar between *ARIS Toolset* and *ARIS Business Architect*, and between *ARIS Easy Design* and *ARIS Business Designer*. However, IDS Scheer has invested a lot of effort into the enhancement and optimisation of the new user interface of their web-based products. We are sure there are many new and useful concepts with which you may be unfamiliar. Furthermore, there are some new facilities in *ARIS Business Designer* and *ARIS Business Architect* you will not be aware of from using the Windows-based products.

We recommend those people who know about ARIS modelling methods and ARIS basics begin reading with Chapters 5 and 6. Leave out Chapter 7, which explains the EPC in detail, and continue from Chapter 8.

# Chapter 3    The Basics of Process Modelling with the ARIS Design Platform

In this chapter we provide a short introduction to the Architecture of Integrated Information Systems (ARIS) concept. We explain the different phases and views of ARIS. We look at some basic principles of business process modelling and introduce ARIS Business Designer and ARIS Business Architect. We also describe the conventions used in this book to describe ARIS commands and operations.

## 3.1    The ARIS Concept

In the preceding chapters we have identified two major parts of a holistic approach to business process management (BPM): a four-phase procedural model for BPM and software such as the ARIS Platform that can be used to support the BPM life-cycle. However, there is an additional, important, aspect we also need in order to implement BPM. It is the reason why tools like ARIS were originally developed and are still successful today: it is the underlying methodology and framework.

### 3.1.1    Why Use a Framework?

ARIS is not just a tool, but a concept or a framework that supports the design, analysis, optimisation and implementation of business processes. The '*Architecture of Integrated Information Systems*' (ARIS) concept was developed by Professor August-Wilhelm Scheer at the *Institute for Information Systems* at the University of Saarland in Saarbrücken, Germany.

ARIS was intended to provide a framework spanning the gap between business requirements and Information Communication Technology (ICT). That is, to provide a way of expressing business processes sufficiently precisely to allow effective communication and detailed analysis, but also to provide an unambiguous basis for the development of the computer-based systems necessary to support them.

The starting point for the development of ARIS was a 1992 joint research project between SAP and the *Institute for Information Systems* based on the implementation and configuration of SAP software in major German companies. The importance of modelling business processes using the ARIS concept has continued to grow from the basic idea of bringing together business and IT. Today, the modelling of business processes using ARIS is also used for purely business-related activities such as: process cost analysis, process re-engineering and optimisation, human resource management, compliance management and quality management.

Different interpretations can be placed on natural language descriptions of complex business issues. Hence, there is a need to define a structured way to describe business processes so they are readily understandable, but structured enough for analysis and optimisation. This is where significant advantage is obtained from using a well-accepted and standardised common framework such as ARIS.

In addition to providing a structured approach to modelling, ARIS is also an '*Architectural Framework*' that provides a specification of how to organise and present all of the information that comprises an enterprise's architecture. Because the discipline of '*Enterprise Architecture*' is so broad, and because the enterprises it describes are often so large, this can result in very complex models. To manage this complexity, an Architectural Framework defines a standard set of model categories called '*Views*' each of which have a specific purpose. Some of the larger Architecture Frameworks define categories of views in terms of the domain they address, e.g. 'business', 'technical', 'information', etc.

An Enterprise Architecture brings together business models (e.g. process models, organisational charts, etc.) and technical models (e.g. systems architectures, data models, state diagrams, etc.). Using these models it is possible to trace the impact of organisational change on IT systems and also the business impact caused by changes to the systems. In addition, the views-based approach of most Architectural Frameworks provides a certain degree of decision support, for instance the decision maker can examine the models and identity critical dependencies and issues.

Using a common notation, based on a clearly defined syntax, different model types can be used to describe, structure and analyse the information in the framework based around different organisational views. These model types are well defined in the '*Architecture of Integrated Information Systems*' (ARIS).

The ARIS framework provides the concept of the '*ARIS House*'; a structuring view for all information on business processes. The core of the ARIS House is the representation of business processes in diagrammatic form as value-added chains or as chains of events and process tasks. We will discuss the different model types, in particular the most important ARIS model: the *Event-driven process chain* (EPC), later in the book.

The ARIS framework not only describes processes, it also includes other important information related to the process flow:

- Organisation and organisational structures,
- Business objectives and strategies,
- IT-systems and software applications,
- Data and data structures,
- Resources (e.g. people and materials),
- Information flow,
- Costs,
- Products and services related to the process,
- Skills and knowledge.

### 3.1.2 What is a Model?

Why should we use a model, especially in diagrammatic form, to represent and analyse our business processes? Imagine you would like to make a remote control model airplane for your children which exactly represents a real-life Beechcraft Bonanza. It would probably be about 31 inches long with a wingspan of about 45 inches; made of wood or other materials and it would have the colour, shape and form of the real airplane. It might be possible to open the cockpit or to remove some parts of the model to see inside. Also some of the instruments in the cockpit might be modelled in detail.

However, it will be obvious to you that this model will not be: life-size, accurate in all details and be usable to transport your family. Nor will it take the same time to build or cost the same as the real airplane, and it can only be viewed from outside. However, such a model has some key characteristics – it is:

- a representation of the real thing,
- built to a certain scale,
- built to a certain level of detail,
- built to show a viewpoint,
- representative of a snapshot in time,
- built for a special purpose.

Exactly the same is true of business models. They are just representations of the real thing, modelled for a particular purpose and hence with a particular viewpoint. A process model of your entire business is not what actually happens; it is a representation of what happens used for a special purpose. This purpose, and the objectives for modelling your business process, has a strong influence on the elements, details and information types you will use. There are many different model types and modelling methodologies, objects and information attributes that can be used for the design and analysis of business processes.

### 3.1.3 The ARIS House

The ARIS House helps you to structure all that complex information by using different views. Returning to our airplane example; the model we described was a single model from a single viewpoint. When we build this model we will use different drawings focused on various, specific, aspects of our airplane model. There would be one drawing for the wings, one for the body, one for the motor and propeller and, perhaps, one focusing on the electrical wiring for the remote control unit. Normally, there is also one overall assembly drawing referencing all the different views of the airplane. So there are different viewpoints for specific aspects of our airplane analogous to the idea of the ARIS House.

Consider a simple process. Let's assume you plan to travel to London for a business trip in a real airplane. What are the different steps you should plan for your travel?

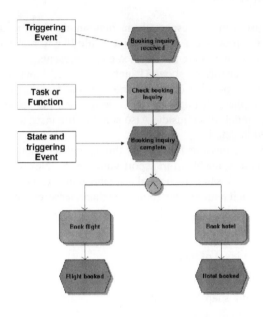

**Fig. 3.1** Flight and Hotel Booking Process Flow

First of all you would make a booking inquiry with your travel agency, tell them about the destination for the flight, your schedule and how many days you plan to spend in London. Triggered by your request, the agency will check your request and start a booking inquiry to find out which flights will be available during your proposed time frame. If the booking inquiry is successful and complete, the flight can be booked and, in parallel, a hotel can be reserved.

As you can see from the Fig. 3.1 above, the process flow for a flight booking can be described using different elements:

- **Events** – used to explain what triggers the process or tasks inside a process. Events can also explain the state of the process,

- **Functions** – used to describe an activity or task,

- **Rules** – used to show the logic of decision branches.

Based on the combination of events, functions and rules the complete process flow can be described. However, this is not, by itself, sufficient to provide a realistic model of a process that can be used as part of BPM for optimisation, simulation, analysis and publishing. What is missing from the example model is information about who is responsible for the specific tasks undertaken in the flight and hotel booking process. So in our model we can allocate **Ms. Maier**, from the call centre department, as being responsible for checking the booking inquiry.

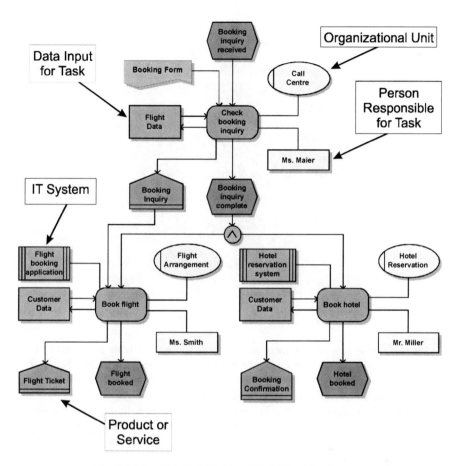

**Fig. 3.2** More Detailed Flight and Hotel Booking Process

***Ms. Smith*** has to book the flight, because she works in the flight booking department, and ***Mr. Miller***, from the hotel reservation department, will place the hotel booking.

To check the booking inquiry ***Ms. Maier*** needs the flight data. The result of this function is a checked booking inquiry which can be seen as the product needed for the next function of the process. This next function is done by ***Mr. Smith*** who has to book the flight based on the booking inquiry; hence he uses the customer's data which he got from the flight booking application.

Based on this example you can easily see how to describe a business process based on a process model and the information it uses (Fig. 3.2). The process model allows us to understand: who is doing what in an organisation and in what sequence, what data and information is needed to execute each business task, which IT-systems will be used and which products or services are generated as a result.

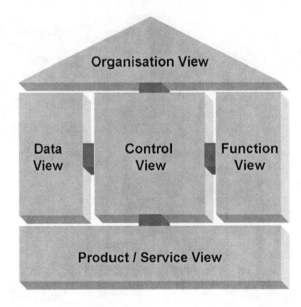

**Fig. 3.3** The ARIS House with 5 Views

Each of these resource objects may have relationships with functions in other processes. For instance, the customer data may also be used in another process model that describes where the customer data is created, updated or needed to fulfil another task. It may occur in a model describing the relation of the customer data to the flight data or to the invoice information regarding that customer. By undertaking an analysis of the occurrences and relationships of objects it is possible to see a detailed view of how the process uses resources and interacts with the business environment.

Consider again our example where we used different kinds of drawings for the assembly of our model airplane. The ARIS House offers the same approach by providing a structure to organise the different model types, objects and to define their relation to each other. The structure of the ARIS House (Fig. 3.3) helps to organise all of the data, but reduces complexity by offering five views:

- **Organisation View** – static models of the structure of the organisation. Includes: departments, people resource and roles in hierarchical organisation charts, technical resources (e.g. equipment, transport etc.) and communications networks.
- **Data View** – static models of business information. Includes: data models, knowledge structure, information carriers, technical terms and database models.
- **Function View** – static models of process tasks. Includes: function hierarchies, business objectives, supporting systems and software applications.

- **Product/Service View** – static models of the structures of products and services. Includes: product trees, products, services.

- **Process (Control) View** – dynamic models showing the behaviour of processes and how they relate to the resources, data and functions of the business environment. Includes: Event-driven process chains, information flow, materials flow, communications diagrams, product definitions, flow charts and value chain diagrams.

The first four views concentrate on the structure of the organisation, while the process view (also called the control view) concentrates on the dynamic behaviour of the business process and brings together all the different elements of other views (Fig. 3.4).

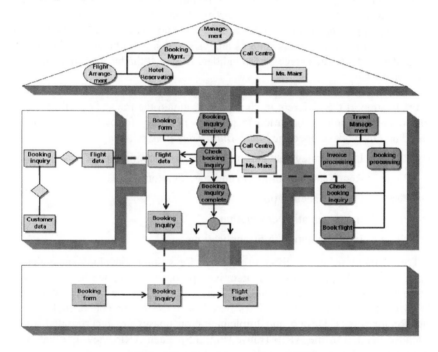

**Fig. 3.4** Integration of Elements in Different ARIS Views

### 3.1.4    ARIS as a Method for Business Modelling

ARIS provides a concept for modelling the different views needed to represent a business. By itself, the ARIS framework doesn't provide a detailed method for how to go about business re-engineering or designing the Information Technology (IT) or Information Systems (IS) necessary to support a business. Such a method was mentioned as part of the BPM lifecycle concept, but ARIS was designed to integrate the ARIS framework into different methods and approaches.

If we look at standard IT or IS projects there are some typical phases required:

- Define objectives,
- Capture requirements,
- Conceptual design,
- Detailed design,
- Implement,
- Validate and verify.

Because of the strong business dependence on IS, similar phases are also needed for business design, Business Process Re-engineering (BPR), other process-oriented methods and Enterprise Architecture frameworks. ARIS was invented with the idea of bringing business requirements into IT implementation; therefore ARIS can support all of the activities needed to support these methods. By using the ARIS Platform, functions such as analysis and simulation are made available to test the model at each stage and to validate it against the business objectives and requirements.

When Prof. Scheer developed the ARIS framework he tried to find different layers to support the different methods. He assumed the translation of a business-related problem into information technology normally follows different phases. Based on this he developed the '*ARIS Build Time Phases*':

- Phase 1: Initial strategic situation and problem recognition,
- Phase 2: Requirements definition and specification,
- Phase 3: Design specification,
- Phase 4: Implementation description,
- Phase 5: Implementation in IT applications.

Today, there are many different methods for systems development which use a phase-oriented approach (or an iterative approach) where we have to rework, refine and make changes between the different phases. Hence, the idea to structure ARIS models inside different views based on these major phases makes sense. The Requirements, Design and Implementation phases are incorporated into an extended version of the ARIS House (Fig. 3.5). Each ARIS view is divided into those phases while the strategic phase sits above the views.

- **Requirements Phase** – contains standardised technical descriptions of the company's concepts and business processes described by typical business users or process owners. Here are the most-used models of ARIS.

- **Design Specification Phase** – includes the description of an application or of the technical requirements in the descriptive language of IT technology.

- **Implementation Phase** – offers the models to describe the hardware and software components used to realise the business objectives and to implement the business processes.

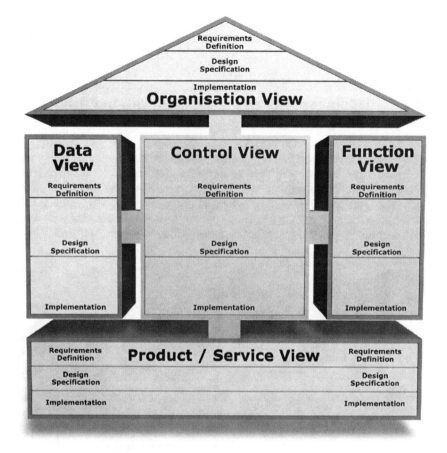

**Fig. 3.5** Extended ARIS House with Views and Phases

The models in *ARIS Business Designer* and *ARIS Business Architect* can now be categorised into a particular view and a particular phase. The phases give a general guide to the order in which to go about things, although you need to keep in mind the possibility of being flexible with your use of the models offered within ARIS. The ARIS framework, with its views and phases, now defines (or very strongly suggests) which models to choose for modelling each aspect of the business and how that model should appear.

Of course, as with any extensive method or powerful tool, there is a great deal of flexibility in how it can be applied. Some models are more useful than others in achieving different purposes and objectives, and some models work together better than others. Thus the ARIS user needs to make choices about which models to use, how to use them and how far to take modelling. The definition and implementation of these structures is one of the most important phases of installing a BPM life cycle in an organisation. Therefore, in the following chapters we will provide more information on the structure of a business process architecture and the modelling conventions. Furthermore we will see how *ARIS Business Designer* and *ARIS Business Architect* provide the necessary functions to support a BPM implementation.

## 3.2    Business Process Modelling with the ARIS Design Platform

When we explained the BPM lifecycle we mentioned that during the design phase of a business process you will need a modelling tool that allows the definition of process models. This modelling tool should be based on a framework or concept which allows all people involved to speak the same language. The products of the *ARIS Design Platform* are developed to support the ARIS framework with professional features for modelling, project management and support (Fig. 3.6).

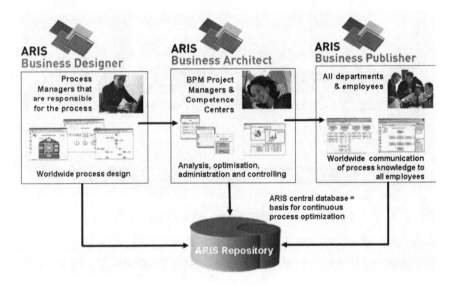

**Fig. 3.6** Typical Setup of ARIS Design Platform Products

### 3.2.1    Typical Scenarios for Using the ARIS Design Platform

Typically an organisation will have '*Process Manager*' or '*Process Owners*' who are responsible for dedicated processes or process areas within an organisation. They define new business processes, analyse and optimise existing processes, and communicate them to all people involved in process execution.

The Process Manager's objective is to describe the process and its related information, so their main role is process modelling for which they use *ARIS Business Designer*.

Process Managers do not want to define the organisation's process hierarchy or the ARIS model types to be used; nor do they want to administer the underlying ARIS database. This is a typical job for *'BPM Project Managers', 'Business Process Experts'* or *'Competence Centres'* who use *ARIS Business Architect*. With *ARIS Business Architect* it is also possible to analyse all the data in the ARIS Database and identify opportunities for optimisation. The BPM Project Managers also organise the data and folder structure of the ARIS Database, define filters and templates and the fonts and languages to be used.

Process knowledge has to be communicated and distributed around the organisation. This publication is usually done by the BPM Project Manager using *ARIS Business Publisher*. The target group for this published process knowledge is potentially all the employees in the organisation and *ARIS Business Publisher* provides users with structured and context-related process information. Its dynamic approach also offers role-based and target group-oriented access to process content.

We have seen from the preceding sections that a business model will consist of many individual models or views using different diagram types with various symbols and connections. *ARIS Business Architect* and *ARIS Business Designer* provide database, method filters, templates, fonts and language support for many different languages.

We may be confusing you with the use of the word *'model'* here so it is important to clarify terms, and this is a good time to introduce the specific terminology used by *ARIS Business Designer* and *ARIS Business Architect* (see Table 3.1).

The ARIS concept underlies all of the ARIS products and its definition within the products is known as the *'ARIS Method'*. The ARIS Method determines the types of *'models'* that are available, the items (*'objects'*) that can be placed in the models and the *'relationships'* between them. All information about an organisation's business processes are stored in a central *'ARIS Database'* based on the ARIS framework concept.

### 3.2.2 Servers, Databases and Models

A business model can be visualised in terms of the ARIS House, populated by those models relevant to the task in hand. In an ideal world we would use ARIS to model every aspect of our business which might involve hundreds of inter-related models. In practice, we tend to break the business model down into bite-sized chunks representing significant areas of interest. In ARIS, those bite-sized chunks are organised as *'models'* within *'databases'* and stored on *'servers'*.

**Table 3.1** ARIS Business Designer and ARIS Business Architect Definition of Terms

| Term | Meaning |
| --- | --- |
| **ARIS Method** | The implementation of the ARIS concept in the ARIS Platform by use of a special product like ARIS Business Designer or ARIS Business Architect. |
| **Model** | An ARIS diagram of a particular type (e.g. a data model, process model, etc.) comprising objects and relationships stored in the underlying ARIS database. |
| **Diagram** | The visual representation of a model in ARIS based on a well defined notation. |
| **Database** | The collection and storage of related ARIS models with all the elements needed to represent a significant business area. |
| **Server** | A file storage system on a PC or networked file server holding a set of ARIS databases. |
| **Business Model** | The collection of all the models and databases that represent the entirety of the business. |

Each model is visualised through a '*diagram*' where the '*objects*' and the '*relationships*' between them can be drawn and viewed. Those models that represent the area of interest are organised into a '*database*'. ARIS databases are held on a '*server*'. This server may be the ARIS **LOCAL** area on a Personal Computer (PC) or a networked ARIS Server. Thus a business model may be held within a single database or in a number of databases held on different servers.

 **Hint** – the major facilities ARIS provides (e.g. access controls, analysis tools, report generators, etc.) only operate across models contained within the same database. Thus for any particular project it is important to define the scope of the work to ensure it is encompassed within a single database.

ARIS models can be moved from one database to another ('*merging*') and databases can be moved from one server to another ('*backup*' and '*restore*'). Thus the physical structure of a business model can be changed as a project progresses or to combine the results of several projects. However, for a business model to be valuable there needs to be consistency and integrity between the models used. Where the same item (e.g. an '*Organizational unit*' object) appears in many models, it is important that it is represented by the same object in the ARIS database. Equally vital, it is important not to re-use an entity (e.g. a process step) because it looks similar to what is wanted when in fact it is something completely different. In complex models, achieving reuse while avoiding duplication is a major challenge. It is much easier to achieve this within a single database than it is across multiple databases.

### 3.2.3      Objects, Occurrences and Relationships

The diagrams of ARIS '*models*' show the '*relationships*' between '*objects*' depicted by their '*symbols*' (see Table 3.2). Objects are representations of the real-world entities (e.g. tasks, organisations, systems, data, etc.) we wish to model and analyse.

**Table 3.2** ARIS Object Related Terms

| Term | Meaning |
| --- | --- |
| **Object** | An ARIS representation of a real-world entity (e.g. task, organisation, system, data item, etc.). |
| **Symbol** | The visual depiction of an object in an ARIS model diagram. |
| **Relationship** | The ARIS representation of the interaction between real-world entities represented by ARIS objects. |
| **Connection** | A visible relationship. The line connecting two objects in an ARIS model diagram denoting an ARIS relationship. |
| **Occurrence** | An instance where an object is used in a model or in different models. |

ARIS has over 270 objects and the ARIS Method defines the range of objects that exist and in which models they can be used. Different types of ARIS objects are represented on an ARIS model diagram by symbols with different appearances (colour, shape, size, etc.). When an object is created by placing a symbol on a diagram, an entry is made in the underlying ARIS database. That object is now available for use within any ARIS model in the database for which it is valid based on the ARIS Method. Thus a model does not contain objects, but simply has '*occurrences*' of them.

An object may occur in many models and more than once in the same model. Any changes made to the object definition will affect all occurrences of the object in the ARIS database, wherever it is used. Any changes made to the symbol representing the occurrence (e.g. colour, shape, size, etc.) will only affect that occurrence.

Objects alone are not enough. What is important is the '*relationships*' between them. Relationships between objects are created by making a '*connection*' between them (drawing a line) on an ARIS Diagram. Connections can be made between objects of the same type or between objects of different types. Not all possible connections are valid and often there are several different connection types representing different relationships possible between two different objects. Those connections that are valid are defined by the ARIS Method. Based on our flight booking example, Fig. 3.7 shows some typical ARIS objects and the relationships between them.

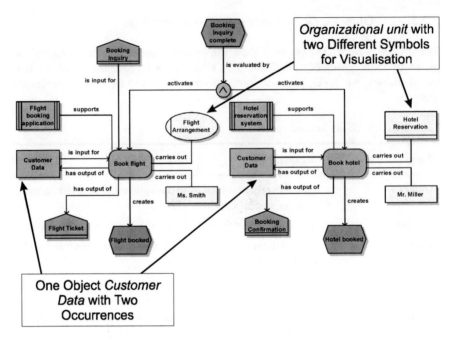

**Fig. 3.7** Typical ARIS Objects and Their Relationships

Relationships between ARIS objects are also stored in the underlying database. Thus it is possible to report on the relationship an object has between all other objects, irrespective of in which models the relationships may have been defined.

### 3.2.4    Attributes and Properties

The totality of all the information the ARIS server stores about objects, models and databases is represented by their '*properties*'. The information includes the appearance of the object, its configuration and specific '*attributes*' (Table 3.3).

**Table 3.3** Information Stored for ARIS Items

| Term | Meaning |
|------|---------|
| **Attributes** | ARIS modelling information stored for different ARIS items (e.g. models, objects, relationships and databases, users, user groups, font formats, etc.). |
| **Properties** | The totality of all information (including attributes) about ARIS items. |

Attributes include information such as the object name, date created, author and free text descriptions (Fig. 3.8). Attributes are populated with values either by the process of drawing the models or by manually entering them.

Some attributes allow additional information to be added to the model for use with *ARIS Reports*, *ARIS Simulation*, *ARIS Business Optimizer*, *ARIS BSC*, *ARIS Audit Manager*, etc. or for exporting to other vendors products (e.g. SAP, Oracle, Fujitsu, IBM, etc.) based on industry standards (e.g. BPEL, XPDL, XML etc.).

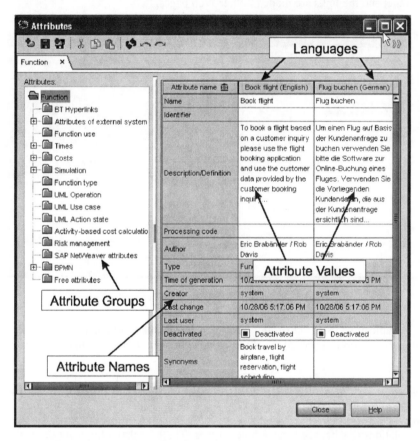

**Fig. 3.8** Typical ARIS Business Architect Object Attribute Display

It is important to realise attributes are used for storing modelling-related information about the objects, models and databases, not for general business information. For instance, if you created an object to represent one of your business systems you would use the attributes to store model-related information about the system that you later need for process analysis; not for your entire organisation's knowledge about the system.

Based on the ARIS Method you can store different kinds of information for different objects. An object representing a business function has, beside some standard attributes like *Name*, *Description/Definition* or *Creator*, additional attributes more specific to a business function such as *Costs*, *Processing type* or *Times*.

However, ARIS also provides special *System Attributes* that enable documents, HTML pages or other applications to be linked to objects, models and databases. Thus, while ARIS does not store all your enterprise knowledge, it can act as a central repository and hub providing easily maintainable links to the most current information. This is particularly valuable when ARIS models are published on the Intranet and the links are made to other Web pages.

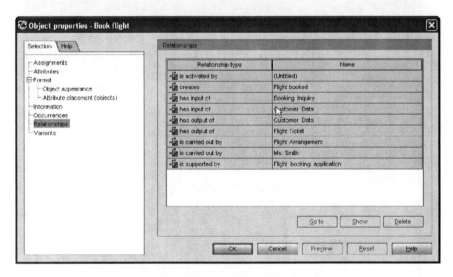

**Fig. 3.9** Typical ARIS Object Properties Dialog Box

A typical ARIS object *Properties Dialog Box* displays all the attributes, relationships, model occurrences of the object along with other useful information (Fig. 3.9).

### 3.2.5    Modelling Conventions with Method Filters and Templates

We have seen that ARIS has many model types, many object types and a variety of relationships between those object types. There is also a large set of attributes available for each. Not every modelling task will need all these models, objects and attributes, so working with all of these would make modelling unnecessarily complicated and prone to error. To simplify things, ARIS provides '*Method Filters*', which limit the number of options available. By limiting the range of models, objects and relationships available to users, the *ARIS System Administrator* can both make the tool easier to use and also enforce corporate modelling standards by implementing modelling conventions.

With such a powerful and flexible tool as ARIS it would be easy for different parts of a large organisation to use the tool in different ways. Method Filters can provide appropriate limiting of this flexibility and purpose-built '*Semantic*

*Checks'* can be used to ensure standards are enforced. ARIS provides a number of standard filters and any number of additional user filters can be defined. Filters can be applied at the database level or be allocated to individual users or groups of users. The combination of user access rights and applied Method Filters can be used to precisely configure how users view and use ARIS.

Managing ARIS modelling conventions by using filters and templates (Table 3.4) is a typical task for the BPM Project Manager or Business Process Expert using *ARIS Business Architect*. It also offers the facility to create new symbols for existing objects and to use so-called *'System attributes'* to describe the user's own information.

**Table 3.4** Methods and Templates

| Term | Meaning |
| --- | --- |
| **Method Filter** | A filter applied to an ARIS database that limits the range of models, objects, relationships and attributes that can be used. |
| **Template** | A graphic template that alters the appearance of ARIS models, but has no effect on the information modelled. |

**Expert Tip** – in ARIS 7 it is possible to create new *'derived'* model types (with user-defined symbols and attributes) based on existing ARIS models. This feature helps the user to create different kind of models for structuring big projects and to guide users by providing models based on pre-defined modelling conventions.

You can also change the appearance of objects and connections (e.g. colour, line thickness, shape, font, etc.) via the *Properties Dialog Box*. The changes made in the object *Properties Dialog Box* only apply to the object or model where the changes were made.

**Expert Tip** – with *ARIS Business Architect* it is possible to create *'Templates'* that allow sets of appearance characteristics to be pre-defined and applied to any model. For instance, a house style can be established or models formatted for a specific purpose (e.g. Web publishing). These templates are for appearance only and have no effect on the actual meaning of the models or objects.

**Warning** – the appearance of ARIS objects (e.g. colour, line thickness, shape, font, etc.) has no semantic significance. Never change the appearance of an object as the sole way of representing important business information. Appearance should only be used as a presentation aid for information that has been formally modelled elsewhere. Even this approach should be used with care, as the appearance will not automatically be updated if the model is changed.

### 3.2.6        A Model is Not Just a Picture

We hope by now you will have gained an initial feel for the concepts behind ARIS
and for the degree of modelling sophistication provided by the products of the
*ARIS Design Platform*. If you are new to ARIS you may be feeling it all looks a
bit complicated and perhaps using pencil and paper might be easier. That's a natural feeling to have when starting to use any new software tool, but persevering
with some of the following chapters will enable the concepts to slot into place.

Nevertheless it is quite common for people to say, "I can do all that in Microsoft PowerPoint or my favourite drawing tool in half the time". Well, you can certainly produce a drawing using those tools; you may even be able to do it more
quickly (although we are not convinced), but it won't be a model. It will only be a
picture. So what's the difference?

The difference between a model and picture is the model follows a method. It
implements a concept that defines what all the objects and connections mean in an
unambiguous way. The models need hardly any explanation and, with some understanding of the business, can usually be understood by anyone familiar with the
method. But if you just have a picture, you always need someone to explain the
real meaning of the picture and the elements in the picture.

Imagine you have to establish a business model for an organisation employing
thousands of people. Imagine also that all the business analysts are drawing pictures which represent their parts of the business and they are all using different
pictures and different kinds of representation. You will quickly get lost trying to
translate the meaning of every picture. The major advantage of using the ARIS
Platform is that it avoids such issues by using a standard method and notation to
underpin its modelling environment.

A model is also capable of analysis. We can run an '*ARIS Report*' to find, for
instance, all the process tasks supported by a particular system or to find all the
departments that update a piece of information. We can generate new models from
a combination of existing models to give a different viewpoint or we can re-use
common elements in new models. We can also publish the models in document
form or on the Web. Finally, and perhaps most important of all, the collections of
models provide a single repository of knowledge about the business.

None of these things can be done with a simple picture and it is difficult and
time-consuming to achieve the same with documents alone. It is difficult to keep
documents up-to-date and, without considerable effort, it is difficult to keep them
consistent and in step with the business. Building a business model using ARIS
also takes time and effort, but if you make the effort, it will enable you to do
things that no picture will.

### 3.2.7        Major Features of the ARIS Design Platform

In the previous sections we have provided an introduction to the ARIS Method,
some of the basic ARIS terms and to the *ARIS Design Platform*. We have also
introduced typical scenarios for the use of the *ARIS Design Platform* products and

the related roles in an organisation. To finish, we will now provide a short over-view of the major features offered by the *ARIS Design Platform* (Table 3.5). We will also include *ARIS Toolset* and *ARIS Easy Design* to give those people already using the Windows-related modelling clients the opportunity to compare them with *ARIS Business Architect* and *ARIS Business Designer*.

**Table 3.5** Feature Comparison of ARIS Design Platform products

| Functionality | ARIS Business Designer | ARIS Easy Design | ARIS Business Architect | ARIS Toolset |
|---|---|---|---|---|
| Explorer (Administration of database content) | X | X | X | X |
| Designer (Creation and editing of objects and models) | X | X | X | X |
| Matrix Editor (Editing of relationships in matrix form) | X | | X | |
| Attribute editing | X | X | X | X |
| Maintenance and display of linked documents and OLE objects | X | X | X | X |
| Automatic ID | X | X | X | X |
| Mass attribute maintenance / attribute inheritance | | | $X^2$ | X |
| Layout | X | X | $X^2$ | X |
| Automatic configuration | X | | X | |
| Definition copies of groups | | | X | X |
| Object consolidation | | | $X^2$ | X |
| Model generation | | | X | X |
| Semantics Generator | | | | X |
| Display of variants | X | X | X | X |
| Creation and comparison of variants | | | X | X |
| Navigation mode | X | | X | |
| Search function | X | X | X | X |
| Expanded search queries | X | | X | |
| Change management / improvement proposals | X | X | X | X |
| Macro definition | | | X | X |

(*Continued*)

**Table 3.5** (*Continued*)

| Functionality | ARIS Business Designer | ARIS Easy Design | ARIS Business Architect | ARIS Toolset |
|---|---|---|---|---|
| Macro functionality | X | X | X | X |
| Execution of event-based macros | X | | X | |
| Predefinition of reports (incl. Editor and Debugger) | | | X | |
| Execution of reports | X | X | X | X |
| Predefinition of semantics checks | | | X | X |
| Execution of semantics checks | X | X | X | X |
| Definition and execution of performance indicator analysis | | | X | X |
| Animation of business cases | | | | X |
| Definition and applications of charts | | | | X |
| Merge (classic) | | $X^3$ | | X |
| Fast Merge | | | X | X |
| User, font and language management | 1 | X | X | X |
| Database administration (DB administration, prefixes, logos) | | $X^3$ | X | X |
| Server administration[4] | | | X | X |
| Database conversion | | | X | X |
| Administration of filters, methodical specifications and templates | | | $X^2$ | X |
| Using filters, methodical specifications and templates | X | X | X | X |
| Editor for creation of own symbols | | | X | X |
| Export / Import in XML format | | | X | X |
| BPEL / WSDL-Interface | | | X | |
| ARIS Process Generator (XLS Import / Export) | | X | X | X |
| Connectivity for Lotus Notes* | X | X | X | X |
| Connectivity for SAP* | X | X | X | X |
| Online help | X | X | X | X |
| Stand-alone-working (local) | | X | X | X |
| Can be installed as desktop application | X | X | X | X |
| Browser-capable front-end | X | | X | |

**Notes:**

**1** Only password change.

**2** Expanded concept compared with ARIS Toolset.

**3** Limited.

**4** ARIS Site Administrator is installed with the server; parts of the server administration functionality are available with ARIS Business Architect and ARIS Toolset.

\* Available as an add-on product to the ARIS Design Platform.

## 3.3      Conventions Used in this Book

We will describe the use of the keyboard and the mouse to operate *ARIS Business Designer* and *ARIS Business Architect* in plain English wherever we can. We will use the English spelling of words like 'reorganise' in the main body of the text, but show the actual spelling and capitalisation used in *ARIS Business Designer* (e.g. US English – "reorganize") in command strings. In order to save space when listing commands, we have used the conventions in the tables below as shortcuts for complex commands (Table 3.6 and Table 3.7).

**Table 3.6** Text Formatting Conventions Used in this Book

| Description in Text | Action Required |
|---|---|
| '*ARIS term*' | First use of a specific ARIS term. |
| *Designer Window* | Reference to one of the ARIS windows or dialog boxes. |
| "*relationship*" | An ARIS relationship. |
| `Userinformation` | Text displayed on screen or to be entered as shown. |
| `<Alt+B>` | Keyboard shortcut for a command. |
| ***Objectname*** | The name of an ARIS object, database or model as shown in an example. |
| Menuitem 1 | Item on menu to be selected. |
| *Dialog Box* | Name dialog box. |
| *Attribute / Field* | Name of ARIS attribute or menu field in which data should be entered or an option chosen. |
| *{MenuGroup}* | Label for items grouped on a dialog box. |

**Table 3.7** Command Descriptions Used in this Book

| Description in Text | Action Required |
| --- | --- |
| Click <u>B</u>utton | Hover the mouse over the button on the displayed window and click the left mouse button. The underlined character shows the shortcut for the button (i.e. Alt+b). |
| Select <u>M</u>enuitem | Hover the mouse over the item on the *Main Menu* or pop-up *Right-Click Menu* and click the left mouse button. |
| Select <u>M</u>enuitem1> Menuitem<u>2</u> | Hover the mouse over item1 on the *Main Menu* (if necessary, click the left mouse button). When a submenu appears click the left mouse button on item2. |
| Select *Object* | Hover the mouse over the object and click the left mouse button. The object should appear selected. |
| Double-Click *Object* | Hover the mouse over the object and rapidly click the left mouse button twice. This will normally open up a new window. |
| Select *Tab* | On window bar, select the tab by hovering the mouse over the tab title and clicking the left mouse button. |
| Right-Click > Menuitem1 [*Dialog Box / Sub Dialog Box*] | With an object already selected, hover the mouse over the selected object and click the right mouse button. When a floating menu appears, hover the mouse over item1 on the menu and click the left mouse button. When the dialog box appears, select the sub-dialog box from the tree view on the left-hand side of the dialog box. |
| Right-Click > Menuitem1 [*Dialog Box* {fieldname}] enter `givenvalue` | Enter the value given into the text field called fieldname in the dialog box. |

# Chapter 4      Business Process Architecture with ARIS

In this chapter we explain the need for a structured Business Process Architecture and introduce the typical model types used in ARIS to represent the architecture.

## 4.1      The Need for a Business Process Architecture

In the previous chapters we looked at BPM and identified the following important elements:

- Setting your BPM targets,
- Using a methodology and a modelling approach such as the ARIS concept,
- Working with an integrated and professional software suite (such as the ARIS Platform) to support the methodology,
- Defining a BPM lifecycle, its organisation and procedure model.

Now we will focus on an additional element necessary for a holistic approach to BPM: the Business Process Architecture of an organisation.

There is a big difference between modelling a small number of processes to be used by a specific department and creating a well-defined BPM structure to manage a huge organisation. Imagine such a large organisation with thousands of employees where every department individually describes their processes using different concepts, different models and with different software tools. This would be a glorious mess. That's why you need to standardise your Business Process Management approach. Standardisation means that not only does everybody speak the same process language, but also there is a common infrastructure for all your BPM projects.

The first step in starting BPM with ARIS is to define your business process architecture. This helps to describe all the processes in the organisation in a structured way so everybody is familiar with the processes, their own role, their tasks and the supporting IT infrastructure. In this chapter we shall look at such an architecture and the typical model types ARIS uses to represent the Business Process Architecture. In Chapter 16 we shall look at modelling conventions and what needs to be standardised in order to effectively implement the architecture throughout the business.

## 4.2      Definition of a Business Process Architecture

So what is a business process architecture?

> **Business Process Architecture** – a hierarchical structure of process
> description levels and directly related views covering the whole
> organisation from a business process point of view. Starts with high-
> level process maps representing a conceptual business view down to
> the detailed process flow descriptions describing specific tasks and
> their relation to roles, organisation, data and IT-systems.

The Business Process Architecture, and the related modelling conventions, will
help us to structure the modelling landscape in our organisation. It describes how
to structure the business process models horizontally by segmenting models into
manageable chunks which link together, and how to structure them vertically in a
hierarchical structure that decomposes each model into increasing levels of detail.
Typically a business process architecture consists of between four and six levels of
process models (Fig. 4.1). Besides the structure of process models, the architecture
will also include other views from the ARIS concept (e.g. organisational diagrams,
data models, objectives diagrams, IT-landscape models etc.).

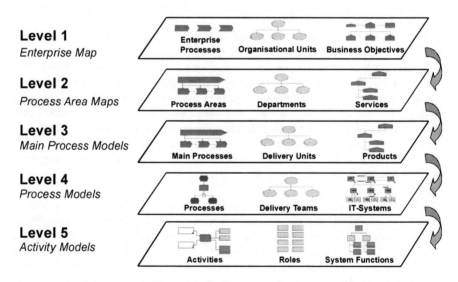

**Level 1**
*Enterprise Map*

**Level 2**
*Process Area Maps*

**Level 3**
*Main Process Models*

**Level 4**
*Process Models*

**Level 5**
*Activity Models*

**Fig. 4.1** Typical Business Process Architecture in ARIS

Once a process architecture is in place it becomes a useful tool for everyone
in the organisation because it helps them to orientate what they do in the process

structure and to identify their own potential improvements. A detailed explanation of how to model and connect process models in a process hierarchy will be described later in Chapter 13.


## 4.3   Architecture as a Necessary Implementation Infrastructure

To better understand the need for a process architecture you can visualise it as the infrastructure for the real, implemented, business processes. The process architecture describes different possible routes that can be taken after an initial process is triggered. Where a customer need triggers a process, we can visualise a 'customer journey' through the organisation's process architecture. An important goal of BPM is to ensure the customer journey meets the customer's need, provides an excellent customer experience and meets business objectives.

The process architecture can be compared with a railway network. In most countries there is a rail system which connects all the country's regions and cities. Some larger cities have more than one station and those stations are also interconnected by the rail network.

If the train operator wants to plan a new route from the south of the country to the north, they will start to identify the route by looking at the overall network and the main routes between the regions. Once an outline route is identified they will next have a more in-depth look at the regional railway network to identify the specific tracks to be used.

Normally, different departments or organisations are responsible for the different regions and the overall network is provided by detailed regional railway system connected at key intersections.

Thus the railway operator planning a new route uses the defined railway architecture. They start at the highest level and drill down to identify the regions, cities and switches needed to connect the starting point with the destination. So the railway architecture shows all possible routes over the whole country and enables the best route to make the new connection to be identified.

A process architecture works in the same way. It shows the different layers of process models that support the organisation and enables the end-to-end process required to meet a customer need or business objective to be identified and implemented.


## 4.4   Typical Models in a Business Process Hierarchy

*ARIS Business Architect* offers more than 115 different model types to support the design of your business. Table 4.1 lists some of the more important models which are typically used to set up a Business Process Architecture.

**Table 4.1** Important ARIS Models

| Model Type | Use |
| --- | --- |
| **Application system type diagram** | At the simplest level, defines a library of the IT systems used by the business. At a more detailed level, models the structure of systems and their constituent modules or provides a hierarchical classification of system types. |
| **EPC** | Detail modelling of processes at various levels in the hierarchy. |
| **EPC as row display** | Modelling processes in row-based swim-lanes. Typically at a fairly high level to show how a process moves from organisational unit to organisational unit or system to system. |
| **EPC as column display** | Modelling processes in column-based swim-lanes. Supports the same scenario as the row-based EPC. |
| **Event diagram** | For defining how a single event (typically a process trigger) modelled at one level in the hierarchy can be broken down into more detailed events when modelled at more detailed levels in the hierarchy. |
| **Function allocation diagram (FAD)** | For defining the relationship between a function and the resources needed to execute it and the data it transforms. |
| **Function tree** | Models the functional structure of a business in a hierarchical way. |
| **eERM entity attribute diagram** | Models the decomposition of data entities showing the attributes they are comprised of. |
| **Entity relationship model (eERM)** | A formal model of the data entities used by the business and the relationships between them. Typically used for representing data used by databases or other systems. |
| **Knowledge map** | Models the knowledge held by different business units. |
| **Knowledge atructure Diagram** | Hierarchical definition of the knowledge held by the business. |
| **Objective diagram** | Models a hierarchy of business objectives along with their critical success factors, and the functions and products supporting the achievement of those objectives. |
| **Office process** | An easy to understand form of the EPC model using pictorial symbols aimed at presenting process flows to people less familiar with standard ARIS models. |
| **Organizational chart** | A hierarchical model of the business organisation. Supports the description of the structure of the organisation by departments and all necessary roles and positions. |

| | |
|---|---|
| **Product/Service tree** | Models the hierarchy of the products and services produced by the business, the processes that deliver them and the Business Objectives their production achieves. |
| **Technical Terms model** | Models the hierarchical and relational structure of information used by the business. |
| **Value-added chain diagram** | Models a hierarchy of high-level functions that add value to the business along with the organisational departments with a role in those functions. |

If you start to define the business process architecture of your organisation, you need to select an appropriate sub-set of all model-types offered by ARIS based on your needs. The following model types are those most commonly used to describe the different ARIS views we introduced in Chapter 3:

- The *Value-added chain diagram* (VAD),
- The *Event-driven process chain* (EPC),
- The *Function allocation diagram* (FAD),
- The *Organizational chart*,
- The *Objective diagram*,
- The *Entity-relationship model* (eERM),
- The *Technical terms model*,
- The *Product/Service tree*.

These different kinds of models help structure the processes, business objectives, organisations, IT landscape and data defined in your Business Process Architecture. Any of the objects used in these hierarchical models can also be used in the EPC process model to show how the business infrastructure supports the process. As we shall see in Chapter 12, you can assign a completed model to an object used in another model. In this way you can create a set of connected models representing vertical process architecture. You can 'drill-down' through the hierarchy to get more detail about the various entities the ARIS objects represent.

## 4.4.1     The Process View

### Value-Added Chain Diagram (VAD)

The *Value-added chain diagram (VAD)* is used to identify the business processes directly involved in the creation of an organisation's added value. These processes are represented by '*Function*' objects in the VAD and can be interlinked by creating a function sequence and thus a 'value-added chain' (Fig. 4.2).

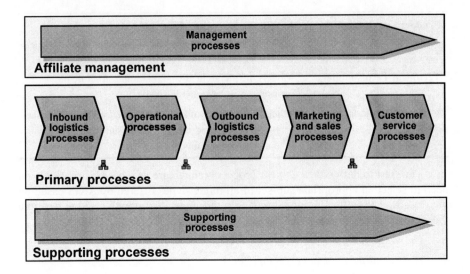

Fig. 4.2 Value-Added Chain Diagram as a Business Overview

The VAD is mostly used at the higher conceptual levels of a process architecture to describe the enterprise business areas or the main business processes in the organisation. It helps to identify the major interfaces between the core business process areas.

The VAD model can also show the hierarchical relationships between value adding processes using superior and subordinate relationships. It can also show links to organisational and information objects at a conceptual level. When allocating organisations to functions or processes we can differentiate between different types of role or responsibility (e.g. ownership, IT responsibility and execution), see Fig. 4.3.

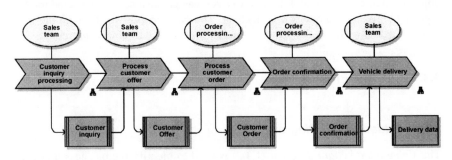

Fig. 4.3 Value-Added Chain for the Sales and Marketing Process

## Event-driven Process Chain

At the more detailed level of the architecture, below the VAD, we use the *Event-driven process chain (EPC)* to describe the detailed process flows and how they are supported by the business infrastructure (Fig. 4.4). The EPC is the most important model in the architecture and we will describe it in more detail in Chapter 7.

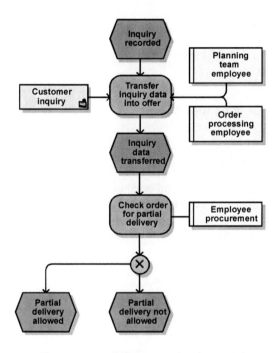

**Fig. 4.4** A Detailed Process Flow in an EPC

## Function Allocation Diagram (FAD)

Every process consists of specific tasks or functions shown in a process flow modelled in an EPC. Often, additional information about the task and its relationship to the business infrastructure supporting it will be described using the *Function allocation diagram (FAD)*(Fig. 4.5).

The FAD helps us to model more detail about an activity, in particular the transformation of input data to output data, without cluttering up the EPC. All the objects which can be allocated to individual functions in an EPC are also available in the FAD (Fig. 4.5). The FAD model can be assigned to the functions in the EPC so users can drill down from the EPC to see the additional detail.  In this way you are able to restrict the detail in the EPC so business processes can be illustrated much more clearly using 'lean EPCs'. The FAD will be described in more detail in Chapter 12.

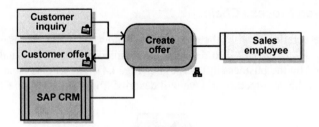

**Fig. 4.5** Function Allocation Diagram (FAD)

## 4.4.2    The Organisation View

### The Organizational Chart

The organisation view shows how an organisation is structured into departments, groups, roles, positions and people. The most commonly used model in this view is the *Organizational chart* which provides a typical way of representing organisational structures. The chart represents the 'Organizational units', as task performers, and their interrelationships (Fig. 4.6).

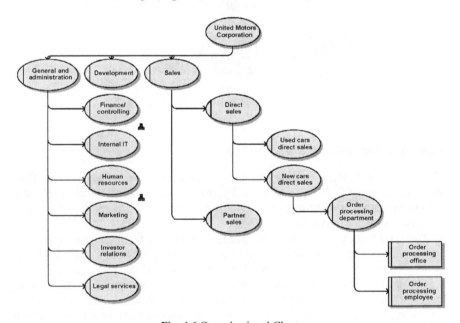

**Fig. 4.6** Organizational Chart

Various connection types are available to link *Organizational unit* objects in ARIS in order to specify the hierarchical relationships more precisely. For instance a connection can have one of the following meanings:

- *"is technical superior to"*,
- *"is disciplinary superior to"*,
- *"is a component of "*.

In order to show individual positions in the organisation with recognised job descriptions, the '*Position*' object type is available. Multiple *Positions* can be assigned to an *Organizational unit* with the connections types described above. A '*Person*' object can be defined to represent actual, named, people who hold *Positions* or belong to *Organizational units*.

In addition, organisational objects can be assigned to object types. For example, in the *Organizational chart* each *Organizational unit* can be assigned to an '*Organizational unit type*' (e.g. "department", "main department" or "group") while a *Person* can be assigned to a '*Person type*' (e.g. "department head", "group leader" or "project manager"). *Organizational charts* can be structured in a hierarchical way by assigning more detailed *Organizational charts* to objects in the chart.

### 4.4.3 The Data View

#### Entity Relationship Model (eERM)

There are a number of different methods for modelling data (e.g. entity-relationship, IEF, object oriented, etc.), but one of the most widely used models in ARIS to describe the data processed by functions is the *Entity relationship model (eERM)* (Fig. 4.7).

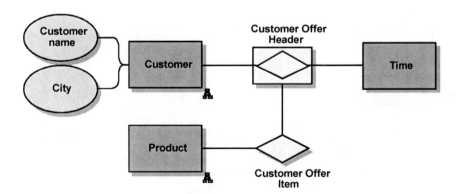

**Fig. 4.7** Entity Relationship Model (eERM)

This modelling method uses a number of specialised terms such as *'Entity type'*, *'Relationship type'*, *'Attribute'*, etc. *Entities* are real or abstract things of interest to the organisation. For instance, examples of *Entities* in the *"Process customer offer"* model in Fig. 4.7 are:

- Customer,
- Product,
- Customer Offer.

*Entities* are described more precisely by certain *Attributes*. This means, for example, a customer can be specified more precisely by their "name", "first name" and "address".

*Entity Relationship Models* are typically used to 'formally' model the data used by the IT systems supporting the business processes.

### Technical Terms Model

As an alternative to the more formal *Entity relationship model (eERM)* described above, the *Technical terms model* (Fig. 4.8), enables a more business view of information to be described. The *'Technical term'* object represents any piece of business information of interest to a process. The precise nature of the *Technical term*

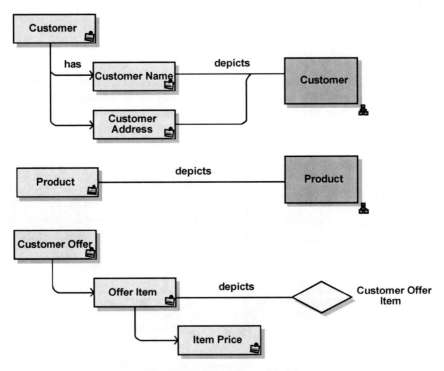

**Fig. 4.8** Technical Terms Model

will depend on the detail at which the process is being modelled. A hierarchy of *Technical terms* can be modelled in the *Technical terms model* to show how high-level information concepts are comprised of more detailed attributes.

If required, it is also possible to include the *Entity type* and *Attribute* objects from the *Entity relationship model (eERM)* in the *Technical terms model* and relate them to *Technical terms*. In this way it is possible to show how business information is actually represented ("*depicted*") by data held within IT systems.

### 4.4.4    The Function View

#### *The Objective Diagram*

Before you start modelling, analysing or optimising business processes, you should define the objectives of your organisation's processes. In the *Objective diagram* (Fig. 4.9) you can define '*Objectives*', create *Objective* hierarchies and assign them to functions representing the new or improved business processes that will achieve the *Objectives.*

You can specify '*Critical factors*' for achieving the *Objectives* and arrange them in a hierarchy. *Critical factors* specify the aspects which need to be considered in order to achieve a particular organisational *Objective* and they are assigned to *Objectives* in the *Objective diagram.*

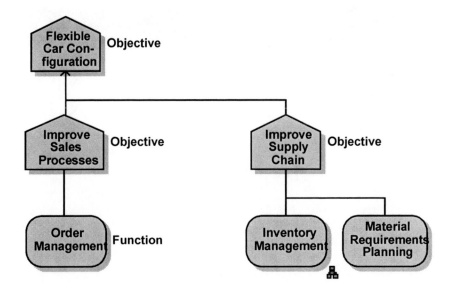

**Fig. 4.9** Objective Diagram

### 4.4.5      The Product/Service View

#### Products/Service Tree

*Products/Services* can be viewed at different levels of abstraction. It is therefore useful to represent these relationships in a model showing the component *Products/ Services* making up a complete *Product/Service*. This relationship is represented in the *Product/Service tree* (Fig. 4.10). For example, a complex product often contains many different sub-assemblies, each of which consists of various components. Each of these items can be represented as a '*Product/Service*'.

The "*has*" relationship between *Products/Services* in the *Product/Service tree* can be used to describe hierarchies of products or other kinds of dependencies. "*Substitution*" relationships to other *Products/Services* show how potential replacement products or services can also be represented, as can the relationships of the *Products/Services* to the organisation's *Objectives*.

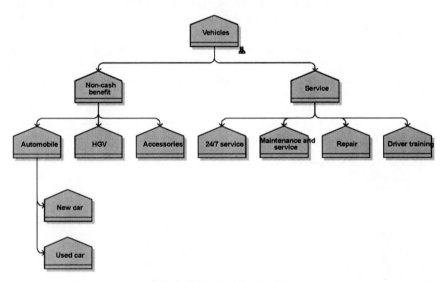

**Fig. 4.10** Product/Service Tree

# Chapter 5     Getting Started with Your First Model

In this chapter we will learn about some differences between ARIS Business Designer and ARIS Business Architect; how to create our first model, place some objects, connect them up and view and print what we have done.

## 5.1     Let's Get Started

In the previous chapters we have learnt about the principles of Business Process Management (BPM), process modelling and the *ARIS Design Platform*. It's now time to get our hands dirty and start some modelling.

We saw in Chapter 2 there are four tools in the *ARIS Design Platform*:

- ARIS Easy Design,
- ARIS Toolset,
- ARIS Business Designer,
- ARIS Business Architect.

In this book we will be describing the web clients: *ARIS Business Designer* and *ARIS Business Architect* that support Internet based modelling. Both of these tools can be run in a web browser (e.g. Microsoft Internet Explorer) or by using the web client installed versions. There is little difference in the function of the two types of client, but some slight differences in their 'look and feel'. In this book we will describe the use of the installed versions.

For the most part *ARIS Business Designer* and *ARIS Business Architect* are very similar when used for process modelling. The main difference is that *Business Architect* has additional '*ARIS Administration*' facilities. However, there is one other important difference we need to understand before we can get started.

### 5.1.1     ARIS Business Servers

*ARIS Business Architect* can be used to create and use '*ARIS Databases*' that reside on the local hard disk of your PC or reside on an '*ARIS Business Server*' hosted on a file server on a corporate network. *ARIS Business Designer*, however, can only be used to access databases on an *ARIS Business Server*; it cannot have any local databases. In practice this means you can only use *Business Designer* if your organisation has an ARIS server and has given you access to it.

**Expert Tip** – experienced users may install an ARIS Business Server on their local PC and access it as if it were on a network. For instructions on how to set this up see the ARIS installation guides.

Because of these differences, the procedure for starting ARIS is slightly different depending on which tool you are using. Section 5.1.2 will describe how to start *Business Designer* and create a new '*ARIS Model*'; Section 5.1.3 will describe the same for *Business Architect*. After that, the rest of the chapter is common to both tools.

**ARIS Business Architect** – In the rest of the book, wherever there are additional facilities in *ARIS Business Architect* we will indicate them with the icon shown on the left.

### 5.1.2    Opening ARIS Business Designer

First ensure your PC is connected to the network so as to have access to the *ARIS Business Server*. Start *ARIS Business Designer* from the shortcut on your desktop or from the Microsoft Windows **Start Menu**. After a few moments you will see the first dialog box of the *Login Wizard* as shown in Fig. 5.1.

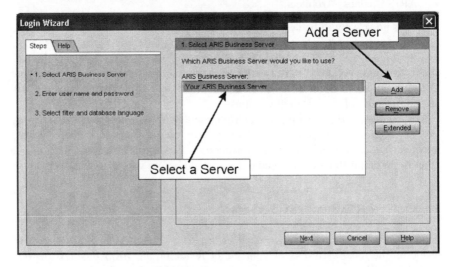

**Fig. 5.1** ARIS Login Wizard: Select ARIS Business Server

Press the **A**dd button and enter the name of your *ARIS Business Server* into the dialog box. If you don't know the name of the server then speak to your '*ARIS System Administrator*'. Once you have entered the name, press OK; select the server name you have just entered from the list and press **N**ext. You will now see the next *Login Wizard* dialog box, Fig. 5.2.

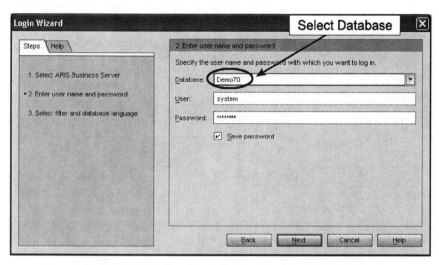

**Fig. 5.2** ARIS Login Wizard: Enter Username and Password

In this dialog box we will use the **DEMO70** database and the default entries in <u>U</u>ser and <u>P</u>assword so you can just press <u>N</u>ext. The final dialog box, shown in Fig. 5.3, asks us for the *Method Filter* we wish to use.

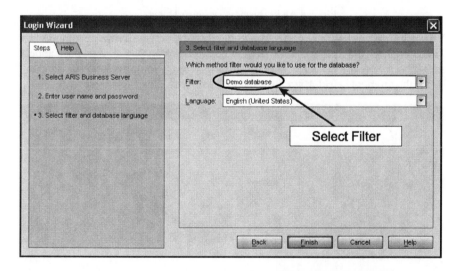

**Fig. 5.3** ARIS Login Wizard: Select Filter and Database Language

Select the **Demo database** from the drop-down list on the <u>F</u>ilter field and press <u>F</u>inish. *ARIS Business Designer* will now open on the *Home Page*, Fig. 5.4. At the bottom right-hand corner of the page the *Your login data* section shows confirmation of the database login information we have just entered in the *Login Wizard*.

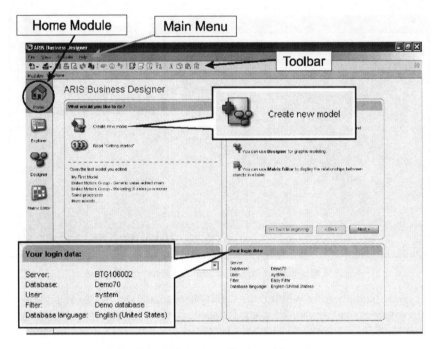

**Fig. 5.4** ARIS Business Designer Home Page

Now we will create a new ARIS Model by clicking on the Create new model icon in the *What would you like to do* area. The *Model Wizard*, Fig. 5.5, now appears asking us to select a '*Group*'. We will look at Groups in more detail in Chapter 8 so for the moment select **Main Group** and press Next.

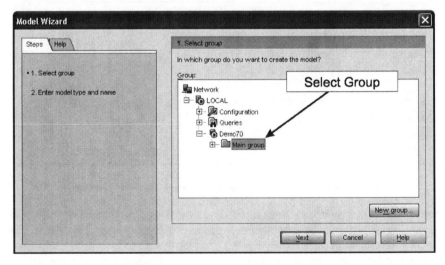

**Fig. 5.5** Model Wizard: Select Group

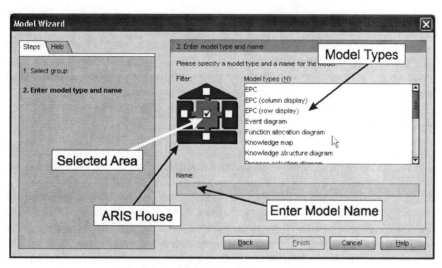

**Fig. 5.6** Model Wizard: Select Model Type

The next dialog box of the *Model Wizard*, Fig. 5.6, asks for the *ARIS Model type*. You can see the different types of model available by clicking in different areas of the '*ARIS House*'. Ticks will appear in the selected areas of the house and the *Model types* list will change to show the available models in those areas of the house (see Chapter 3 for more information on the ARIS House).

If at any time you need more help when using the ARIS wizards or dialog boxes you can click on the *Help* tab on the left-hand side of the wizard or dialog box window. Context-sensitive help will be now be displayed. For instance, selecting the *Help* tab on the left-hand side of *Enter model type and name window* and

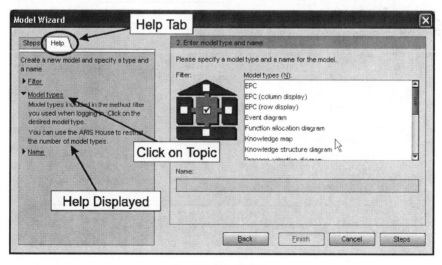

**Fig. 5.7** Wizard Help

then selecting *Filter* will display useful help on how to use the ARIS House to filter the list of available ARIS model types (Fig. 5.7).

Let us chose a model. Make sure the centre part of the ARIS House is selected (it should be ticked) and chose **EPC** from the list. Enter a suitable name for your model (e.g. My First Model) into the *Name* box and press Finish. The *Designer Module* of *ARIS Business Designer* now opens. We shall see how to use it in Section 5.2, but first let us see how to go through the same process with *ARIS Business Architect*.

### 5.1.3    Opening ARIS Business Architect

When we started *Business Designer* in Section 5.1.2 we were asked a number of questions about servers, databases and filters. This is because *Business Designer* can only connect to one of these when it starts. *ARIS Business Architect* has more flexibility and all of these items can be selected once the application has started. This means that starting *Business Architect* is much quicker and all we have to do is select it from the shortcut on the desktop or from the Microsoft Windows Start Menu. After a few moments you will see the *Home Page* shown in Fig. 5.8.

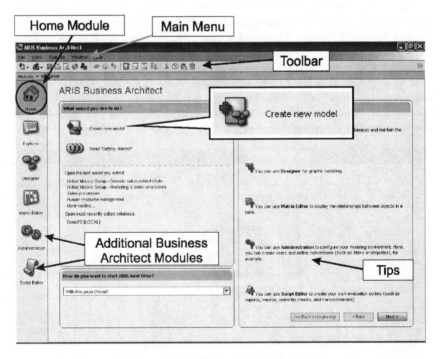

**Fig. 5.8** ARIS Business Architect Home Page

To create a new ARIS Model click on the Create new model icon in
the *What would you like to do* area. The *Model Wizard* starts just as it did
with *Business Designer,* but because we didn't have to tell *Business
Architect* which servers, databases and filters to use when we started it up, we now
have to do that so it knows where to put our new model.

In the *Select group Dialog Box,* first double-click on **LOCAL**. This will now
start the standard database system
that resides on the hard disk of your
PC (it may take a few moments).
The **LOCAL** entry will expand to
show the available ARIS Databases
and you can now click on **DEMO70**
which is probably the only one
shown (Fig. 5.9). Once again there
will be a short pause while the database opens. Select **Main group**
and press Next.

We now see the rest of the
*Model Wizard* dialog boxes which
are exactly the same as those described for *Business Designer* (Fig.
5.6). Select **EPC** from the list of
*Model types.* Enter a suitable name
for your model into the *Name* box
(e.g. `my first model`) and press
Finish. The *Designer Module* of
*ARIS Business Architect* will now
open (see Section 5.2.1).

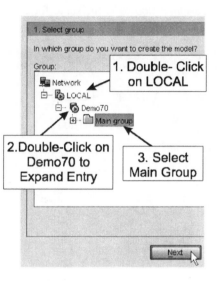

**Fig. 5.9** Model Wizard: Select Group
(Business Architect)

## 5.1.4    Menus and Toolbars

At the top of the *Business Designer Window* or *Business Architect Window*, below
the *Title Bar* (see Fig. 5.4 and Fig. 5.8), are the *Main Menu* and the *ARIS Toolbar.*

The *Main Menu* contains command groups such as File and View and is similar
to most Microsoft Windows applications. We will introduce some of these commands in this chapter and the rest later on.

The *Toolbar* contains icons that give you quick access to many of the more frequently used *Main Menu* commands. The visible icons will change depending on
which '*ARIS Module*' you are using.

Once we start using the *ARIS Modules* we will also see when we select an item
we can right-click and display a pop-up *Right-Click Menu.* This pop-menu will
provide context-sensitive access to the most useful commands from the *Main
Menu* relevant to the item selected.

## 5.2      Starting Modelling

### 5.2.1      The ARIS Designer Module

The *Designer Module* is the same for *Business Architect* and *Business Designer* and looks like Fig. 5.10.

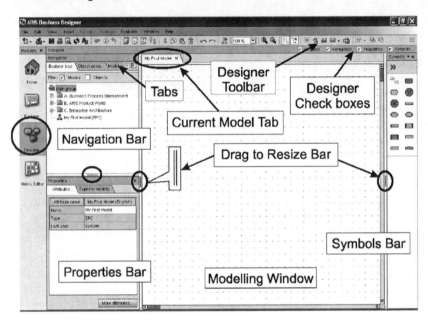

**Fig. 5.10** ARIS Designer Module

Depending on whether you have used *Business Designer* before you may not see all of the various '*Bars*'. The visibility of bars can be controlled by a set of '*Checkboxes*' at the top right of the *Designer Window* (Fig. 5.11).

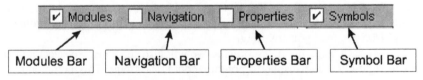

Click on a Box to Make the Bar or Window Visible

**Fig. 5.11** ARIS Designer Checkboxes

**Hint** – to give yourself more modelling space you can turn off the first three checkboxes, but make sure you have the *Symbols Checkbox* ticked so the *Symbols Bar* is visible.

## 5.2.2    Adding Objects

We can now add some '*ARIS Objects*' to our model. The pallet of available objects is shown on the *Symbols Bar* (sometimes called the *Modelling Toolbar*) (Fig. 5.12).

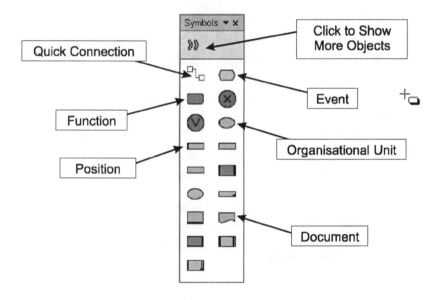

**Fig. 5.12** ARIS Symbols Bar

To place an object from the *Symbols Bar* on the model, click on the required object (e.g. chose the green '*Function*' icon) and then move your cursor over the *Modelling Window*. The cursor will change to a small rectangle with a cross above it. Move the cursor to the position where you want the object and left-click.

The function object will now appear with a white box highlighted at the centre with the label "*Function*" in it. You can now overtype this label with your own label (e.g. "Enter Order").

Remember, you have to select an icon and then click on the model, you cannot 'drag and drop' the symbols from the *Symbols Bar* onto the model.

Now chose the purple '*Event*' object and place this above the green function.

You can label it "Order Request". We now want to connect these two objects together to create an '*ARIS Relationship*'. On the *Designer Toolbar* at the top of the *Business Designer* window make sure the Toggle connection mode Button is highlighted. If not just click on it.

Now hover your mouse over the purple event object. The cursor will change to a cross. If you drag the cursor to the edge of the object you will see it changes to a small square with a jagged line attached (the full set of cursor shapes is shown in

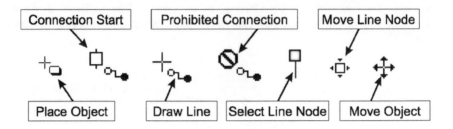

**Fig. 5.13** ARIS Designer Cursor Shapes

Fig. 5.13). This indicates you are hovering over an attachment point. Left-click the mouse and as you drag the cursor a connecting line appears.

Drag the cursor to the edge of the green function object until you see the attachment cursor and click again to complete the connection. If you have lined up the connection points you will have a nice straight line. If not, then it will have some corners in it. Don't worry, we can tidy this up later. Place another event below the function and label it "Order Entered". It should now look like Fig. 5.14.

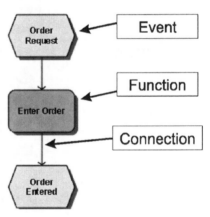

**Fig. 5.14** Some Connected Objects

### 5.2.3    Saving Your Model

You may wish to save your model at this point. Click on File > Save from the *Main Menu* or click on the Save Button on the *Toolbar*.

 **Warning** – ARIS has no automatic save or file backup facility so you should regularly save your model while you are making changes. There is also no **Save as...** option so if you want to save different versions of your model, then make a copy of it first in the *Explorer Module*. We will see how to do this in Chapter 8.

### 5.2.4 Placing and Connecting Objects

We will now add another function below the last event, but this time we will use a quicker way to place and connect objects. First select the last event by clicking on it (you will see the object highlighted as shown in Fig. 5.15) and, with it still selected, move your mouse to the *Symbols Bar* and click a function icon. A pop-up window appears showing the two possible '*rela-* 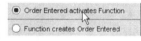 *tionships*' between the two objects. We will use the default "*Order Entered activates function*" option so just click on it.

Move your mouse back onto the model (the cursor changes to a small square and cross again) and click beneath the event where you want the centre of the function to appear. The new function now appears already connected up and with its name highlighted so you can give it a new name (e.g. "Obtain Delivery Date"). After entering the name and pressing the <Enter> key the object remains highlighted. You can then click on another icon on the *Symbols Bar* and place it the same way (e.g. place and connect an event called "Delivery Date Obtained").

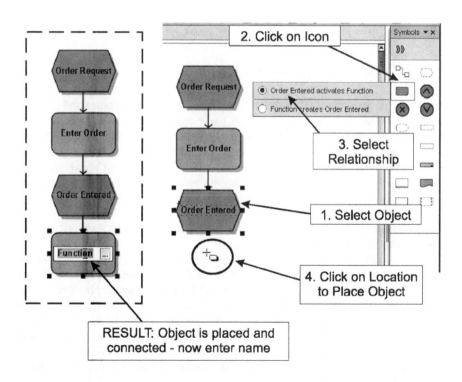

**Fig. 5.15** Place and Connect an Object

Using this technique you can rapidly place and connect objects to draw a process flow very quickly. Have a go at this now. Don't worry, you can remove objects or connections by selecting them and clicking on Edit > Delete from the *Main Menu* or from the Right-Click Menu.

### 5.2.5    Process Flows and Decisions

Real processes don't just contain tasks (functions), but they also have decisions and parallel paths. To create changes in flow we use the '*Rule*' objects shown in Fig. 5.16.

**Fig. 5.16** ARIS Rule Objects

We will revisit rules in Chapter 7, but for now we will use an *XOR* (exclusive OR) object to represent a decision. Place a new function under  the last event and label it "Check Customer Credit". Now place and connect an *XOR* to it and underneath it place and connect two events. Label one "Credit Good" and the other "Credit Refused". After placing and connecting the first event you will have to reselect the *XOR* in order to place and connect the second event using the quick method we described above. Alternatively, make sure no objects are selected (click anywhere in the white space of the model) and place the two events and manually connect them up.

Under each of the events place and connect two functions. Place a second *XOR* beneath them and connect them up to a final event and label them all so your model looks like Fig. 5.17.

We now have a simple order handling process that makes a decision about the customer's credit worthiness represented by the function **Check Customer Credit** with two possible outcomes: **Credit Good** and **Credit Refused** represented by the events. The logic of the possible outcome is shown by the *XOR* exclusive-OR rule which means one or other of the outcomes is possible, but not both. This representation may look strange to you if you are used to drawing processes using flow charts that use diamonds to represent decisions. However, this more rigorous approach in ARIS more clearly defines the decision-making logic, and is better able to handle many outcomes.

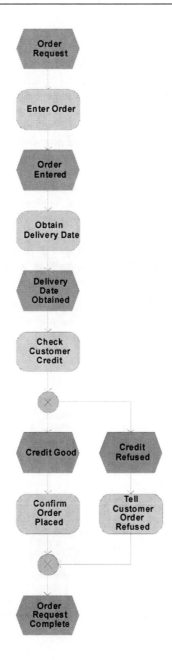

**Fig. 5.17** A Simple Process Flow

### 5.2.6     Other Object Types

You will have noticed there are other objects on the *Symbols Bar*. These represent some of the resources a process may use. For instance select the **Enter Order** process step and then select the circular yellow '*Organizational unit*' icon on the *Symbols Bar*. You will see three possible relationships appear; select the middle "*Organizational unit carries out Enter Order*". Now click on the model to the right of the function **Enter Order** so the object is placed and connected. Enter the name "Order Handling Dept". This object represents the department that carries out the task. You could also use the yellow rectangle '*Position*' object to represent a particular role that carries out the tasks (e.g. "Order Entry Clerk"). Typically each function in a model should have an *Organizational unit* or *Position* associated with it.

Now try selecting **Enter Order** again and this time choose the grey '*Document*' icon. Place and connect it and give it the name "Order Form". This now represents the order form that "*provides input for*" the function. Fig. 5.18 shows these new object types added to our process.

 **Hint** – to see what relationship one object has with another, hover your mouse over the connecting line and after a moment a '*tooltip*' will appear showing the relationship type.

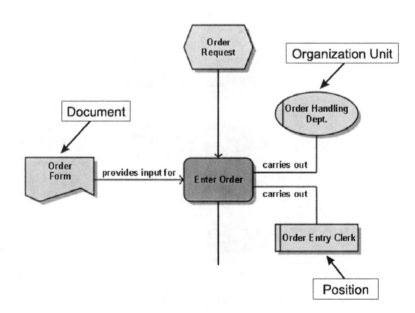

**Fig. 5.18** Other Object Types

# 5.3 Viewing and Printing Your Model

### 5.3.1 Model Layout

We have now created a small process, but you may have had some trouble getting the objects and connections to line up to look exactly like Fig. 5.17. Well don't worry, there is no need to spend time manually adjusting the layout as you would in a drawing tool. Instead we can use the *ARIS Layout* facility.

On the *Main Menu* select Arrange > Layout to bring up the *Layout Dialog Box* (Fig. 5.19).

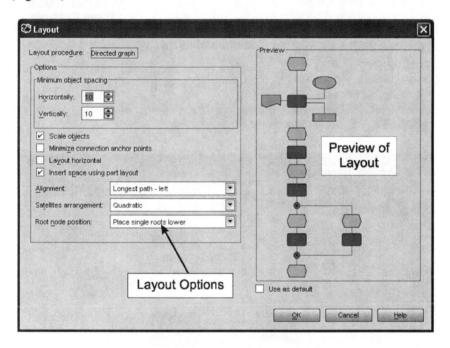

**Fig. 5.19** Layout Dialog Box

On the right-hand side is shown a preview of what the model will look like after automatic layout while on the left are various layout options. We will describe these in more detail in Chapter 10, but try experimenting now, for instance by selecting "*Longest path – left*" in the *Alignment* box, as shown in Fig. 5.19. If you don't like the layout you can press Cancel to leave the layout at it was before. Alternatively press OK to change the model layout to match the preview.

It is good practice to always use the automatic layout facility to arrange your models, rather than spend time manually laying it out. This helps avoids the temptation for people to read unintentional meaning into the arrangement of objects.

## 5.3.2    Zoom and Scaling

The model should look much more tidy now, but you may not be able to see it all. The size of the representation of the model on the screen can be changed using the zoom and scale controls on the *Designer Toolbar* or the associated commands in the View menu (Fig. 5.20).

The View > Fit to window command adjusts the scale so the whole model can be viewed in the modelling area in the *Modelling Window* while the View > Reset zoom restores the scaling to 100%. With very large models and high zoom factors it can be difficult to visualise where the visible area is in relation to the whole model. This can easily be seen, however, by using the *Model overview window Tab* (Fig. 5.21) selectable in the *Navigation Bar*.

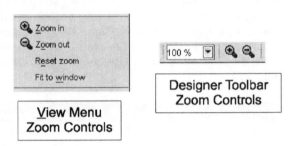

**Fig. 5.20** Zoom and Scaling Controls

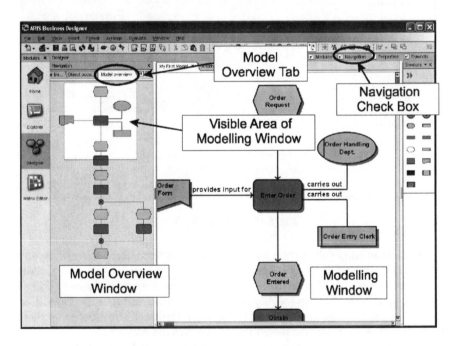

**Fig. 5.21** Model Overview Window Tab

To make the *Navigation Bar* visible, click on the *Navigation Checkbox* at the top right of the *Designer Window* (see Fig. 5.10)  and scroll round the tabs in the *Navigation Bar* and select the *Model overview window Tab*. You can increase the size of the *Navigation Bar* by dragging on the window boundary.

The *Model overview window* shows a white shaded area representing the visible area of the model. As you scroll around the main model, or zoom in or out, the shaded area will also move around the *Model overview window* to show you where you are. Better still, if you drag the shaded area around the *Model overview window* the visible part of the model in the *Modelling Window* will also move around. This makes it quick to locate a particular part of a zoomed model.

You can close the *Model overview window* at any time by un-checking the *Navigation Checkbox*.

### 5.3.3    Printing Your Model

ARIS models can be quite large so before printing it is important to preview how the model will be represented on the page sizes your printer can support. To preview the print layout select File > Print preview from the *Main Menu* or select the Print preview Button.

The *Print preview Window* (see Fig. 5.22) will show one or more printer preview pages with the model spread across them. You can use the Zoom in and

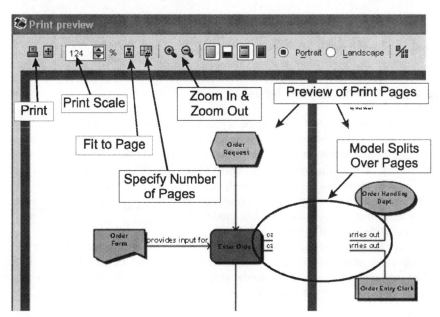

**Fig. 5.22** Print Preview

Zoom out icons to make this easier to view (Note: the Zoom icons do not affect the print layout, only the magnification of your view of it).

There are a number of ways to adjust the layout of the model on the pages. Perhaps the easiest way is to start is by pressing the Fit to Page icon which will show the entire model on a single page. You can then use the *% selection box* to increase or decrease the size of the model on the pages. Alternatively you can use the *Specify number of pages* dialog box and drag the sliders to achieve the same effect. You can also toggle the Portrait and Landscape buttons to change the page orientation.

Once you are happy with the layout of the model you can either press the Print icon to print the model immediately or press the Close button to return to the *Designer Window* and print later using File > Print from the *Main Menu*.

 **Hint** – the type of printer and size of paper (e.g. A4) that will be used for printing will be the default printer and paper size set in Microsoft Windows. To change this, close the *ARIS Preview Window*, and select Start > Printers and Faxes in Microsoft Windows. Select your default printer, or make another printer the default, and Right-Click > Printer Preferences to make the change to the printer settings (e.g. the page size). When you are finished, return to the *Designer Window* in ARIS and select View > Refresh (F5) from the *Main Menu*. You can then re-open the *Print preview Window* and the new print settings will have taken effect.

## 5.4      Finishing Off

### 5.4.1      Closing Your Model

When you have finished working on a particular model you can close it by clicking on the small cross on the tab at the top of the *Model Window*. It is possible to have more than one model open at a time, in which case there will be several tabs at the top of the window. The currently visible model has a light coloured tab while other open models (not currently visible) have dark tabs. You can make a different model visible by clicking on its tab in which case the currently visible model will be hidden (but still open).

My First Model  ✕   Another Model ✕

You can click on the cross on any tab and close the model irrespective of whether the model is visible or not so be careful to select the right one. If any changes have been made to the model since you last saved it you will be prompted to save it before the model closes.

You can close the currently visible model by selecting File > Close from the *Main Menu*. You can also close all the currently open models by selecting File > Close all.

## 5.4.2    Closing ARIS

You can close *ARIS Business Designer* or *ARIS Business Architect*  by selecting File > Close from the *Main Menu* or by clicking on the cross at the top right-hand corner of the ARIS window. If any changes have been made to any models open at the time you close ARIS, you will be prompted to save them before ARIS closes.

**Warning** – if you have models open in the *Designer Module*, but no changes have been made to them since you last saved them, then if you click on the window close icon (the cross at top right-hand corner) ARIS will close without any confirmation. You will not lose any data, but it can be irritating if you have a number of models open that you are working on, so take care.

# Chapter 6      More About the ARIS Interface

In this chapter we learn about the ARIS Modules, Toolbars and Menus. We find out how to change the operation and appearance of ARIS and how to get help. We look briefly at ARIS Properties and Attributes.

## 6.1      The ARIS Modules

When we work with ARIS we use one or more of the *ARIS Modules*. We can quickly switch between modules to do different tasks and then switch back to continue with what we were originally working on. There are six modules, four are available in *ARIS Business Designer* and a further two are available in *ARIS Business Architect* (see Table 6.1).

**Table 6.1** ARIS Modules

| Module | | Description |
|---|---|---|
| **Home Page** | Home | This is the default page when ARIS starts. It provides information on the last few edited models (and for *Business Architect*, the last databases opened), a quick link for creating a new model and useful tips. |
| **Explorer** | Explorer | This is the navigation window for ARIS enabling you to create, manage and view the *ARIS Group* (folder) structure and its contents. It enables models, objects and databases to be created, opened, renamed, deleted and moved. |
| **Designer** | Designer | This is the graphical modelling window for ARIS. It enables objects to be placed in models and connected together. It enables object *Properties* and *Attributes* to be set and the layout of the model to be changed and viewed. |
| **Matrix Editor** | Matrix Editor | The is a spreadsheet-like interface the enables objects and their *Relationships* to be created, modified and viewed in a table without the need for a graphical model. |
| **Administration** | Administration | Only available in *Business Architect*, this window provides administration for servers, databases and users. It allows databases to be maintained, reorganised and backed-up. |
| **Script Editor** | Script Editor | Only available in *Business Architect*, this window allows the maintenance and development of *ARIS Scripts* (in JavaScript) that can be used for generating *ARIS Reports*, running *Semantic Checks* and creating *Macros*. |

Initially ARIS starts up in the *Home Page* (Fig. 6.2). We can select operations directly from the *Home Page* (e.g. Create new model), from the *Main Menu* or *ARIS Toolbar*. We can also select a different module from the *Modules Bar* on the left-hand side of the window (see Fig. 6.1) or by using Vi̲ew > M̲odules from the *Main Menu*. The main area of the ARIS window will change to the window for the chosen module and the range of commands available from the *Main Menu* or *Toolbar* will change to match the context of the module.

At any time we can select a different module without losing the work in our original module. When we want to return to the original module we just select it and we can carry on from where we left off.

You can turn the *Modules Bar* off by clicking on the small cross at the top right-hand corner of the *Modules Bar* or by selecting Vi̲ew > M̲odules > H̲ide from the *Main Menu*. You can alter the size of the module icons either by selecting the small down arrow at the top of the *Modules Bar* or by selecting Vi̲ew > M̲odules > S̲mall icons / L̲arge icons from the *Main Menu*.

**Fig. 6.1** ARIS Modules Bar

 **Question** – why can't I see the *Modules Bar*?
**Answer** – it is possible to turn off the *Modules Bar* to provide more modelling area. To turn it back on select Vi̲ew > M̲odules > S̲how from the *Main Menu*, or in any of the modules except the *Home Page* you can turn on the *Modules Checkbox* (see Section 6.5.3).       ☑ Modules

## 6.2     ARIS Home Page

The *Home Page* is the default starting page for *Business Designer* and *Business Architect* (see Fig. 6.2). We have already seen in Chapter 5 that we can create a new model directly by clicking on Create new model in the *What would you like to do* area. We can also see a list of the models we have recently edited in the *Open the last model you edited* area (the list will be empty if this is the first time you have used ARIS). If you want to open an existing model that isn't listed here, you can select it from the *Explorer Module* which we will look at in Section 6.3.

 **ARIS Business Architect** – also allows you to Open most recently edited database from the *Home Page*. This is not available from *Business Designer* because you can only open one ARIS Database when you start *Business Designer*.

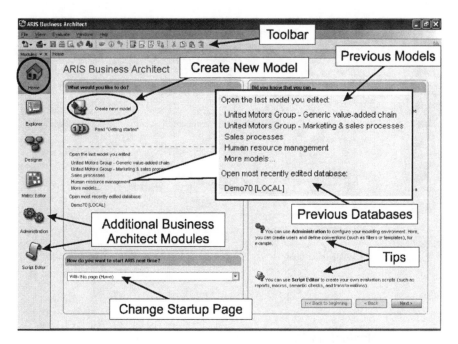

**Fig. 6.2** ARIS Home Page (Business Architect)

On the right-hand side of the *Home Page* are a set of Tips. You can scroll through the various pages of tips by using the **Next >** and **< Back** buttons. Des pite what you might expect you can't click on the tips to get any more information although some of the them have hyperlinks (underlined blue text) that will take you to the appropriate item in the *ARIS Help Window* (see Section 6.8).

Once you have been using ARIS for a while you may find the *Home Page* is no longer very useful. In that case you can change the default start-up page using the *How do you want ARIS to start next time*? drop-down box at the bottom left of the *Home Page*. Setting it to "*With Explorer*" is a good option.

## 6.3 Explorer Module

The *Explorer Module* is the main window you will use for creating, managing and viewing the structure of *ARIS Models* and *Objects*. We will look at *ARIS Explorer* in more detail in Chapter 8, but for now we will have a brief overview. The window is split into two vertical panels (Fig. 6.3).

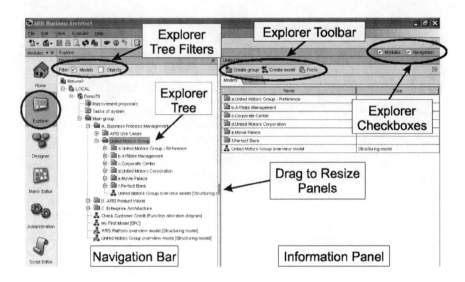

**Fig. 6.3** ARIS Explorer Module

## 6.3.1    Navigation Bar

The left-hand panel, the *Navigation Bar* (Fig. 6.4), has a hierarchical browser, or *Explorer Tree*, similar to that used in Microsoft Windows.

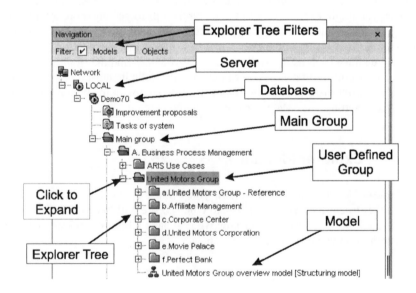

**Fig. 6.4** Explorer Navigation Bar

It displays folders containing items such as *Improvement Proposals* or folders containing *ARIS Models* and *Objects*. The folders containing *Models* and *Objects* are known as *Groups*. The *Explorer Tree* normally displays the groups and the models in those groups. You can alter the display to also show the objects in the groups (or just the objects or neither) by selecting the Models Checkbox or Objects Checkbox in the *Explorer Filter Checkboxes* area at the top of the *Navigation Bar*.

If you select a group, model or object and chose an edit command from the *Main Menu*, or the Right-Click Menu, you can undertake various tasks such as Open, Copy and Paste, and Delete (Fig. 6.5). You can also select more complex tasks such as E̱valuate > Sta̱rt Report.

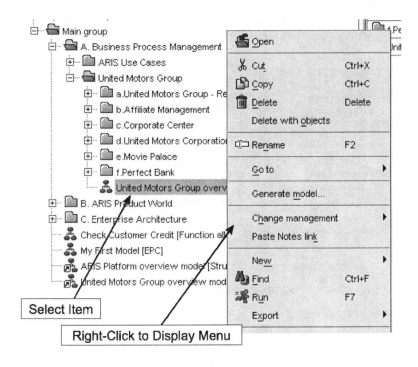

**Fig. 6.5** Explorer Right-Click Menu

 **Hint** – most commands are always available from the *Main Menu*, but the pop-up *Right-Click Menu* is often more useful as it gives quick access to the context-sensitive commands appropriate to the item selected.

The *Explorer Tree* can be turned on and off by selecting the [✔ Navigation] *Navigation Checkbox* at the top right-hand corner of the *Explorer Window* or in the V̱iew menu. If the *Explorer Tree* is turned off, the *Information Tabs* (Section 6.3.2) occupy the whole window area.

**ARIS Business Architect** – allows servers and databases to be shown in the *Explorer Tree*, while *Business Designer* is limited to showing the groups, models and objects within the single database selected at start-up.

### 6.3.2    Information Tabs

The right-hand panel (Fig. 6.6) provides more information on any item (server, data-base, group, model or object) selected in the *Explorer Tree* on the left-hand side. The *Information Tabs* are context-sensitive so will display different information depending on what item has been selected.

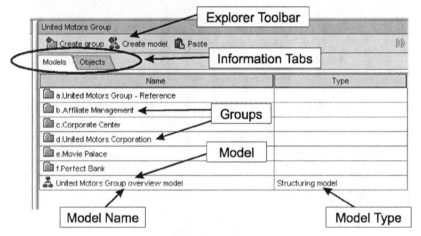

**Fig. 6.6** Explorer Information Tabs

Typically, if a group is selected, the *Information Tabs* will contain two tabs: *Models* and *Objects*. The *Models Tab* shows any models and sub-groups in the group selected; the *Objects Tab* shows objects and sub-groups. The information displayed is the name of the item and its type.

If other types of item are selected in the *Explorer Tree* (e.g. models or objects), other sorts of information are displayed in the *Information Tabs* (e.g. *Occurrences* or *Variants*). We will look at these other types of information in later chapters.

There is also a small context-sensitive *Explorer Toolbar* above the *Information Tabs* providing commands such as Create group, Create model, etc.

### 6.3.3    Using Explorer

The most common commands you will initially want to perform with *Explorer* will be to create and delete groups and models (Table 6.2)

**Table 6.2** Basic Explorer Commands

| Task | Description |
|------|-------------|
| **Create New Group** | Select an existing group (e.g. **Main Group**). Right-Click > New > Group. Type the name for the group in the highlighted box. |
| **Rename Group** | Select the group. Right-Click > Rename or press F2. Type the new name and press Enter. |
| **Delete Group** | Select the group. Right-Click > Delete. A confirmation message will be displayed, select Yes if you are sure. **Note**: another confirmation message will be displayed if the group is not empty. |
| **Create New Model** | Select a group where you wish to store the model. Right-Click > New > Model. Chose the Model type from the *New Model Wizard* and enter a name. |
| **Rename Model** | Select the model. Right-Click > Rename or press F2. Type new name and press Enter. |
| **Open a Model** | Select the model and double-click, or Right-Click > Open. The *ARIS Designer Module* will automatically be selected with the chosen model open. |
| **Delete a Model** | Select the model and Right-Click > Delete. A confirmation message will be displayed, select Yes if you are sure. **Note**: avoid selecting Delete with objects; we will see the significance of this command in Chapter 9. |
| **Copy a Group or Model** | You can copy items in the *Explorer Tree* in the normal way using Copy and Paste commands. However, there is special significance to copying ARIS items which we will investigate in more detail in Chapter 15. |

## 6.4     Designer Module

The *Designer Module* provides the graphical modelling environment for creating *ARIS Models*. As we shall see, when we create models we are doing much more than creating a drawing. As well as creating a visual graphical representation, we are also creating *ARIS Objects* in the underlying *ARIS Database*, and establishing *Relationships* between those objects. The *Designer Module* therefore has facilities for creating objects, relationships and properties as well as drawing facilities to layout, visualise and change the appearance of the model.

The *Designer Module* has the most functions of all the modules. We had a brief introduction in Chapter 5 and we shall look at it again in more detail in Chapter 9. For now we will summarise some of its windows and toolbars.

### 6.4.1     Designer Window

In its default state the main area of the *Designer Module* is taken up by the modelling area, or *Modelling Window*. To the right of the *Modelling Window* is the *Symbols Bar* or *Modelling Toolbar* (*ARIS Help* is not very consistent in its use of names for window items, for instance it uses both of these terms, we shall use *Symbols Bar*).

At the top and to the right of the *Designer Module* window are four checkboxes that control the visibility of the *Modules Bar*, *Navigation Bar*, *Properties Bar* and *Symbols Bar*. You can also select what is visible using the <u>V</u>iew menu on the *Main Menu*. See Fig. 6.7.

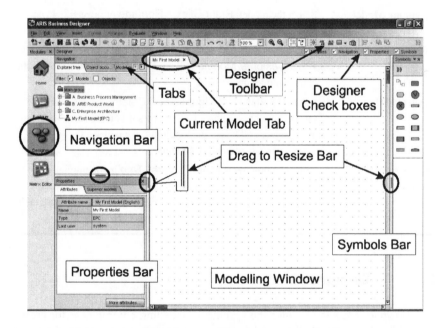

**Fig. 6.7** ARIS Designer Module

Turning off the *Modules Bar* can provide additional modelling space. Turning off the *Symbols Bar* also increases the visible model area which is useful if you are just viewing the model.

## 6.4.2      Symbols Bar

As we saw in Chapter 5, we can select the *Symbols* that represent
*ARIS Objects* from the *Symbols Bar* and place them on the model.
We can also quickly connect them up using the '*place and connect*'
facility.

The *Symbols Bar* normally only shows a sub-set of the more
commonly used objects that the chosen Method Filter allows in the
model. If you wish to use an object not currently visible, click
on the Add symbols Button at the top right of the *Symbols Bar*.
The *Add symbols Dialog Box* (Fig. 6.8) appears and you can
select one or more objects and press A̲dd.

You can alter the size of the symbol icons on the *Symbols Bar* by
selecting V̲iew > Symbols > S̲mall icons / L̲arge icons from the *Main
Menu*.

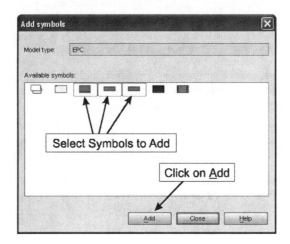

**Fig. 6.8** Add Symbols Dialog Box

## 6.4.3      Navigation and Properties

Turning on the *Navigation Bar* or the *Properties*   ✔ Navigation   ✔ Properties
*Bar* (select the *Designer Checkboxes* at the top right-hand side of the *Designer
Window*) splits the *Modelling Window* into two vertical panels. To the right-hand
side is a reduced-size modelling area, while on the left-hand side is an area to display the *Navigation Bar* and *Properties Bar*. If both are selected, the *Navigation Bar*
is at the top with the *Properties Bar* beneath it. You can alter the sizes of the left
and right-hand panels by dragging the vertical division left or right.

## Navigation Bar

The *Navigation Bar* has three tabs that display different information about the model (Fig. 6.9):

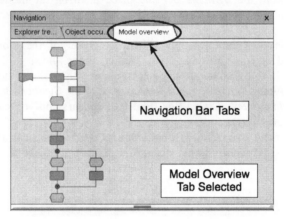

**Fig. 6.9** Designer Module Navigation Bar

- **Explorer Tree** – a version of the *Explorer Tree* from the *Explorer Module*. This can be used to open additional models, select existing objects for re-use or models for '*assignment*' (see later chapters).

- **Object Occurrences** – shows all the objects currently being used in the model and their type. Selecting an object will cause it to be selected in the *Modelling Window* which will automatically scroll so the object is visible.

- **Model Overview** – shows a representation of the entire model with the area currently visible in the *Modelling Window* shown as a white square. Dragging the square will cause the *Modelling Window* to scroll in synchronisation.

## Properties Bar

The *Properties Bar* is context-sensitive and will display different tabs depending on what item is selected in the *Modelling Window*.

 **Hint** – to display information about the current opened model, ensure nothing is selected by pressing the ESC key or by clicking on any unused area in the model.

With an object selected the following tabs are available (Fig. 6.10):

- **Attributes** – the basic *ARIS Attributes* for that object and their values. To see more attributes, click on the More attributes Button at the bottom right-hand corner and select an attribute from the dialog box.

- **Assignments** – displays the name and type of any model '*assigned*' to that object. We will cover assignments later in Chapter 12.

- **Relationships** – shows the *ARIS Relationship* (typically the connections) between the selected object and any other object in the database (not just the objects in the current model).

- **Occurrences** – shows all models in which the selected object appears including the current model. If the object appears in a model more than once it will be shown in the list more than once. You can open the model and go to the selected object by clicking on the <u>O</u>pen model Button at the bottom right-hand corner. This display is similar to the *Object Ooccurrences Tab* in the *Navigation Bar,* but the display is from an object perspective rather than a model perspective.

**Fig. 6.10** Designer Module Properties Bar

### 6.4.4   The Matrix Editor

We have briefly seen that we can establish a *Relationship* between two objects by making a connection between them in the *Designer Module*. For instance, in our example in Chapter 5 we connected an *Organizational unit* (**Order Handling Dept**) and a *Document* (**Order Form**) to the **Enter Order** *Function* with the "*carries out* " and "*provides input for* " relationships.

We can view these relationships by hovering our mouse over the connection and viewing the tool tip that appears or by selecting an object and viewing its relationship in the *Relationships Tab* of the *Properties Bar* (see Section 6.4.3). However, when there are large numbers of objects and relationships, creating and viewing them in this way is not ideal. The *Matrix Editor* provides an alternative table view enabling relationships to be created and viewed without the need for a graphical model.

An advantage of the *Matrix Editor* is that in one table it is possible to create and view a variety of different relationships that cannot be accessed from just one type of model. You can also export this table view into Microsoft Excel.

Fig. 6.11 shows an example of the *Matrix Editor,* but further description is beyond the scope of this 'getting started' book.

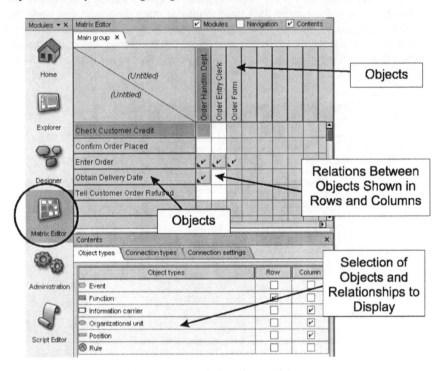

**Fig. 6.11** The Matrix Editor

### 6.4.5    Administration Module

The *Administration Module* is only available in *ARIS Business Architect.* It is intended for advanced ARIS users to manage the *ARIS Databases,* the structure of their *Groups, Models* and *Objects,* and the *Users* of those databases. Its other main use is the configuration of the modelling conventions that will be used and the maintenance of the ARIS *Method Filters* that implement those conventions.

The appearance of the *Administration Module* is very similar to the *Explorer Module.* In the left-hand panel is an *Explorer Tree* and the right-hand panel is an *Information Panel.* The *Explorer Tree* shows *ARIS Servers,* the *ARIS Databases* on those servers and the *ARIS Groups* within the databases. However, it also shows additional *Configuration* folders for the servers that contain details of the *ARIS Conventions* and *ARIS Methods* used on that server. There are also additional folders within the databases for items such as *User, Font Formats* and *Languages.*

**Question** – when I select a group from my database in the *Explorer Tree*, why don't I see any models or objects listed in the *Information Tabs*?

**Answer** – you are probably in the *Administration Module* instead of the *Explorer Module*. Selecting a group in the *Explorer Tree* of the *Administration Module* only results in any sub-groups being shown in the *Information Tabs*. It doesn't show any objects and models. Select the *Explorer Module* from the *Modules Bar* or <u>V</u>iew > <u>M</u>odules from the *Main Menu*.

Selecting an item in a *Configuration* folder (e.g. a *Font Format* or *Template*) presents context-specific information in the *Informational Panel* and provides access to commands to maintain the configuration item from the *Main Menu* or Right-Click Menu.

The facilities and commands of the *Administration Module* are beyond the scope of this book.

## 6.4.6 The Script Editor

ARIS has several types of programming scripts for automating the production of document reports, validating and modifying models, and performing other operations (see Table 6.3).

**Table 6.3** ARIS Automation Scripts

| Task | Description |
|------|-------------|
| **Macros** | *Scripts* that alter database contents or model appearance. Can be triggered by events that occur in ARIS (e.g. an object is created or a model is saved). *Macros* can be defined that run other *ARIS Scripts* and can be assigned to icons on the *Toolbar*. |
| **Scripts** | Analyses database contents and extracts information in a variety of formats (e.g. Word, Excel, HTML). |
| **Semantic Checks** | Analyses database contents and model structure for conformance against a set of configurable modelling rules and conventions. Generates reports in formats such a Word and Excel. |
| **Transformations** | Transforms one object or model type into another (e.g. creates a data class from a data entity type). |

 **Expert Tip** – in addition to the standard *Scripts* provided with ARIS, experienced users can create their own scripts using the *Script Wizard* or the JavaScript programming environment.

The *Script Editor Module* is used to create and maintain the various automation scripts. These scripts can be used locally or made available on an *ARIS Server* for use by other users. Creating your own scripts requires good knowledge of the ARIS Method as well as programming skills and is beyond the scope of this book.

## 6.5    Menus and Toolbars

### 6.5.1    Main Menu

At the top of the *Business Designer Window* or *Business Architect Window*, below the *Title Bar*, are the *Main Menu* and the *ARIS Toolbar*.

The *Main Menu* contains command groups such as <u>F</u>ile and <u>V</u>iew and is similar to most Microsoft Windows applications. We will introduce some of these commands in this chapter (see Table 6.4) and the rest as we come across them.

**Table 6.4** ARIS Main Menu (Typical Commands)

| Task | Description |
|---|---|
| <u>F</u>ile | • Commands for creating, deleting and opening servers, databases and models, |
| | • Find models and objects matching the search criteria, |
| | • Import and export files in XML format, |
| | • Page setup, print preview and print (*Designer Module* only with model open), |
| | • Model history – a list of recently opened models, |
| | • Exit ARIS. |
| <u>E</u>dit | • Copy, paste, delete and rename groups, models and objects, |
| | • Display attributes and properties for groups, models and objects, |
| | • Undo and redo last commands (*Designer Module* only). |
| <u>V</u>iew | • Select module, |
| | • Configure *Modules Bar* visibility, |
| | • Configure window and bar visibility, |
| | • Refresh database, |
| | • Configure *ARIS Options,* |
| | • Zoom in, zoom out and window resize commands (*Designer Module* only). |
| <u>I</u>nsert | • Insert graphical objects and text (*Designer Module* only). |

| Format | • | Format model appearance (*Designer Module* only), |
| | • | Apply template *(Designer Module* only), |
| | • | Edit attribute placements (*Designer Module* only). |
| Arrange | • | Arrange layout and appearance of model (*Designer Module* only). |
| Evaluate | • | Run *Report Scripts* and *Macros.* |
| Window | • | Lists open models, matrix diagrams or scripts. Selecting item will select the appropriate *ARIS Module* and display the open window, |
| Help | • | Selection of *Topic Help* or *Method Help*, |
| | • | Enter new *licence key.* |

### 6.5.2     Toolbars

The *ARIS Toolbar*, located below the *Main Menu*, contains buttons that give you quick access to many of the more frequently used *Main Menu* commands. The *Toolbar* is context-sensitive and the buttons that are visible will change depending on which module you are using. Some of the more commonly used buttons we will come across are shown in Fig. 6.12.

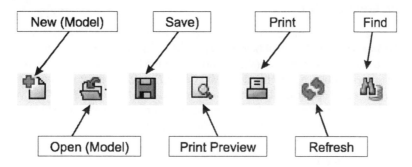

**Fig. 6.12** ARIS Toolbar Buttons

In addition to the main *Toolbar*, the *Information Tabs* in the *Explorer Module* have their own toolbar that appears when groups, models or objects are selected in the *Explorer Tree.*

### 6.5.3    Filters and Checkboxes

The *Explorer Module* and *Designer Module* both have checkboxes in the top right-hand corner that control which bars are visible (Fig. 6.13).

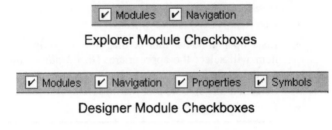

Fig. 6.13 Explorer and Designer Checkboxes

*Modules Checkbox*

The *Explorer Module* and *Designer Module* have a *Modules Checkbox* that controls the visibility of the *Modules Bar* on the left-hand side of the window. The *Modules Bar* can also be turned on and off using View > Modules > Show / Hide from the *Main Menu*. The size of the module icons can be controlled from the same menu.

*Navigation Checkbox*

The *Explorer Module* and *Designer Module* both have a *Navigation Checkbox*. In the *Explorer Module* the checkbox turns on and off the *Explorer Tree* that appears in the left-hand *Navigation Bar* (see Section 0). In the *Designer Module* the *Navigation Checkbox* allows a simplified version of the *Explorer Tree* to be made visible in the *Navigation Bar* at the left-hand side of the *Designer Modelling Window* (see Section 6.4.3). This can be used to open additional models, select existing objects for re-use or models for assignment (see later chapters).

*Properties Checkbox*

The *Designer Module* has a *Properties Checkbox* that allows the *Properties Bar* to be made visible at the left-hand side of the *Modelling Window*. The *Properties Bar* has tabs for displaying *Attributes, Relationships, Assignments* and *Occurrences* (see Section 6.4.3).

*Symbols Checkbox*

The *Designer Module* has a *Symbols Checkbox* that allows the *Symbols Bar* to be turned on or off at the right-hand side of the *Modelling Window* (see Section 6.4.2). Normally turned on while modelling as it contains the palette of symbols for ARIS objects, it can be turned off when viewing models to provide a larger *Modelling Window* area.

### 6.5.4      Right-Click Menus

Once we start using the ARIS modules we will also see that when we select an item we can right-click and display a pop-up *Right-Click Menu*. This pop-up menu will provide context-sensitive access to the most useful commands from the *Main Menu* relevant to the item selected. Fig. 6.14 shows the Right-Click Menu for an object selected in the *Designer Module*.

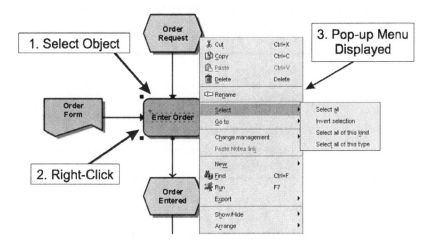

**Fig. 6.14** Right-Click Menu for an Object

### 6.5.5      Menu Icons

Many of the commands on the *Main Menu* and the Right-Click Menu have some icons beside them to help you quickly select the right command. Many of these icons are the same as the buttons on the *Toolbar* (see Section 6.5.2), but some only appear on the menus. Some of the less familiar icons are shown in Table 6.5.

**Table 6.5** ARIS Icons

| Icon | Use | Icon | Use |
|------|-----|------|-----|
| ⊏⊐ | Rename | ⠿ | Attribute Placement |
| ⊞ | Page Setup | 🗑 | Delete |
| ⓘ | Attributes | ⚗ | Run Link |
| ☞ | Properties | ⚙ | Model |
| ↻ | Refresh | ⬆ | Superior Model |

## 6.6       Properties and Attributes

### 6.6.1     ARIS Properties

The totality of all the information ARIS stores about objects, models and data-bases is represented by their *Properties*. The information includes the appearance of the object, its configuration and specific *Attributes* (see Table 6.6).

**Table 6.6** Information Stored for ARIS Items

| Term | Meaning |
| --- | --- |
| **Attributes** | ARIS Modelling information stored for ARIS items (e.g. models, objects, relationships and databases, users, user groups, font formats, etc.). |
| **Properties** | The totality of all information (including attributes) known about ARIS items. |

### *Properties Dialog Box*

The *Properties* of an ARIS item can be viewed and modified using the *Properties Dialog Box*. To display the dialog box, select the item in the *Explorer Module* or the *Designer Module* and do any of the following:

*   Select Edit > Properties from the *Main Menu*,
*   Right-Click and select Properties from the pop-up menu,
*   Press <ALT><ENTER>,
*   Click on the *Properties Icon* in the *Toolbar*,   ⓘ
*   Double-Click on an object in the *Explorer Module* or *Designer Module*.

A typical object *Properties Dialog Box* is shown in Fig. 6.15. Clicking on the various entries in the *Selection Tab* will display *Attributes*, *Relationships*, all *Occurrences* of the object and other information. We will look at *ARIS Properties* in more detail in Chapter 14.

### *Properties Bar*

In the *Designer Module* it is possible to use the *Properties Bar* to view a sub-set of the *Properties* shown in the *Properties Dialog Box* (the *Attributes*, *Assignments*, *Occurrences* and *Relationships* properties of an object, or the *Attributes* and *Superior models* properties of a model). To make the *Properties Bar* visible, select the *Properties Checkbox* at the top right-hand corner of the *Designer Window* or select the <u>V</u>iew > Properties checkbox in the *Main Menu*. We looked at the *Properties Bar* earlier in Section 6.4.3 and will look at *Properties* in more detail in Chapter 14.

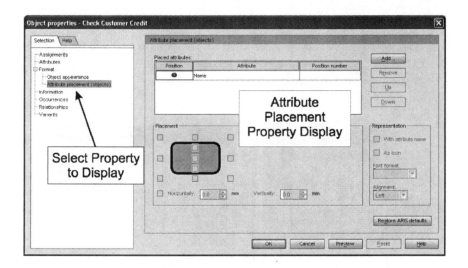

**Fig. 6.15** ARIS Properties Dialog Box

## 6.6.2    ARIS Attributes

Most ARIS items (databases, users, models, groups, objects, etc.) have *Attributes* associated with them. *ARIS Attributes* include information such as the item name, date created, author, a description, remarks and free text descriptions. Attributes are populated with values either automatically when the item is created or by a user manually entering values into them. Some attributes allow additional information to be added to the model and objects for use with analyses, simulation, Web publication or other specialist tools.

It is important to realise that attributes are used for storing modelling-related information about the objects, models and databases, not for general business information. For instance, if you created an object to represent one of your IT systems, you would not use its attributes to store every bit of information you know about that system. However, ARIS does provide special *System Attributes* that enable documents, Web pages or other applications to be linked to objects, models and databases. Thus, while ARIS does not store all your enterprise knowledge, it can act as a central repository providing easily maintainable links to the most current information. This is particularly valuable when models are published on the Intranet and the links are made to other Web pages.

### Attribute Window

Attributes can be viewed and edited using the *Attributes Window* (see Fig. 6.16). To display the window, select the item to be inspected in the *Explorer Module* or the *Designer Module* and do any of the following:

- Select Edit > Attributes from the *Main Menu*,
- Right-Click and select Attributes from the pop-up menu,
- Press <F8>,
- Click on the *Attributes Icon* in the *Toolbar*.

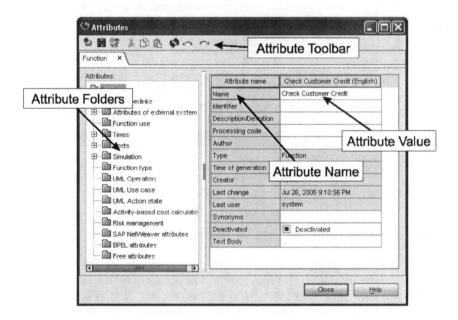

**Fig. 6.16** ARIS Attributes Window

The *Attributes Window* is split into two vertical panels. The left-hand panel has an *Explorer Tree* style interface which shows a set of folders into which the attributes are grouped. The most used attributes (e.g. *Name*, *Description/Definition*, etc.) are listed in the top-level folder. The right-hand panel shows the attributes in the selected folder along with their values. Values in white boxes can be edited (type in a value and press Enter) while those in grey boxes are set automatically by ARIS. Attribute values may be text fields, numbers or drop-down lists. The set of attributes that is visible, and the set of values they can contain, is set by the ARIS Method Filter in use. For more information on *Attributes* see Chapter 14.

### Attributes Tab

In the *Designer Module* it is possible to view the *Attributes* of the model and its objects using the *Attributes Tab* in the *Properties Bar*. To make the tab visible, select the *Properties Checkbox* at the top of the *Designer Window* or select the <u>V</u>iew > Properties checkbox on the Main Menu. Select the *Attributes Tab* and you will see a list of attributes as shown in Fig. 6.17.

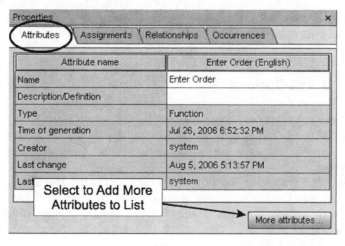

**Fig. 6.17** Properties Bar – Attributes Tab

Unlike the *Attributes Window* that displays all attributes arranged in folders, the *Attributes Tab* displays just a sub-set of those attributes that have values set (i.e. they are '*maintained*'). To see an attribute not listed, click on the More attributes … button at the bottom of the tab. The *Insert attributes Dialog Box* (Fig. 6.18) shows the remaining attributes listed in their folders. Select one or more attributes and press OK to add them to the *Attribute Tab* display.

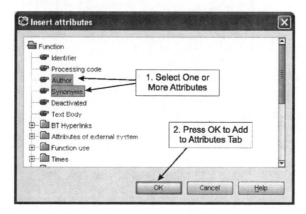

**Fig. 6.18** Insert Attributes Dialog Box

**Hint** – to select a single attribute from the *Insert Attributes Dialog Box* just double-click on it and it will inserted into the list in the *Attributes Tab*.

If you no longer want to see an attribute listed on the tab, select the attribute name in the left-hand column, Right-Click > Hide and chose whether to always hide the attribute, or only hide it if its value is not maintained.

If you click on the attribute name header of the left-hand column in the *Attribute Tab* you can chose whether to sort the list in the order determined by the ARIS Method (the header then has a small *ARIS House* in it) or in alphabetical order.


## 6.7    ARIS Options

Various settings and preferences for how ARIS operates (e.g. the default username and password, or the background colour for models) can be set from the *ARIS Options Dialog Box*. To view and modify options select V̲iew > O̲ptions... from the *Main Menu*.

The *ARIS Options Dialog Box* (Fig. 6.19) has two panels. The left-hand panel show a hierarchical grouping of the options while the right-hand panel shows various options settings. For instance the Model > Layout Option has different settings for the layout of models. You may recall from Chapter 5 we could also set these using the *Layout Wizard*.

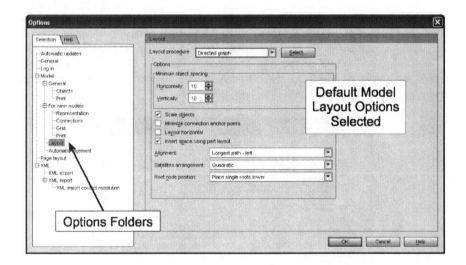

**Fig. 6.19** ARIS Options Dialog Box

The *Layout Wizard* controls the settings for the particular model where the *Layout Wizard* is being used where as the Model > Layout option sets the default settings for all new models (you will notice there is no preview of the model in the *Options Dialog Box* because that would only be relevant for a specific model).

## 6.8      How to Get Help

Help is available in a number of ways:

- Help on ARIS topics – select Help > Help Topics from the *Main Menu*,
- Help on the ARIS Method, that is the *Models*, *Objects* and *Attributes* used in ARIS – select Help > Method help from the *Main Menu*,
- Context-sensitive help – press F1 for *Topic Help* or CTRL + F1 for *Method Help* for a model, object or attribute.

### 6.8.1      ARIS Topics

Selecting the *ARIS Topics Help* will display the *Help Window*. Similar to help in many Microsoft Windows applications there are three tabs in the window: *Contents, Index* and *Find* (Fig. 6.20).

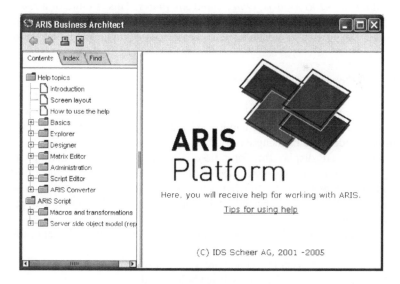

**Fig. 6.20** ARIS Topic Help

## Contents

The *Contents* tab provides useful information topics:

- *Introduction* – a basic introduction to the topic,
- *Procedure* – step by step instructions to perform a particular operation,
- *Valuable information* – additional background information.

## Index

The *Index* tab provides an alphabetical list of all key items of help. Clicking on the item will display more detail in the right-hand panel.

## Find

The *Find* tab initially shows a blank display, but if you enter the name of something you wish to search for in the *Find* box, and press Enter, all items that have the search string in the topic will be displayed. Clicking on the item will display more detail in the right-hand panel.

### 6.8.2    ARIS Method

Selecting *ARIS Method Help* displays a different help screen that has an alphabetical list of all the *ARIS Models*, *Objects* and *Attributes*. This is more of a reference manual for experienced users than help, but the entries for models do show all the objects that can be used in the model and some example graphics of typical models.

### 6.8.3    Context-sensitive Help

While you are working with ARIS you can get help on the item you are working with by selecting the item (e.g. window, object, connection or select nothing for the current model) and pressing F1 or CTRL + F1.

Pressing F1 will display the *Topic Help Window* with the right-hand pane displaying help about the item you selected. The left-hand pane with the *Contents*, *Index* and *Find* tabs is just set to wherever it was last time you used it and doesn't relate to the help in the right-hand pane, but you can use the tabs to navigate to other help topics.

Pressing CTRL + F1 will display the *Method Help Window*, again set to display help on the item you selected.

So if you select an event object and press F1 you will get general help on objects, while if you press CTRL + F1 you will see help specifically on events.

# Chapter 7      The Event-driven Process Chain

In this chapter we look at the Event-driven process chain that forms the core
of the ARIS Method. We explore how it is built using events, functions and
rules and how to model decisions, parallel paths, loops and process flows.

## 7.1      Introduction

The *Event-driven process chain* (EPC) is the main ARIS model for representing
processes. It is a dynamic model bringing together the static resources of the business
(systems, organisation, data, etc.) and organising them to deliver a sequence of tasks
or activities (*'the process'*) that adds business value. There are several varieties of
the EPC (row, column, etc.), but in this book we will concentrate on the basic
EPC. The majority of other models in ARIS give views of the basic information
and relationships presented in the EPC.

## 7.2      The EPC Objects

Essentially there are four types of objects used in the EPC:
- Events,
- Functions,
- Rules,
- Resources (data, organisation, system, etc.).

Fig. 7.1 shows an example EPC model of a process fragment using the four object
types above. In this chapter we will look at the first three types and show how they
are used to model process flow. In Chapter 11 we will see that by adding resource
objects we can show how the process interacts with its environment.

### 7.2.1      Events

ARIS *Events* represent the changing state of the world as a process proceeds:
- External changes that trigger the start of the process
  (e.g. "*customer order received*"),
- Internal changes of state as the process proceeds
  (e.g. "*product manufactured*"),
- The final outcome of the process that has an external effect
  (e.g. "*order delivered to customer*").

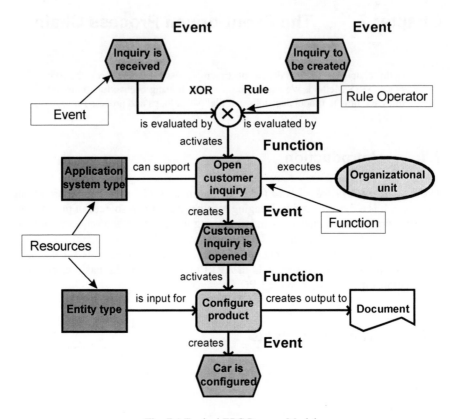

**Fig. 7.1** Typical EPC Process Model

To borrow a software engineering term: events represent the '*pre-conditions*' and '*post-conditions*' for each step in the process. Pre-conditions are those things that must be present, or must have happened, before an activity can start. Post-conditions represent what has changed as a result of doing the activity. Events can occur as a result of things people do or as a result of an IT system operation. The final event in one process can be the trigger for another process and in that way we can link sections of processes together to form a larger '*end-to-end*' process.

To describe events, we typically use the convention '*noun–verb*' or, more specifically in an IT environment, '*information item – action*' (see Table 7.1).

**Table 7.1** Naming Events

| Description | Noun (information item) | Verb (action) |
| --- | --- | --- |
| "Order Entered" | Order | Entered |
| "Cost Calculated" | Cost | Calculated |

## 7.2.2 Functions

ARIS *Functions* represent the activities or tasks carried out as part of a business process; ideally with each one adding some value to the business. Functions may be carried out by people or by IT systems. They have inputs (information or material), create outputs (different information or a product) and may consume resources.

In Chapter 11 we shall look in more detail at the exact nature of processes, activities and functions. We shall see they are in fact '*transformations*', but for the moment we can just think of functions as 'doing something'.

To describe functions we use the convention '*verb–noun*' or more specifically, '*action – information item*' (see Table 7.2).

**Table 7.2** Naming Functions

| Description | Verb (action) | Noun (information item) |
|---|---|---|
| "Enter Order" | Enter | Order |
| "Calculate Cost" | Calculate | Cost |
| "Sell Product" | Sell | Product |

 **Expert Tip** – it is quite common to use terms such as "*sales*" or "*marketing*" to represent high-level business operations. However, it is too easy to confuse these with the names of business departments. It is better to use the '*verb–noun*' approach to describe what is really done (e.g. "*Sell Product*").

It is important not to use ambiguous or long-winded descriptions for functions. In more detailed process models functions will represent specific, well-understood, activities (e.g. "*Enter Order*"). However, when modelling high-level operations it can be tempting to have long descriptions (e.g. "*Receive order, validate, process and inform customer*"). It is better to have one succinct title or split the function into several separate functions.

## 7.3 The Event-driven Process Chain

Functions are triggered by one or more events. In ARIS terminology an event "*activates*" a function and a function will always "*create*" one or more new events. So events trigger functions, and functions produce new events which in turn trigger further functions, and so on, to produce a chain of functions and events – the *Event-driven process chain* (Fig. 7.2). In fact the *Event-driven process chain* should really be called the *Event-driven function chain*.

**Hint** – in the previous chapters we showed example EPC fragments exactly as they appear in the *Designer Module*. We will be looking at many EPC examples in this chapter so to make them easier to read on the printed page we have turned off the background colours of the objects and made the connecting lines bolder.

In reality processes are not a simple chain of events and functions and we need to introduce the concept of process flow. Process flows are built around decisions and parallel paths.

Decisions that change the process flow are always taken by functions, but to represent the logic of the possible outcomes we need to introduce '*Rules*'. We briefly introduced those in Chapter 5, but we shall look at them in more detail in Section 7.4.

People who are used to other modelling methods and tools that don't have the concept of the *Event-driven process chain* often wonder about the value of introducing events. They are more used to just stringing functions together one after another. We shall see in Section 7.3.2 that the addition of events to the process model introduces a degree of rigour that makes ARIS models a more accurate representation of the 'real world' and hence increases their value.

The important rules to bear in mind when using the *Event-driven process chain* are:

- Every model must have at least one start event and one end event,
- Functions and events always alternate.

**Event**

Order Received

**Function**

Enter Order

**Event**

Order Entered

**Function**

Calculate Cost

**Event**

Cost Calculated

**Fig. 7.2** Event-driven Process Chain

Functions should not normally connect to another function and events should never connect to other events. With simple models it is easy to ensure the '*greens*' and '*purples*' always alternate, but in larger models, with many rules, it can be a bit trickier to ensure this rule is followed. The easiest way to do this is just to follow each path, ignore the rules, and check that the functions and events alternate.

**Expert Tip** – creating an appropriate Method Filter can be used to enforce modelling conventions such as not allowing functions to connect to other functions.

### 7.3.1    Naming Events in the EPC

The naming of events in the EPC requires some additional explanation. The way we view the events depends to a large extent on whether they are at the start of the process, the end of the process, or in the middle (Fig. 7.3).

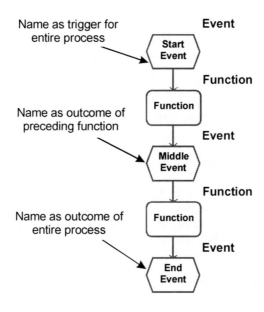

**Fig. 7.3** Naming Events

### Start Event

The event at the top of a process represents the change in the external world that causes the entire process to be initiated. It triggers the first function in the process and its name is normally chosen to be something meaningful and significant to the process as a whole, rather than just something relevant for the first function. Thus we might call the event "*Customer Order Received*" rather than "*Envelope in Post Tray*".

### End Event

The event at the end of the process represents the completion of the whole process (or that part of it described in the model). The end event may often be the trigger for a further process in another model, so it is wise to choose a name that is meaningful when viewed at the end of the model or at the start of another. Its name is not, therefore, necessarily directly related to the function that created it which may be of little importance.

In the example shown in Fig. 7.2, the last event was **Cost Calculated**. In reality, there would probably be further functions and events after this step, but if it really were the end of the process, we would probably give it a more significant name such as "*Order Entry Complete*".

### Internal Events

Events in the middle of a process, those connecting the sequence of functions together, are both trigger events for the following function and outcome events for the preceding function. That gives us a problem; do we label them to reflect what has just happened or what is about to happen? The normal convention is to name them to reflect the outcome of the previous function. As we shall see below, this helps us to establish that we have correctly described what the functions do and how the process flows.

In processes where there is a long sequence of functions and events without any change in control flow, the names of the intervening events will be trivial and will not add much value. Some people are tempted to miss these events out, but this can be dangerous as we shall see later. However, occasionally, an event may denote that a significant stage in the process has been reached. In this case, it is perfectly acceptable to give the event a more significant name, just as we did with the 'end event'. Such naming should be used sparingly to create more effect.

### 7.3.2    Why Use Events?

People new to ARIS, especially those who have used other flowcharting or modelling tools, often wonder about the value of adding events between every function. Why not just connect functions directly together as shown in Fig. 7.4a? In ARIS it is possible to connect functions together, if this is enabled in the Method Filter. However, there are good reasons not to do this because adding and naming events is:

- a good check of correct definition of the function,
- a good check of correct process flow.

The first reason for not directly connecting functions together is that the discipline of working out what event follows a function is an extremely good check that the function has been correctly described:

- Does the function really occur as a consequence of the event?
- Does the event always trigger the function or are there other conditions that must also be met?

Also look at the event following the function:

- Does it describe what has changed as a result of executing the function?
- Is it the only outcome or are there several alternatives?

If you can't work out what has changed, it is likely that the definition of the function is not correct. If rather a lot seems to have changed, did all this change as a result of this one activity? It may be that what the function is representing is not really just one activity, but a number of activities (parallel or sequential) wrapped up together that would be better shown separately. Check if the granularity and importance of this function is similar to those in the rest of the model.

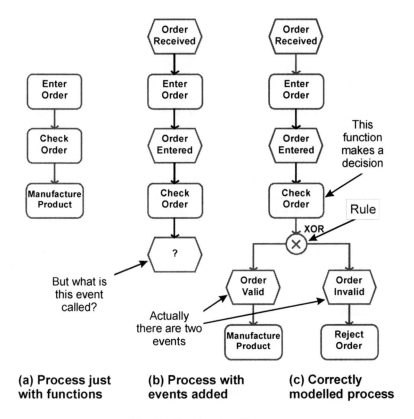

**Fig. 7.4** The Benefit of Events

The second reason for using events is that the careful consideration of the event following a function will make it clear where decisions are being made that affect process flow. Look again at the process just using functions in Fig. 7.4a. The process looks like a straightforward chain of activities: **Enter Order**, **Check Order** and **Manufacture Product**. But now look at the process in Fig. 7.4b where events have been added between the functions. In particular, look at the event following the function **Check Order**. What should this be called? It is tempting to label it "*Order Checked*". At first sight this looks correct, but look again; does it really make sense? What has changed as a result of checking the order? It is too simplistic to say the order has been checked. Why has the order been checked?

The step adds no value unless there is a reason for checking the order and hence more than one possible outcome. People often make this mistake when first starting to use ARIS. If asked "why was the order checked?" modellers nearly always know why (e.g. to see if the order is valid or if it is above a certain monetary value) yet they have not reflected this knowledge in the model. As a result, they miss the obvious fact that there is more than one outcome from executing the function. The function not only carries out the check, but also makes a decision about what should happen next.

If we now look at the correct process model in Fig. 7.4c we can see there is a rule after the function which is followed by two events. These events now represent the two possible outcomes of the decision taken by the **Check Order** function. The rule represents the logic of the outcome (e.g. with an *XOR* only one of them can occur at any one time). We will look at rules in detail in Section 7.4.

In the simple example above we assumed there was only one outcome from **Enter Order**, but two outcomes from **Check Order**. Of course, it is also possible there may be more than one outcome from **Enter Order**. For instance, order entry might fail and alternative action may be necessary. It is a matter of judgement how much detail you will need to model. Remember:

> **"Don't model the universe!"**
> **"Know when you have done enough."**
> **"Define standards and stick to them."**

Thus, far from being an unnecessary effort, the addition of events between functions adds a degree of rigour to process modelling. This helps ensure the models are a more accurate reflection of what really happens. The disadvantage is the models become larger, which makes concise presentation more difficult.

If you really must, you can remove the 'trivial' events between strings of functions, particularly in high-level models. However, we would strongly recommend you initially build your models with all the events in place. Only once you are confident the model is correct should you delete the trivial events

## 7.4 Rules and Process Flow

As we said above, real processes do not just consist of sequential steps. The need to cope with parallel paths, decisions, multiple triggers and complex flows is the reason we use modelling tools to represent processes. To model a process flow we add '*Rules*' to the functions and events previously described. We saw an example of this in the previous section (Fig. 7.4c) where there were two possible outcomes from a decision, only one of which can be true at any one time.

### 7.4.1 Rules

There are three basic types of rule, as shown in Table 7.3, and they have slightly different usage depending on whether they follow or precede functions.

Understanding the flow of process models requires an understanding of how rules combine with functions and events to represent decisions and parallel paths. Decisions (see Section 7.5) use *OR* and *XOR* rules, while parallel paths (see Section 7.6) use *AND* rules. Some combinations are not valid in any circumstances while others are valid, but are confusing so we will not show them. If you use the rules as defined above and in the examples that follow, you will be able to correctly model the majority of process flow situations.

**Table 7.3** ARIS Rules

| Operator | Following a Function<br>(*single input, multiple outputs*) | Preceding a Function<br>(*multiple inputs, single output*) |
|---|---|---|
| **OR** | **OR** *– Decision*<br>One or many possible paths will be followed as a result of the decision. | **OR** *– Trigger*<br>Any one event, or combination of events, will trigger the Function. |
| **XOR** | **Exclusive OR** *– Decision*<br>One, but only one, of the possible paths will be followed. | **Exclusive OR** *– Trigger*<br>One, but only one, of the possible events will be the trigger. |
| **AND** | **AND** *– Parallel Path*<br>Process flow splits into two or more parallel paths. | **AND** *– Trigger*<br>All events must occur in order to trigger the following Function. [1] |

**Note 1**: It may be necessary to consider a time period during which all the events must occur in order for the AND trigger to be valid.

**Expert Tip** – to change a rule to one of a different type (e.g. *OR* to *XOR*), select the operator, Right-Click > Properties [*Format / Object Appearance*] and select the new operator from the *Symbol* field scroll box. Then select the *Attributes Tab* on the *Properties Bar* and change the *Name* attribute of the operator.

# 7.5      Decisions

In the ARIS EPC modelling method decisions are made by functions; the name of the function describing the decision being taken.

### 7.5.1      Modelling Decisions

The function makes the decision and connects to a rule which determines the logic of the possible outcomes (e.g. *OR* or *XOR*). The rule has a single input and two or more outputs. The outputs lead to events that indicate which particular outcome of the decision has triggered that path of the process (see Fig. 7.5b).

You should avoid having *OR* or *XOR* rules following an event because there is no function to make the decision about which path to follow. You do sometimes see this in top-level models. For instance, in Fig. 7.5a an event **Order Received** connects to an *OR* which connects to parallel paths that each process a different type of order. The assumption here is that when the order is received it is routed to the appropriate path of the order-handling process.

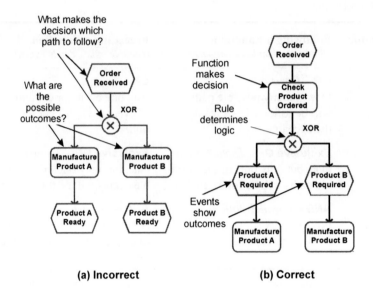

**Fig. 7.5** Modelling Decisions

Although this shorthand approach keeps the model simple, it can give a false impression of what is actually happening. If the order is actually routed to different processes, it is better to model the function that representing the routing decision, even if it is automatic (Fig. 7.5b). If, on the other hand, the orders aren't routed to the particular process, but the customer sends the order to a different address depending on the product, then they are in fact entirely separate processes and it is a mistake to model them as if they were one.

Incorrect modelling of decisions is one of the most common mistakes people make using ARIS (after not modelling decisions at all!). Typically people don't model what actually happens, but some idealised version of it. This only leads to problems later during implementation, analysis or re-design.

### 7.5.2    Decision Rules

There are two rules we can use to represent decisions:

- *OR* – Any combination of paths,
- *XOR* – One path or the other, but not both.

It is very tempting to model everything using an *OR* operator because this is the term we use in everyday language. However, in practice most decisions can only take one of the possible outcomes and hence should be modelled using the *XOR*.

The exceptions to this are situations similar to the order-processing example above. For example, imagine a business with different processes for delivering each different product it sells. When an order arrives it might be for just one product, or it may be for a combination of products. To model this situation you should use an *OR* operator after the function to allow for any combination of processes flows to be initiated. However, you should remember that later in the process there must be a step that makes sure the correct combination of products has been assembled before final delivery (see Fig. 7.6). These situations are not that common, so we can state the general rule:

- Always model decisions with an *XOR* unless you are certain multiple combinations can actually occur.

### 7.5.3    Joining Decision Paths

The result of a decision is to send the process down one or more alternative paths. Sometimes one of those paths may be a dead-end where the process stops but, normally, the paths join back together at some point to complete the process. The join should always be made using the same rule used to make the split after the decision, as shown in Fig. 7.6.

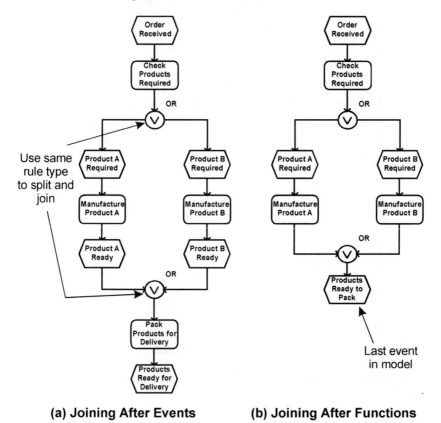

**(a) Joining After Events**            **(b) Joining After Functions**

**Fig. 7.6** Joining Decision Paths

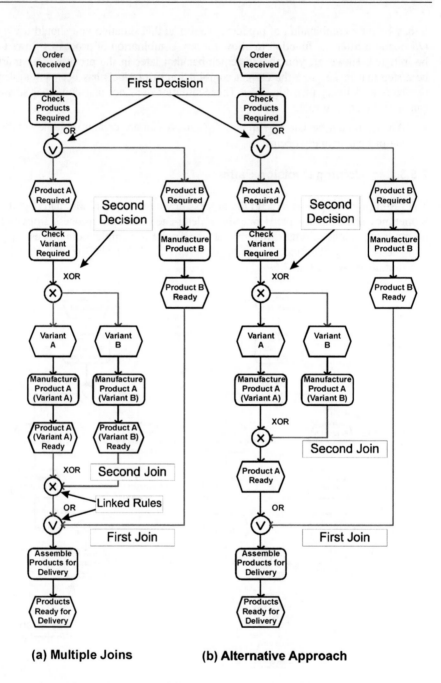

**(a) Multiple Joins**          **(b) Alternative Approach**

**Fig. 7.7** Multiple Joins

The question arises: should the join be made after the events in the alternative paths or after the functions? Provided you ensure the functions and events correctly alternate, it doesn't really matter. Normally it is better to have the join after the events (Fig. 7.6a) so the event at the end of each path marks the completion of the path. The '*joining*' rule is then followed by a function.

If you need to make the join at the very end of a process, often there are no other functions after the join and before the final event. In this case you will have to put the rule before the final event and the paths must end in functions (Fig. 7.6b). Often, paths split from several different decisions will join at the same point. In that case, although you can bring all the joining paths together at the same rule, it is good practice to use individual rules and join the rules as in Fig. 7.7a. This is essential if the rules are of different types (e.g. *OR* and *XOR*).

Fig. 7.7b shows an alternative approach. The *OR* rule that joins the path from the **Product B Required** flow is separated by an event (**Product A Ready**) from the *XOR* rule that combines the paths from the **Product A Required** flow. This is possible because the **Variant A** and **Variant B** paths in the **Product A Required** flow have been modelled ending in functions. Although we said it was generally better to end paths in events, this representation probably leads to a clearer model. This just goes to show there is no single correct way to model a process. Provided you follow the alternating event–function chain you may choose the representation that seems to make the most sense in terms of the process you are modelling.

### 7.5.4    Do-nothing Decision Paths

You make think paths resulting from decisions where nothing subsequently happens would be pointless, but in fact they occur quite often. Look at the example in Fig. 7.8a. If the paint is still wet we have to wait for it to dry before applying the second coat. If the paint is already dry we can carry straight on to apply the second coat so there is no need for a task, and hence a function, in the "paint dry" path.

Fig. 7.8b shows an alternative way to represent this. This time there is no event or function in the "paint dry" path, but just a connecting line. The left-hand example has the advantage that the events after the rule make it clear what the outcome of the decision is. On the other hand, the right-hand example looks cleaner and it is very obvious nothing happens in the "paint dry" path. However, it is not so clear which outcome triggered the "do nothing" path and we have had to resort to putting a label on the path to make it clear. Once again you have to choose the most appropriate method for the process you are modelling.

**Warning** – if you should need two events with the same name, it is essential you create two separate events. On no account should you copy the event object. In any case, it is good practice to make the names of similar events slightly different.

If we didn't need a second coat and **Paint Dry** was the end of the process, we would have no choice but to use the right-hand representation, because we need to end the process in an Event.

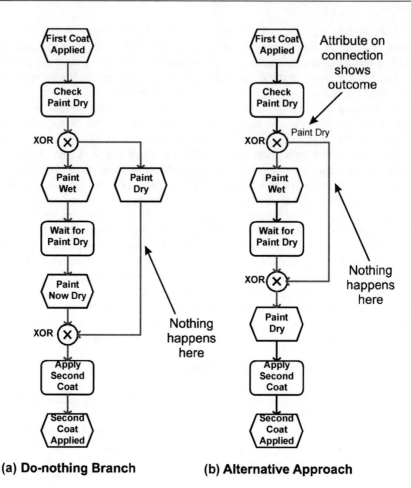

**(a) Do-nothing Branch**          **(b) Alternative Approach**

**Fig. 7.8** Do-nothing Paths

## 7.6 Parallel Paths

Parallel paths use the *AND* rule which separates the process into two or more paths. The paths normally re-combine in an *AND* later on in the process. When they re-combine, the process cannot continue until all the paths joining at the *AND* have been completed. In the example in Fig. 7.9 we now have to complete both the **Manufacture Product A** and **Manufacture Product B** flows for every order.

The *AND* split is normally made after an event, and best practice is to re-combine after the last event in the parallel paths. Again this is not a hard and fast rule. You can re-combine after functions and put a single event after the *AND* which represents all the paths being completed.

The former is better for long complex process paths and the latter for simple parallel tasks.

Splitting the process into parallel paths implies they can be done at the same time because they have no dependence on each other. Of course, just because you have modelled it that way, doesn't mean they will actually happen at the same time. There may be no process dependence, but if the same person has to do both tasks, then only one can be done at a time. Even if different people do the tasks, there is still no guarantee they will work in parallel; there could be a significant gap between the one branch completing and the other even starting. Collecting real process data will enable you to check if the process is being executed as you intended. Simulating the process with *ARIS Simulation* will enable you to check if the allocated resource can achieve what you intended.

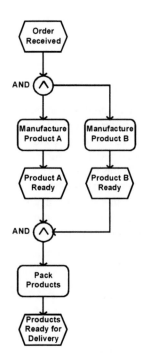

## 7.7     Triggers

### 7.7.1     Basic Triggers

**Fig. 7.9** Parallel Paths

Most of the examples so far have a single event triggering the start of the process. The event represents a change of state in the external environment that requires the process to start.

When defining trigger events it is important to make sure the event, by itself, is sufficient to trigger the process. For instance, an order received by telephone is an obvious trigger. The telephone rings, someone answers it and takes the order. Similarly, an order received by FAX also seems to be a trigger. If you were modelling the sales process at a high-level you would certainly show telephone and FAX as alternative triggers. However, at a more detailed level, they may not be equivalent. There is no guarantee that when a FAX arrives anyone will notice and process the order. It may be necessary to design a process where, periodically, someone checks the FAX and deals with the orders.

Processes often fail because tasks that are 'so obvious' are not modelled and as a result no one does them; everyone assumes someone else does it. A good example is an Internet web site that gives an e-mail address for making contact, but when you send a message no one ever replies!

Always scrutinise your events and apply the following tests:

- Does the event represent an external 'change of state'?
- Does the change of state itself directly trigger the process as opposed to just influencing it?

- Is the event sufficient to trigger the process or are there other conditions that must be met?

## 7.7.2    Multiple Triggers

Often a process can be triggered by several different events; Fig. 7.10 shows three examples modelled with different rules. As we saw with decisions, the use of the *XOR* is more common than the *OR*. However, it is very important to work out the correct logic for triggering the process.

In the first example, Fig. 7.10a, we can see the start of an order entry process triggered by the customer making a telephone call or by sending a FAX. At first sight this seems fairly straightforward and it is modelled with an *XOR*. But, what happens if the customer telephones to place an order, but also sends a FAX confirmation? In that case either or both events will trigger the process.

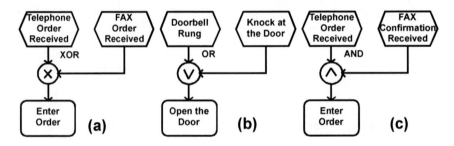

**Fig. 7.10** Multiple Triggers

To handle this situation we might be tempted to replace the *XOR* with the *OR*, but is this correct? The telephone call would always trigger the process, but if it is common for customers to also send a FAX confirmation, then when a FAX is received it would be necessary to associate the FAX with any previous telephone order to make sure the order was only placed once. This means the process for handling receipt of a FAX is slightly different from receiving a telephone call and needs to be modelled differently.

We can now see that modelling triggers using an *OR* can be a bit awkward. If you do use the *OR* you should think very carefully about what it means. In the example in Fig. 7.10b the triggers are **Doorbell Rung** *OR* **Knock at the Door**. This means any combination of those events can trigger the process. Either event will trigger the process by themselves and it is pretty obvious a visitor may knock on the door and ring the bell at the same time and it stills triggers you to open the door in the same way. Well maybe you might answer it just that bit more quickly, but you still only open it the once.

To make valid use of the *OR* we have to be certain if both events occur at the same time they have exactly the same triggering effect as either one occurring by itself. If we decide they never occur simultaneously then, provided they both have the same triggering effect, we should use *XOR*. If they have different effects then we need more complex logic; we also have to think about what time period counts as being '*simultaneous*'. These different scenarios are summarised in Table 7.4.

**Table 7.4** Event-triggering Logic

| Occurrence | Effect | Model with |
|---|---|---|
| Non-simultaneous events | Each have same effect. | *XOR* |
| Non-simultaneous events | Each have different effect. | More complex logic required. |
| Simultaneous events | Same effect as when they occur individually. | *OR* |
| Simultaneous events | Different effect from when they occur individually. | More complex logic required. |
| Simultaneous events | Both required to trigger. | *AND* |

The third example, Fig. 7.10c, shows triggers combined with an *AND*. Both events have to occur before the function is executed. In this example we have insisted the customer confirm telephone orders by FAX before we process them. However, we come across the problem of time periods again. If the customer places the telephone order, but we never receive the FAX, the process just stalls. In practice we might prefer to give the customer a call if we haven't received the FAX by the next day. Therefore, we need to consider during what time period the events combined by an *AND* must arrive for the process to be triggered and, if not all the events arrive during that period, what we do instead?

The above examples are rather contrived, but they help to make the point that you need to think carefully about how multiple events combine to trigger a process. The use of a single rule may seem an easy way out of describing an awkward scenario, but it may cause you to gloss over vital detail that should be modelled in a more complete way.

## 7.8    Loops

To cope with more complex process flows and decisions we need to introduce the concept of loops. A loop returns a process to an earlier stage to re-run that part of the process again. Fig. 7.11 shows a slightly more complex version of our order-handling process. The process requires a FAX confirmation to be received before the original telephone order can be processed. Because there might be a delay before the FAX is received, the process checks to see if the order is still valid, i.e. the price is still correct. If the order is OK, the **Order Current** event will link to the rest of the order-handling process (not shown). If the order is no longer valid, the customer is asked if they want to re-order with the revised prices. If they do, the process loops back to the top of the process to go through the order and confirmation activities again.

To link the loop into the process we have broken the connection between the first event and function and inserted an *XOR* operator to make the connection for the loop. You will notice it is an *XOR* and not an *OR* because, logically, the initial trigger and the loop trigger could never occur together. A new order and a re-order may arrive at the same time, but one would have to wait its turn.

The process continues exactly as before with the customer still needing to confirm by FAX. Of course, if the customer once again delays sending the FAX, the order may go out of date again and so we would go around the loop another time. If this continues to happen, we could go around the loop forever; that's the problem with loops – they loop! So in practice we would need an escape route. Perhaps if the order goes out of date twice we would just cancel it.

You do need to be sure when you send the process flow back to an earlier point, that the same process does repeat in exactly the same way. Often when process exceptions or errors occur, and the process loops back to an earlier point, it will get special attention the next time around and it may not be true to model it as if it were exactly

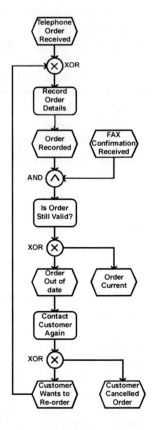

**Fig. 7.11** Loops

the same as the first time. In our example, (Fig. 7.11), we have shown the **Record Order Details** step being repeated. However, in practice it would not be necessary to re-enter the whole order again, but just to update the prices. Typically, there is some special processing in the loop back which then joins the main process later than might be first thought. It is a matter of judgement whether to draw attention to the detailed differences occurring after a loop back.

## 7.9      Horizontal or Vertical Layout?

The *Event-driven process chain* can be drawn either horizontally or vertically. As we have seen in Chapter 5, we can have ARIS automatically layout the model and one of the options we can chose is horizontal or vertical orientation. All the examples in this book are shown in vertical format as they fit the page better. Although some people prefer to lay out processes horizontally, so they can see the process flowing from left to right, experience has shown that EPCs are easier to follow in a vertical format.

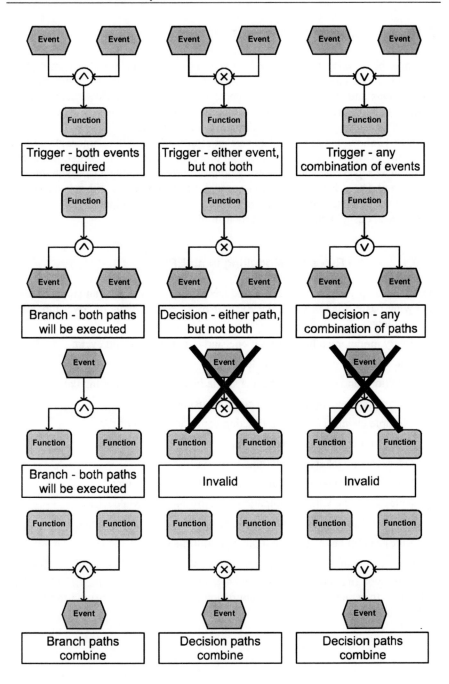

**Fig. 7.12** Function, Event and Rule Combinations

## 7.10      Putting it All Together

You may be thinking the *Event-driven process chain* is really rather complicated. However, all we have been doing is combining the three basic object types (*Functions*, *Events* and *Rules*) together to represent various process flow scenarios. It is possible to combine these objects together in many different ways. Some of these are valid and some are invalid, as summarised in Fig. 7.12.

Fig. 7.13 shows a more complete version of our order-handling process incorporating many of the scenarios introduced in this chapter. But don't forget, not everything can be represented as a process. Complex project planning, tasks with multiple options and data driven systems don't model well as processes, either because they can be better represented in other ways or because they use a high degree of human intelligence, design and planning in their implementation.

### 7.10.1     The Rules for Modelling in an EPC

Based on the principles we have introduced in this chapter we can summarise the following basic rules of using the *Event-driven process chain* to cover modelling process flows:

- Every model must have at least one start event and one end event,
- Functions and events always alternate,
- Functions and events only have a single incoming and outgoing connection,
- Process paths always split and combine using rules,
- Multiple events triggering a function combine using a rule,
- Rules cannot follow a single event,
- Decisions are taken by functions,
- Functions that take decisions are always followed by rules,
- Rules show the valid combination of paths that follow a decision,
- Events following rules indicate the actual outcomes of decisions,
- Rules cannot have multiple input and multiple outputs.

These rules follow the ARIS Method, but in some cases are more prescriptive than those you may come across in an ARIS training course or in *ARIS Help*. This is in order to remove some of the confusion that occurs when people use rules in ambiguous ways.

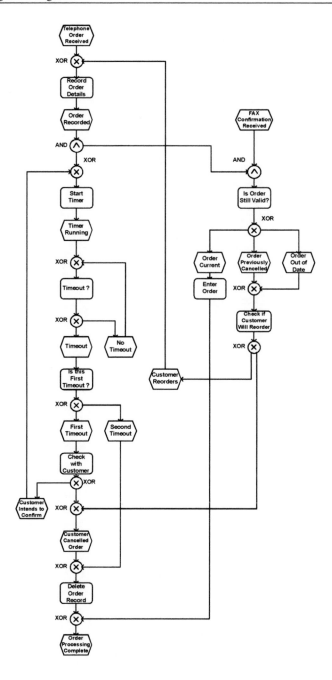

**Fig. 7.13** Putting it All Together

# Chapter 8　　ARIS Explorer Module

In this chapter we look in detail at the facilities available in the ARIS Explorer Module. We look at the group hierarchy, how to manipulate items in the groups, when and why you need a user name and password to log into a database and how to set your default passwords.

## 8.1　　Introduction

The ARIS *Explorer Module* (Fig. 8.1) is similar to Microsoft Windows Explorer; it is used for creating, viewing and manipulating ARIS databases, groups, models and objects. It comprises the *Explorer Toolbar*, the *Explorer Checkboxes* and the *Explorer Window* with the *Navigation Bar*.

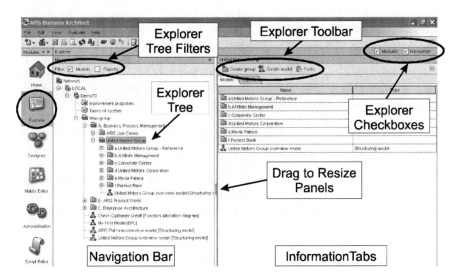

**Fig. 8.1** ARIS Explorer Module

## 8.2　　Explorer Window

The ARIS *Explorer Window* has two main areas, the left-hand *Navigation Bar* with its *Explorer Tree* and the right-hand area with *Information Tabs*. You can adjust the relative width of the areas by clicking and dragging the centre partition. You can also toggle the left-hand *Navigation Bar* on and off by clicking on *Navigation Checkbox* at the top right-hand corner of the *Explorer Window*. To the left of the *Explorer Window* is the *Modules Bar* (see Chapter 6) which can also be toggled on and off using the *Modules Checkbox*.

### 8.2.1 Navigation Bar

The *Navigation Bar* at the left-hand side of the *Explorer Window* displays an *Explorer Tree* with a hierarchical list of ARIS items including: ARIS servers, databases, models, objects and their directory structure (*'groups'*). When you select an item in the *Explorer Tree*, the *Information Tabs* on the right-hand side display its contents and information about the selected item.

### 8.2.2 Information Tabs

The *Information Tabs* on the right-hand of the *Explorer Window* show the contents of the item selected in the left-hand *Explorer Tree*. Different types of item will be displayed (model, object, occurrence, etc.) depending on what has been selected. The label at the top of the tab shows what is being displayed. For some items, the display will have several tabs so you can switch between different views of its contents. For instance, select a group in the *Explorer Tree* and the *Information Tabs* display either the models or objects in that group.

### 8.2.3 Explorer Toolbar

The *Explorer Toolbar* is located at the right-hand side of the *Explorer Window* above the *Information Tabs*. It contains context-sensitive buttons whose action depends on the item selected in *Explorer Tree* and *Information Tabs* (see Table 8.1 and Fig. 8.2).

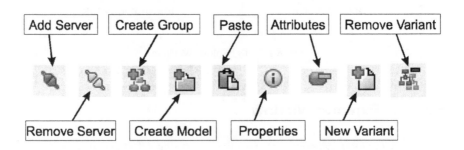

**Fig. 8.2** Explorer Toolbar Buttons

**Table 8.1** Explorer Toolbar Buttons

| Selected item in Navigation Bar | Selected Information Tab | Buttons |
|---|---|---|
| Network | Server | Add server..., Remove server. |
| Server | Server Contents | |
| Database | Database Contents | |
| Group | Models | Create group, Create model, Paste. |
| | Objects | Create group, Create object, Paste. |
| Model | Occurrences | Properties, Attributes (These relate to objects and require an object occurrence to be selected in the tab). |
| | Variants | New..., Remove. |
| Object | Variants | New..., Remove. |

 **Question** – why are the Properties and Attributes buttons greyed out on the *Explorer Toolbar*?
**Answer** – it's because you haven't selected an object occurrence in one of the *Information Tabs*.

## 8.2.4 Explorer Filters

The *Explorer Filter Checkboxes* are located above the *Navigation Bar* and control whether models or objects are displayed in the *Explorer Tree*.

## 8.2.5 Left-Click Operations

As you would expect, a left-click on an item selects it. In the *Explorer Tree*, a left-click may also do more than that. If you left-click on an ARIS server then ARIS will try to make a physical connection to the server. Left-click on a database and ARIS will attempt to log into and open the database.

## 8.2.6 Right-Click Operations

A right-click on an item brings up a pop-up *Right-Click Menu* (Fig. 8.3) showing many of the valid operations for that item. These normally duplicate options that can be selected from the *Main Menu*, but the *Right-Click Menu* is often more useful as it gives quick access to commands appropriate for the item selected. Two of the most useful *Right-Click Menu* options are:

- Right-Click > Attributes…,
- Right-Click > Properties.

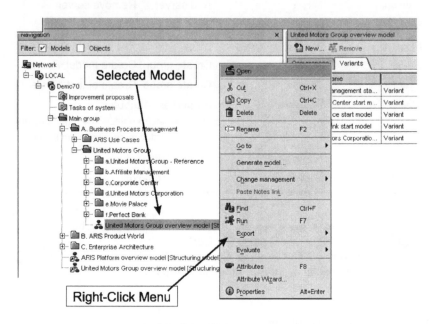

**Fig. 8.3** Right-Click Pop-up Menu

A right-click operation can also be associated with a drag and drop. If you select a group, model or object, right-click and drag it to a new group, when you release the mouse the *Right-Click Menu* will display move, copy or paste options.

## 8.3     The Navigation Bar

The hierarchy of items that can be viewed and manipulated in the ARIS *Explorer Module* comprises:

- Servers     (Business Architect only),
- Databases  (Business Architect only),
- Folders,
- Groups,
- Models,
- Objects.

The hierarchy is displayed in the *Explorer Tree* in the left-hand *Navigation Bar* (Fig. 8.4). You can drill down the hierarchy by double-clicking the item names or clicking the adjacent "**+**" sign until there are no more levels to drill down.  You can quickly go up to the previous higher level of the hierarchy by clicking on the Up Button on the *ARIS Toolbar*.

**Hint** – *ARIS Help* is inconsistent in its use of the terms *Navigation Tree* and *Explorer Tree*. We shall use the term *Explorer Tree*.

In Chapter 5 we saw that when you start *ARIS Business Designer* you are asked to select a server and a database. As a result, when you use the *Explorer Module* in *Business Designer* you will not see any servers or database in the *Explorer Tree* which starts at the group level. On the other hand, the *Explorer Module* in *Business Architect* displays the full hierarchy of ARIS items, as shown in Fig. 8.4.

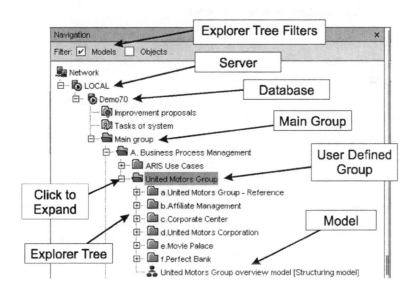

**Fig. 8.4** Explorer Hierarchy

When a group is selected in the *Explorer Tree*, in addition to sub-groups, the *Explorer Tree* can also show the models and object in these groups. The visibility of models and objects is controlled by the *Explorer Filter Checkboxes* just above the *Explorer Tree*. Toggling these checkboxes on and off will allow the display of models, objects, both or neither. Typically, the most useful setting is to have *Models* turned on and *Objects* turned off. Displaying objects does allow some specific information about objects (e.g. their variants) to be displayed in the *Information Tabs,* but it does cause the *Explorer Tree* display to be rather cluttered.

## 8.4      The ARIS Network of Servers

At the top of the hierarchy is the ARIS **Network** containing all the '*ARIS servers*' you can connect to on your local PC or via a network. You will have a **LOCAL** server which contains databases on your PC's hard drive and, if your PC is connected to a network, you may also be able to connect to one or more networked ARIS servers.

**ARIS Business Architect** – allows databases to be stored in a **LOCAL** server on the PC's hard disk in addition to a networked ARIS Server while *ARIS Business Designer* only allows access to databases on an ARIS server.

### 8.4.1      Connecting to a New Server

To make a new connection to a networked ARIS server:

1.   Select **Network**,
2.   Right-Click > <u>A</u>dd server…,
3.   Type in the name of your server, or its Internet Protocol (IP) address, into the *Server name or IP address* field of the *New server Dialog Box*,
4.   Press OK.

You may need advice from your *ARIS Server Administrator* on exactly how to connect to the server. If you are actually connected to the network when you are defining the connection, tick the *Text connection Checkbox*. ARIS will attempt to connect to the server and give you an error message if a server with the specified name is not available. You may still define a connection even if you are not currently connected to the network. In this case, leave *Test connection* unchecked.

You may remove a server definition by selecting the server name and using the Right-Click > Rem<u>o</u>ve server command.

### 8.4.2      Using a Networked Server

To connect to a networked server, click on the name of a server listed under **Network**. If the server is available, the little computer symbol next to the server name will change to show a green arrow and ARIS will display a list of all the databases on the server. If ARIS cannot make a connection, an error message will be displayed and the computer symbol will show a red dot. If this happens, you should check your network connection is working and you have entered the correct server name or IP address. If you cannot get this to work, seek help from your *ARIS Server Administrator*.

**Warning** – when using an ARIS server you may intuitively feel you should log out or disconnect from the server before exiting from ARIS. Thus is not necessary and you should avoid using the Right-Click > Remove server command as this completely removes the server connection definition and the next time you want to use the server you will have to make the definition again. Provided you have logged out of all the databases on the server (Right-Click > Log off), it is quite safe just to exit from ARIS.

Once you have connected to a networked server you can access its databases in exactly the same way as described in the next section for the *LOCAL* server.

### 8.4.3    The LOCAL Server

When using *Business Architect* you can see what databases are available on your PC's hard disk by clicking on the *LOCAL* server name. The little computer symbol next to the name will change to show a green arrow. To expand the hierarchy display, either double-click on *LOCAL* or click on the "**+**" sign next to the name just as you would in Microsoft Windows Explorer. A list of databases should appear represented as blue cylinders (e.g. *DEMO70*).

### 8.4.4    Databases

To open a database in *LOCAL*, click on the database name. You will be logged in automatically with a default user name and password.

Once the database opens, the blue database symbol next to the database name will change to show a little green arrow. To expand the hierarchy display, either double-click on *LOCAL* or again click on the "**+**" sign next to the name. A list of folders should appear. You don't actually have to open the database and expand the hierarchy as two separate operations; you can do it all in one go by double-clicking the database name or clicking on the "**+**" sign.

Each ARIS database contains, by default, a set of folders at the top-level. For the moment we are only interested in the folder labelled *Main Group*. In ARIS, the term *Group* is used to denote those folders containing models, objects and other groups (sub-groups). *Main Group* is the top-level group under which all other sub-groups are located. If you wish, the name of *Main Group* can be changed by selecting it and Right-Click > Rename (or press <F2>).

### 8.4.5    Database Usernames and Passwords

To open a database, either in **LOCAL** or on a networked ARIS server, click on the database name. One of two things will now happen. Either the database will open or your will be asked to enter a *User name* and *Password* (Fig. 8.5). If the database is on a networked ARIS server, you will almost certainly be asked for a user name and password. If you are working locally this will only happen if you have deliberately set things up this way.

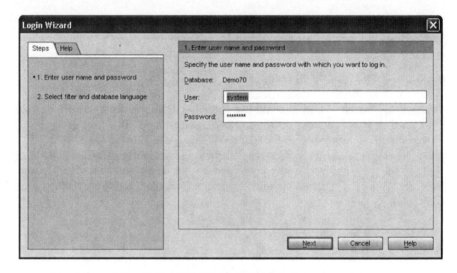

**Fig. 8.5** Login Wizard

In all the examples so far we have assumed the database opens directly, however it is important to understand why sometimes you will be asked for a user name and password, and sometimes not. All ARIS databases, whether in **LOCAL** or on a server, have one or more *User Accounts*. By default all new databases are created with a single **system** user account. Additional accounts can be created by someone who has appropriate administration privileges.

### The System Account

All new ARIS databases are created with a **system** account with the following default user name and password:

- **system**      default *User name* = "system",
- **system**      default *Password* = "manager".

To change the password of the **system** account:

1.   Login using the **system** account,

2.   Select the database name in the *Explorer Tree*,

3.   Eile > Database > Change password...  or Right-Click > Change password...,

4.   Enter the existing and new passwords into the *Change password Dialog Box* (Fig. 8.6).

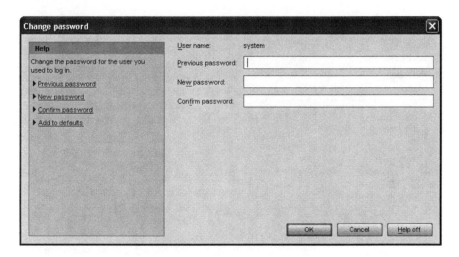

**Fig. 8.6** Change Password Dialog Box

The **system** account is very powerful because it has all the user privileges and access rights enabled. It is recommended you change the password of this account to prevent access by unauthorised users; this is essential for databases on a networked ARIS server.

 **Warning** – if you change the **system** account password and make a mistake or subsequently forget it you will be unable to access the database again. If this happens you would need to contact IDS Scheer for them to unlock the database. One way around this is to create a second account with system privileges with a different name and password.

### Default Login

When you are working on a **LOCAL** database you may only ever log into it using the **system** account. To save you having to enter the user name and password each time, ARIS allows you to store a default user name and password that will be used for automatic log in.

Initially these defaults are set to the default **system** account user name and password (i.e. "system" and "manager"). If you try to open a database where the

***system*** password has not been changed you will be logged straight in. If the ***system*** account password has been changed, ARIS will display a *Login Wizard* for you to enter a different user name and password (see Fig. 8.5).

To change the default log in user name and password:

5.  Select View > Options... [*Log in*] from the *Main Menu*,

6.  Change the values in {*User Defaults: User name*} and {*User Defaults: Password*} see Fig. 8.7). These values are case sensitive.

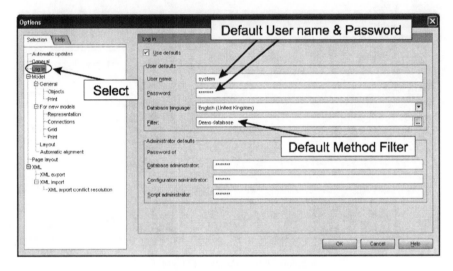

**Fig. 8.7** Log In Options Dialog Box

### *Accessing Server Accounts*

If you access a networked ARIS server, the *ARIS Server Administrator* will almost certainly have changed the ***system*** account password and allocated you a specific user name and password of your own. You will, therefore, always be asked to enter that user name and password when you log in. If you frequently log into the same server database (or all your databases have the same user name and password), you can change the default values in the *User name* and *Password* fields in View > Options... [Login] to match. Now ARIS will use these values as the default log in and you won't see the *Login Wizard*.

 **Warning** – setting the default *User name* and *Password* fields to automatically log you into a server database means anyone using your copy of ARIS can open the database without knowing a user name and password. This could be a serious security breach and may contravene your company's security policy.

**Hint** – if *User Accounts* have been defined for a database, but the password for the **system** account has not been changed you can force ARIS to ask you to log in with a user name and password rather than just automatically logging you into the **system** account. Instead of clicking on the database name to open it, right-click and select the Log In... command. To force manual log in for all databases, deselect *Use Defaults* in View > Options... [*Log in*].

## 8.4.6      Logging Off a Database

Logging into a database was a bit involved, but logging out is simplicity itself. Just close any models you may have open, select the database name and Right-Click > Log Off. The green arrow on the blue database symbol now disappears. You can tell which databases are open by looking for the green arrow on the database symbols. You can close all open models in one operation by selecting the Window > Close all command from the *Main Menu*; you will be prompted to save any unsaved models.

## 8.4.7      Method Filters

In Chapter 3 we looked at the underlying ARIS concepts. The implementation of these concepts in the ARIS product range is known as the '*ARIS Method*'. The ARIS Method is very comprehensive with over 150 models, 200 objects and 1500 attributes. It is unlikely that any single modelling project would need to use all elements of the ARIS Method so ARIS provides '*Method Filters*' that restrict which ARIS items are available at any one time.

A number of Method Filters are provided with ARIS and users with appropriate access rights can define their own filters. Filters are available at the server level and are applied to databases and users of that database. Thus filters can be used to define which models can be created and used in a specific database. Different users of the database can be given access via different filters to provide them with different views of the information and also to restrict which items can be edited.

### Effects of Method Filters

The restricting effect of Method Filters can often be confusing to new users.

**Question** – why can't I see my models when I open a database, where have they gone?

**Answer** – if you open a database with a specific Method Filter, but the database contains models not defined in the filter, they won't be visible; nor will any objects not in the filter. Make sure you are using the correct Method Filter.

If you open a model in the *Designer Module* containing objects not in the Method Filter, they will be greyed-out and you won't be able to perform any operations on them. If the objects are defined in the filter, but not the connections between them, you won't be able to connect them up. So whenever you think all your models have been deleted or ARIS isn't working properly – don't panic – check to see if you are using the correct filter!

### Selecting A Method Filter

If you are accessing ARIS databases on a server, when you log into the database, the Method Filter (or a limited choice of filters) will normally have been defined for you by the *ARIS System Administrator*. When you are using databases in the **LOCAL** area on your PC, normally you will have free choice over which filter to use.

To check which filter you are currently using with a database:

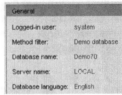

1.  Select the database name in *ARIS Explorer*,

2.  Right-Click > Properties [*General*],

3.  View the entry in the *Method filter* field.

 **Hint** – for a quick way to find out which Method Filter is in use for the database you are logged into, hover your mouse over the database name in the *Explorer Module Explorer Tree*. A Tooltip will appear showing database details including the user name and current Method Filter.

If this is not the filter you wanted:

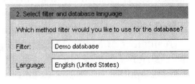

1.  Close all open models,

2.  Log out of the current database (select the database name in the *Explorer Tree*, Right-Click > Log off),

3.  Select the database name in the *Explorer Tree*,

4.  Right-Click > Log in,

5.  On the second page of the *Login Wizard*, select the appropriate Method Filter in the *Filter* field.

Where a database allows you a choice of Method Filters you can set the default Method Filter that will be used when you log into a database in a similar manner to setting the default user name and password:

1.  Select View > Options... [*Log In*] (see Fig. 8.7),

2.  Change the Method Filter using the *Select filter Dialog Box* (Fig. 8.8) that is triggered when you click on the Browse Button (...) to the right of the *Filter* field in the *User Defaults* area.

**Hint** – when you use the *Select filter Dialog Box* to change the default Method Filter, you may be surprised to find no filters are listed. You first have to select a server (e.g. **LOCAL**) from the *Server* drop-down box at the top of the dialog box.

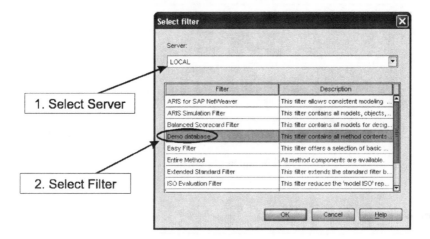

**Fig. 8.8** Select Filter Dialog Box

### The Importance of Method Filters

When you first install ARIS, the default will be to log in using the **Easy Filter** Method Filter. This is a very restrictive filter and only displays a very limited number of models and objects. This is useful when you first start using ARIS, but very soon you may wish to change to using the **Entire Method** filter to see the full capability of ARIS.

Although useful for experimentation the **Entire Method** is not restrictive at all. We don't recommend you undertake any significant modelling work with the **Entire Method** filter selected because it is too easy to find yourself being inconsistent about which objects you use and what they represent. It is important to have a set of models and objects which are sufficient to model your requirements, but not so expansive that they cause confusion and error.

There are other standard Method Filters available which you can investigate to see if they meet your needs, and experienced users can create their own.

## 8.5     The Information Tabs

Table 8.2 shows the information available in the *Information Tabs* (see Fig. 8.9), depending on which item has been selected in the *Explorer Tree*.

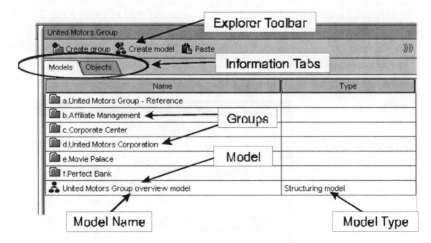

**Fig. 8.9** Explorer Information Tabs

**Table 8.2** Explorer Module Information Tabs

| Selected in Navigation Bar | Selected Information Tab | Contents |
|---|---|---|
| Server | Server Contents | List of databases on server. |
| Database | Database Contents | List of folders in database (Improvement Proposals, Tasks on system, Main Group). |
| Group | Models | Sub-groups and models. |
| | Objects | Sub-groups and objects. |
| Model | Occurrences | List of all occurrences of objects in the model. |
| | Variants | List of models that are variants of the selected model. |
| Object | Variants | List of objects that are variants of the selected object. |

### 8.5.1    Groups

Selecting a '*Group*' in the *Explorer Tree* will display the contents of the group in the *Information Tabs*. The contents can include sub-groups, models and objects. These are displayed in two tabs: the *Models Tab* and the *Objects Tab* (see Fig. 8.9). The *Models Tab* displays sub-groups and models; the *Objects Tab* displays sub-groups and objects. Most of the time we use the *Models Tab*. The display of groups, models and objects in the tabs echoes the structure in the *Explorer Tree*, but in addition, shows the *type* of model or object. You can sort the *Information Tabs* by *Name* or *Type* by clicking on the column header.

You can only select a single item in the *Explorer Tree*, but you can select multiple items in the tabs. Having selected an item you can either double-click on it to open it or right-click to bring up the pop-up *Right-Click Menu* of commands that can be performed on the item.

 **Hint** – it is advisable to only have a single model in the **Main Group**. This should be a model providing an overview and introduction to all the models in your database that can be used a starting point for navigation of your model structure. This approach is particularly recommended when the database is to be published on the Internet using *ARIS Web Publisher*.

## 8.5.2     Models, Objects and Occurrences

We saw in Section 8.5.1, if you select a group in the *Explorer Tree*, the *Information Tabs* display either the models or objects in the group. Using the same logic, you might expect that if you select a model in the *Explorer Tree*, the *Information Tabs* would display the contents of the model (its objects). If you try selecting a group you will see there are actually tabs for *Occurrences* and *Variants* (see Fig. 8.10). We will delay looking at variants until later (Chapter 15), but why do we see a display of occurrences rather than objects?

The answer is objects don't exist inside models; reference is only made to them in models. There is only a single definition of each object in an ARIS database. For convenience these definitions are organised into groups, which is where we see the objects displayed in the *Explorer Tree*. When we place an object into a model diagram, ARIS puts a graphical representation (a '*symbol*') of the object in the model and creates a pointer to the underlying database object definition.

The symbol represents an '*occurrence*' of that object in the model. The power of

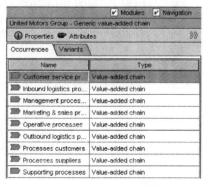

**Fig. 8.10** Occurrences Tab

ARIS is that objects can be re-used. For instance, if the object represents the department carrying out a task, the *Organizational unit* object representing that department can be re-used in all the models where the same department is involved with other tasks.

When an object is re-used in another model, a new occurrence of the object is represented by placing its symbol in the model. The occurrence points to the original object definition in the ARIS group. Thus an object has a single definition and may have multiple occurrences represented by symbols in ARIS models. Different types of symbol can also be used for different occurrences. For instance the same function used in a *Value-added chain diagram* has a different type of symbol if copied and pasted into an *EPC*.

So, when we select a model in the *Explorer Tree*, the *Occurrences Tab* lists all the individual occurrences of objects in the model. If an object has been used more than once in the model there will be more than one entry for that object in the list.

The important point to realise is the occurrence display has nothing to do with the group structure. The list of occurrences refers to objects that may be anywhere in the group structure and similarly there is not necessarily any direct relationship between the models and objects located in the same group. By default, when a new model is created it will be placed in the currently selected group. Any new objects placed in the model will also be placed in that group. However, existing objects can be re-used in models in other groups, and models and objects can be independently moved to other groups using the *Explorer* commands (see Section 8.6.5). Thus, after a while, models and objects will become spread around the group structure and occasional housekeeping is needed to tidy up.

You can demonstrate this to yourself using the **DEMO70** database. Activate the *Models* and *Objects* checkboxes above the *Explorer Tree* and try selecting models in different groups. The *Explorer Tree* will include all the objects in the group, while the *Occurrences Tab* will show you all the object occurrences for the selected model. Compare the two lists.

 **Hint** – there is no way to display the group in which an object shown in an occurrence list is actually located, but for a quick way to find out – right-click on the object occurrence in the *Occurrences Tab* and select Go to > Occurrence in Explorer. The *Explorer Tree* will open up the group structure and show the location of the selected object.

### 8.5.3     Attributes and Properties

Information about all the items able to be viewed in ARIS Explorer can be displayed through the *Attributes Window* and *Properties Dialog Box*. These are described in more detail in Chapter 14.

### *Attributes*

To display the attributes of an item, select it and do any of the following:

- Edit > Attributes,
- Right-Click > Attributes,
- Press <F8>,
- Select the Attributes Button from the *ARIS Toolbar*.

Specifically for objects:

7.   Select a model containing the object in the *Explorer Tree*,

8.   Select the appropriate object from the *Occurrences Tab*,

9.   Select the Attributes Button from the *Explorer Toolbar*.

### *Properties*

To display the properties of an item, select it and do any of the following:

*   <u>E</u>dit > P<u>r</u>operties,

*   Right-Click > P<u>r</u>operties,

*   Press <ALT-ENTER>,

*   Select the Properties Button from the *ARIS Toolbar*.

And specifically for objects:

10.  Select a model containing the object in the *Explorer Tree*,

11.  Select the appropriate object from the *Occurrences Tab*,

12.  Select the Attributes Button from the *Explorer Toolbar*.

### 8.5.4      Names, Identifiers and the GUID

The names given to groups must always be unique. Model names only have to be unique for the same type of model within the same group. Object names don't have to be unique at all. The uniqueness of items in ARIS is maintained by an internal '*Global Unique Identifier (GUID)*'. The GUID is a string of the form:

**"B8BAA395-0C72-11D3-845F-00005A4053FF"**

The GUID is guaranteed to be unique across all ARIS databases, world-wide. You can view the GUID for an object by:

13.  Selecting the object in the *Explorer Tree*,

14.  Right-Click > P<u>r</u>operties [*Information*].

The GUID is displayed in the *GUID* field. However, it is not very useful for day-to-day management; instead the *Identifier* attribute can be used. If enabled by the *ARIS Database Administration*, the *Identifier* consists of an alphanumeric pre-fix and an automatically allocated serial number that can be viewed in the *Attributes Window* or *Attributes Tab* of the *Properties Bar*.

*Identifier* attribute values are allocated for items within a database and are not globally unique. Thus it is quite possible to copy an object from another database that has the same *Identifier* as an object already in the database. It is also possible to manually change the value of the *Identifier* attributes. However, under normal circumstances, *Identifier* attributes will be unique within a database and are a very useful management tool.

**Hint** – because *Identifier* attributes automatically provide an almost unique reference to ARIS objects, people are often tempted to use them to make reference to objects in documentation or in other models. We strongly advise against this. Because they are such useful aids to database administration you may find your *ARIS Database Administrator* will periodically re-index all the *Identifier* attributes in the database without warning, thus losing any references you have made. For the same reason, you should not manually enter values into the *Identifier* attributes.

Although ARIS will allow different objects to have the same name, for the most part this should be avoided.

## 8.6      ARIS Explorer Commands

There are many useful commands in the *Explorer Module* that can be used to manipulate ARIS items. Commands can be issued from the *Main Menu,* the *ARIS Toolbar*, the *Explorer Toolbar*, from shortcut keys (e.g. <CTRL-C>) or by selecting an item in *Explorer Window* and right-clicking. You can also drag and drop items in the *Explorer Tree* or *Information Tabs*. The commands available from the pop-up *Right-Click Menu* (see Fig. 8.3) vary depending on what item was selected.

### 8.6.1      New Item Commands

Commands for creating new databases, groups, models and objects can be issued in several ways.

### *New Database*

To create a new database (*ARIS Business Architect* only):
1.   Select **LOCAL**,
2.   Right-Click > Ne<u>w</u> > <u>D</u>atabase…,
3.   Enter the database name into *Create database Dialog Box*.

### *New Group*

To create a new group in a database, select an existing group in the database and do any of the following:
* <u>F</u>ile > Ne<u>w</u> > <u>G</u>roup…,
* Right-Click > <u>N</u>ew > <u>G</u>roup,
* Click on the Create group Button in the *Explorer Toolbar*.

A new group called **New group** will be created in the selected group. You can rename the group by selecting it and executing the Right-Click > Rename command pressing <F2>.

### New Model

To create a new model in *Explorer* you can do any of the following:

*   File > New... > Model,
*   Click on the File new Button and choose Model,
*   Right-click on a group name and select New > Model,
*   Select a group and click on the Create model Button.

The last two commands recognise the context of the database and group structure you are working in and will create the new model in that group. The first two are context free and will ask you to specifically select a database and group. ARIS will then display the *Model Wizard* (see Chapter 5) which will enable you to choose the model type and specify its name.

### New Object

Previously (in Chapter 5) we described creating new objects by selecting an object symbol from the *Symbols Bar* in the *Designer Module*. This operation creates a new object definition and places an occurrence of the object in the model. However, you can also create object definitions directly within *Explorer*. We don't normally create individual objects this way, but the facility can be very useful when you need to create large numbers of objects at one time (e.g. to create a library of *Organizational unit* objects).

To create new objects in ARIS Explorer:

1.   Select the group where you wish to create the new object definitions,
2.   Right-Click > New > Object....

Or

1.   Select the *Objects Tab*,
2.   Click on the Create object Button in the *Explorer Toolbar*.

The *Create objects Dialog Box* will appear as shown in Fig. 8.11. At the top of the dialog box the *Object type* field has a drop-down list from which you can select the type of objects you wish to create. Enter the name of the new object into the empty cell in the *Names* field. When you have entered the name, press <Enter> or <Tab>. The cursor now moves to a new empty cell and you can enter another name. You can continue in this way to enter any number of new objects.

You can copy and paste the name of a new object into ARIS from other applications running under Microsoft Windows. This is very useful if, for instance, you

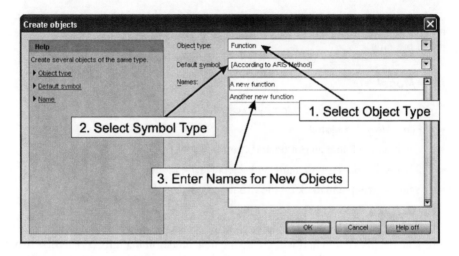

**Fig. 8.11** The Create Objects Dialog Box

have a list of business departments in a Word document or Excel spreadsheet, and you wish to create ARIS *Organizational unit* objects to represent them.

You cannot create objects of more than one type in a single operation. While the *Create objects Dialog Box* is open, all the objects created will be of the type shown in the *Object Type* field drop-down box. If you select a different entry in the box, it will apply to all the objects shown in the list.

If you wish to create objects of a different type, select OK to save the objects created so far and select Right-Click > New > Object... to open the dialog box again. You can now select a different *Object Type* and create new objects of this type. Repeat this process for each set of object types you require.

You can place occurrences of these newly created objects into models in *Designer* by dragging them from the *Explorer Tree* to the *Designer Module Modelling Window* (see Chapter 9).

 **Warning** – objects created in *Explorer* that do not have an occurrence in a model will be deleted if the Reorganize command is run. If you create objects in the *Explorer Module*, it is strongly recommended you immediately place them all in a '*library model*' to ensure they are not accidentally deleted.

### 8.6.2    Open Model

You can open an existing model for viewing or editing in the *Designer Module* using any of the following:

• File > Open > Model,

- Click on the Open Button on the *ARIS Toolbar* and select Model,
- Select model name in the *Explorer Tree*, Right-Click > Open > Model,
- Double-click on the model name in the *Explorer Tree*.

The double-click method is the quickest.

### 8.6.3    Find

Selecting File > Find from the *Main Menu* (or the *Right-Click Menu* or  pressing <CTRL-F>) will bring up the *Find Dialog Box*. This is a very powerful facility but is outside the scope of this book.

**Question** – I can't locate the Find > Objects with Identical Names... command, where has it gone?

**Answer** – users of *ARIS 6 Toolset* may be familiar with using this command from the ARIS menus. In *ARIS Business Architect* this has now been incorporated into the Find command. The option to find *Objects with identical names* can be selected from the drop-down box in the *Find what* field.

### 8.6.4    Model History

The File > Model history command shows a list of models recently opened in the *Designer Module*. Click on the name of a model listed and ARIS will open the model again for editing. If you are not already logged into the appropriate database, ARIS will log you in first.

A similar list of recently opened models is also shown on the *ARIS Home Page* (see Chapter 6).

### 8.6.5    Copy, Cut and Paste Commands

There are a number of different sorts of copy and paste in ARIS: *Occurrence Copy*, *Definition Copy*, *Variant Copy* and *Shortcut*. It is very important to understand the distinction between '*occurrences*' and '*definitions*' and we discuss these in detail in Chapter 15.

### Copy

You can make a copy (an occurrence copy) of an item in ARIS by selecting the item and doing any of the following:

- Edit > Copy,
- Right-Click > Copy,

- `<CTRL-C>`,
- Click on the Copy Button on the *ARIS Toolbar,*
- Right-Click, drag the item to a new group, release the mouse key and select Copy here.

### Cut

You can remove an ARIS item and make it available for pasting by selecting the item and doing any of the following:

- Edit > Cut,
- Right-Click > Cut,
- `<CTRL-X>`,
- Click on the Cut Button on the *ARIS Toolbar.*

### Paste

In addition to the right-click drag and drop command which automatically does a copy and paste at the same time, you can paste a previously copied item by selecting the ARIS group where you want to place the copy and executing any of the following commands:

- Edit > Paste  or  Right-Click > Paste,
- Edit > Paste as > Copies  or  Right-Click > Copies,
- `<CTRL-V>`,
- Click on the Paste Button on the *ARIS Toolbar*
  or *Explorer Toolbar.*

If you make a copy of an item in ARIS into the same group as the original, the copy will have the same name as the original with a number appended at the end (e.g. "sales function" copied becomes "sales function (1)"). You can rename the item to something else if you wish.

Executing the paste command, as described above, for models or objects will make an '*occurrence copy*'. By using the Paste as command from the *Main Menu* or *Right-Click Menu,* or by using the right-click drag and release method, it is possible to make '*definition copies*' or '*variant copies*'. We will discuss the difference between these types of copies in Chapter 15.

### Paste as Shortcut

A shortcut of a model or object can be created in another group by either:

- Right-Click > Paste as > Shortcuts,
- Right-Click, drag and release the item, select Create shortcuts here.

The definition of the object or model stays in its original group, but a pointer to the item called "shortcut to *itemname*" is placed in the new group. The icon for the shortcut has a small arrow attached to it to show it is a shortcut in the same way the Microsoft Windows displays shortcuts.

This is very useful for models as it enables quick access from a single group to sets of models that may actually be located in various locations across the group structure. Thus is particularly useful for creating different views or classifications of the models you have created. You can double-click on the model's shortcut to open the original model.

You can rename the shortcut using the normal Rename (F2) command (the pointer icon will still indicate it is a shortcut). You can also copy, paste and delete the shortcut without affecting the original model.

You can also make a shortcut of an object definition. This is not as useful as model shortcuts, but can be used for creating libraries of objects and allowing an object to appear in several different libraries.

### Delete

You can delete an ARIS object by selecting it in the *Explorer Tree* and executing any of the following:

- Edit > Delete,
- Right-Click > Delete,
- Click on the Delete Button on the *ARIS Toolbar*,
- Press the keyboard <Delete> key.

A *Confirm delete Dialog Box* will always be displayed before the item is actually deleted. If you delete a model, all the object occurrences in the model will be deleted, but the object definitions will remain in their original groups. The definitions can be re-used in other models. If all the occurrences of an object have been deleted from models, the object's definition will remain in the group structure until the next time the database is reorganised.

 **Hint** – the Reorganize command deletes the definitions of all unused objects. If you wish to keep an object definition even though it is not currently being used, create a 'library model' (any model type the object is valid for) and place the object in it as a temporary measure.

 **Warning** – if you try to delete an object that has occurrences in any models, a second *Confirm delete Dialog Box* will be displayed. If you say yes to this message the object definition will be deleted along with all its occurrences in all models. This operation is not recommended unless you are certain of what you are doing.

### Delete with Objects

Normally, when you delete a model the model itself will be deleted along with all references to the object occurrences in the model. The object definitions themselves will not be deleted, even if the objects are not used elsewhere. Unused object definitions are only deleted by running the Reorganize command.

The Edit > Delete with objects command allows you to delete a model and, at the same time, delete the object definitions for all the objects with occurrences in the model, provided the objects do not have occurrences in other models. This is particularly useful for deleting temporary or test models where the objects are unlikely to be used elsewhere. It prevents the database filling up with object definitions that are no longer required.

You can select multiple models for deletion, and you will be asked to confirm that you wish the deletion to take place. The command is also available from the *Right-Click Menu.*

### 8.6.6      Move Commands

An ARIS object or model can be moved from one group to another by selecting it with the left mouse key and dragging and dropping it into a new group. In addition, specific move commands are available by dragging and dropping the item with the right mouse key pressed. When the key is released  to drop the item into the new group, a *Right-Click Menu* will appear providing additional move commands as well as copy and paste commands. Using right-click drag and drop is always safer as it gives you the option to choose what action you want to take at the point you release the mouse key.

### Move Here

The Move Here command moves the selected objects or models from the current group location to a new group:

1.   Select the models or objects in the *Explorer Tree,*

2.   Hold down the right-hand mouse key and drag the selected items to the new group,

3.   Release the mouse key,

4.   Select Move here from the pop-up menu.

Exactly the same effect can be achieved by dragging models or objects to the new group with the left-hand mouse key held down. However, the right-mouse drag operation is more useful (and safer) because, when you release the mouse key, the pop-up menu gives you the option to move the object or model, make one of the various forms of copy, or cancel the command.

## Move Here with Objects

When you move a model to a new group using drag and drop or the Move here command described above, the object definitions for objects that have occurrences in the model remain wherever they are in the group structure. The Move here with objects command allows you to move a model into a new group and, at the same time, have the object definitions for those objects with occurrences in the model also moved to the same group:

1.  Select the model in the *Explorer Tree*,

2.  Hold down the right-hand mouse key and drag the model to the new group,

3.  Release the mouse key,

4.  Select Move here with objects from the pop-up menu.


### 8.6.7     Rename

To rename a group, model or object, select the item and do any of the following:

*   Edit > Rename,

*   Right-Click > Rename,

*   Press the <F2> key.

   Group names must always be unique. Model names only have to be unique for the same type of model within the same group. Object names don't have to be unique at all although it is recommended you keep them unique.


### 8.6.8     Refresh

The View > Refresh (or <F5>) command updates the display of *ARIS Explorer* and *ARIS Designer* to reflect the outcome of any recent operations. Normally, the display is updated automatically, but it may not always happen. If you modify *Font Formats* or *Templates*, you will often need to issue the View > Refresh (or <F5>) command to make the change visible in any models already open.

> **Hint** – if a change you have just made in *ARIS Explorer* or *ARIS Designer* does not seem to be visible, press <F5> to refresh the ARIS window displays.


### 8.6.9     Change Password

To change the *Password* of the *User Account* you have used to log into an ARIS database:

1.  Select the database name in the *Explorer Tree*,
2.  File > Database > Change password... or Right-Click > Change password...,
3.  Enter the existing and new passwords into the *Change password Dialog Box* (Fig. 8.6).

### 8.6.10    Backup and Restore

Database administration is outside the scope of this book, but some of the more useful administration commands accessible from the *Explorer Module* are summarised below:

### Backup

Select the database, then:

1.  File > Database > Backup... or Right-Click > Backup...,
2.  Use the *Select file Dialog Box* to chose where to save the file.

### Restore

Select the ARIS server, then:

1.  File > Server > Restore... or Right-Click > Restore...,
2.  Use the *Select file Dialog Box* to locate the previously backed-up file.

### Reorganize

The database Reorganize... command can only be executed from the *Administration Module* in *ARIS Business Architect*. Select a database and:

•   File > Database > Reorganize... or Right-Click > Reorganize....

# Chapter 9  ARIS Designer Module

In this chapter we look in detail at the ARIS Designer Module. We look at
the editing and drawing facilities; how to place objects, re-use them, connect them together, resize and move them

## 9.1  Introduction

The ARIS *Designer Module* (Fig. 9.1) is used for creating, editing and viewing
ARIS models and their objects. Its comprised of the *Modelling Window* with one or
more tabs for each opened model and the *Designer Checkboxes* which control the
visibility of the *Symbols Bar,* the *Navigation Bar* and the *Properties Bar.*

## 9.2  Creating and Opening Models

### 9.2.1  Creating New Models

In the last chapter we saw how to create a new model from the *Explorer Module* by
doing any of the following:

- File > New… > Model,
- Click on the File new Button and choose Model,
- Right-click on a group name and select New > Model,
- Select a group and click on the Create model Button on
  the *Explorer Toolbar.*

  The last two commands recognise the context of the database and group structure you are working in and will create the new model in that group. The first two
are context free and will ask you to specifically select a database and group. ARIS
will then display the *Model Wizard* (see Chapter 5) which will enable you to
choose the model type and specify its name. ARIS will then automatically switch
to the *Designer Module* and display a new, empty model.

### 9.2.2  Opening Existing Models

You can open an existing model for viewing or editing using any of the following:

- File > Open > Model,
- Click on the Open icon on the *ARIS Toolbar* and select Model,

- Select the model name in the *Explorer Tree*, Right-Click > Open > Model,
- Double-click on the model name in the *Explorer Tree*.

The first two options will ask you to choose a database and a model; the last two will open the selected model. You can access the *Explorer*  *Tree* either from the *Navigation Bar* in the *Explorer Module* (see Chapter 8) or directly in the *Designer Module* by ensuring the *Navigation Checkbox* is ticked.

> **Hint** – you can open several models in one operation by selecting all the required models in the right-hand *Information Tab* of the *Explorer Module* and clicking Right-Click > Open. Each model will be opened in a separate *Designer Module* Window.

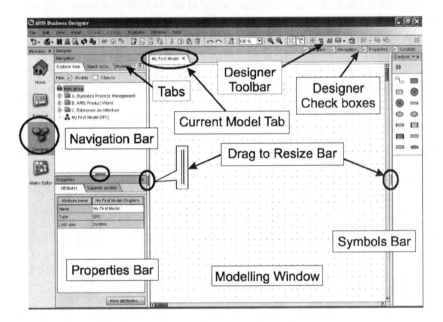

**Fig. 9.1** ARIS Designer Module

### 9.2.3    Saving and Closing

An ARIS model is not saved unless you explicitly save it by using any of the following:

- File > Save,
- File > Save all,
- Clicking the Save icon.

You can close a model by:

- <u>F</u>ile > C<u>l</u>ose,
- <u>F</u>ile > Close a<u>l</u>l,
- Clicking the Close Button (**x**) on the *Modelling Window* tab.

If you try to close an unsaved model, ARIS will ask you if you want to save it before the window closes. ARIS has no automatic background save or recover facility so you should frequently save your models as you work on them. By contrast, you don't have to worry about saving the database because it is being updated continuously as a result of saving models and attributes.

 **Question** – how do I save my model with a different name?
**Answer** – there is no <u>S</u>ave As... command in ARIS so if you want to save different edited versions of your model you will need to first make a copy of the model in the *Explorer Module* (see Chapter 8) and rename it as appropriate.

## 9.3 The Designer Window

The *Designer Window* (Fig. 9.1) has one main display area, the *Modelling Window*, with three additional bars that can be toggled on and off as needed. On the right of the *Modelling Window* is the *Symbols Bar* which can be toggled on and off with the *Symbols Checkbox*. On the left-hand side of the *Modelling Window* are the *Navigation Bar* and *Properties Bar* which can also be toggled on and off with the *Navigation Checkbox* and *Properties Checkbox*.

When these bars are enabled you can adjust their relative widths by clicking and dragging the centre or edge partitions. To the far left of the *Designer Window* is the *Modules Bar* (see Chapter 6) which can also be toggled on and off using the *Modules Checkbox*. In addition, the *ARIS Toolbar* at the top of the window now displays additional buttons specific to the *Designer Module*.

### 9.3.1 Modelling Window

The *Modelling Window* provides a drawing area in which a graphical representation of a process model can be created by placing objects, connecting them up and adjusting the layout. The window will have one or more tabs for each open model. You can select which model to work on by clicking on the tabs at the top of the *Modelling Window*. The currently visible model has a light coloured tab while other open models (not currently visible) [My First Model ✕ Another Model ✕] have dark tabs. You can make a different model visible by clicking on its tab in which case the currently visible model will be hidden (but still open).

You can click on the Close Button (**x**) on any tab and close the model irrespective of whether the model is visible or not so be careful when clicking on the tabs. If any changes have been made to the model since you last saved it you will be prompted to save it before the model closes.

You can make a grid visible on the *Modelling Window* by clicking on the Toggle grid Button on the *Designer Toolbar*. When the grid is visible, placed or moved objects will automatically align to the grid. We will see how to set up the grid and other aspects of the model's appearance in Chapter 10.

### 9.3.2    Designer Toolbar

The *Designer Module* does not have its own toolbar (unlike the *Explorer Module*), but additional buttons are added to the *ARIS Toolbar* (see Fig. 9.2). For clarity we will use the term *Designer Toolbar* to refer to this extended *ARIS Toolbar*.

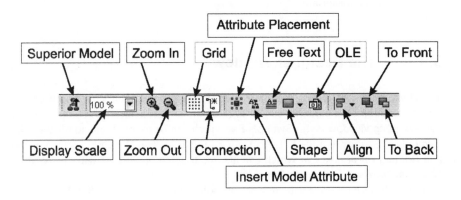

**Fig. 9.2** Designer Toolbar Buttons

### 9.3.3    Left-Click Operations

A single left-click on a graphical item (e.g. an object or connection) will select the item. A double left-click will normally bring up the *Properties Dialog Box* (see Chapter 14). A double-click on the assignment icon (see Chapter 12) will open the assigned model.

### 9.3.4    Right-Click Operations

A right-click on a graphical item (e.g. an object or connection) will select the item and bring up a context-sensitive *Right-Click Menu*.

### 9.3.5 Tooltips

If you hover your mouse over an object or connection in the *Modelling Window,* a tooltip box will appear displaying some of the key attributes of the item including the *Name, Type* and *Description* attributes.

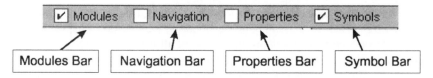

 **Question** – why don't I see any tooltips when I hover my mouse over an object?

**Answer** – you can enable the display of tooltips from

<u>V</u>iew > <u>O</u>ptions...[*General / Objects*] and check the *Show tooltips* box.

### 9.3.6 Designer Checkboxes

The visibility of the *Modules Bar,* the *Symbols Bar,* the *Navigation Bar* and the *Properties Bar* can be controlled by a set of *checkboxes* at the top right-hand of the *Designer Window* (Fig. 9.3).

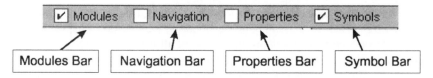

Click on a Box to Make the Bar or Window Visible

**Fig. 9.3** ARIS Designer Checkboxes

 **Hint** – to give yourself more modelling space you can turn off the first three checkboxes, but make sure you have the *Symbols Checkbox* ticked so the *Symbols Bar* is visible.

### 9.3.7 Symbols Bar

The *Symbols Bar* (also called the Modelling Toolbar) provides a pallet of available objects that can be used within the model. The range of objects provided on the toolbar is restricted by the ARIS Method Filter selected when you log into the database. The toolbar can be further configured by the user to just show the most frequently used and useful objects. We shall see how to use the *Symbols Bar* in Section 9.4.1.

The *Symbols Bar* can be turned off by removing the checks from the *Symbols Checkbox*. This can be useful if you just wish to view the model. You can alter the width of the *Symbols Bar* by dragging the left-hand edge of the bar. Alternatively you can minimise the bar and set it to appear automatically when you move your mouse to the far right-hand side of the *Modelling Window*.

To set the visibility of the *Symbols Bar*, click on the down arrow next to the *Symbols* label in the *Symbols Toolbar* title area, select from the Show, Hide, and Sho<u>w</u>/Hide automatically options.

### 9.3.8     Navigation Bar

The *Navigation Bar* can, optionally, be displayed by clicking on  the *Navigation Checkbox*. The bar has three tabs which display:

*   Explorer Tree,

*   Model Overview,

*   Object Occurrences.

The *Explorer tree Tab* is very similar to the tree in the *Navigation Bar* of the *Explorer Module*. It can be used to select additional models to be opened or objects for re-use in the current model (see Section 9.5.3).

The *Model overview window Tab* provides a view of the complete model and can be used to visualise the scaling of the *Modelling Window* (see Chapter 10).

The *Object occurrences Tab* provides a list of all the objects used in the model and visually shows their symbol types. When you select an object occurrence in the list, the *Modelling Window* automatically scrolls so the object is visible. The selection can be used for viewing the attributes and properties of the objects as well as making copies and assignments.

### 9.3.9     Properties Bar

The *Properties Bar* can, optionally, be displayed by clicking on the *Properties Checkbox*. The bar has context-sensitive tabs with different displays depending on the item selected:

*   Attributes          (Model, Objects, Connections),

*   Assignments        (Objects),

*   Relationships      (Objects),

*   Occurrences        (Objects),

*   Superior Models    (Model).

**Question** – why can't I see the *Properties Bar* even though the *Properties Checkbox* is checked?

**Answer** – if the dividing bar between the *Navigation Bar* and the *Properties Bar* has been dragged to the bottom of the window, the *Navigation Bar* will occupy all of the bar space and the *Properties Bar* will not be visible. To rectify this, drag the dividing bar back to the middle of the window.

The *Attributes Tab* shows a list of the most important attributes for the selected object (or the current model if no object is selected). Those attributes not set automatically by ARIS can have their values set and edited in the *Attributes Tab* (see Chapter 14). The user can control which attributes are visible in the tab by clicking on the More attributes... Button.

The *Assignments Tab* shows any models assigned to the selected object. Assignments can be created or deleted by clicking on the buttons at the bottom of the tab (see Chapter 12).

The *Relationships Tab* shows all the connections between the selected object and other objects in the database (not just those in the current model). See Chapter 11 for more information on relationships.

**Hint** – you can tell if the relationship is in the current model by selecting it in the *Relationships Tab*. If the Go to Button is enabled then it is in the current model and if you click on the button, the connected object will be selected in the *Modelling Window* which will scroll so it is visible.

The *Occurrences Tab* shows a list of all the occurrences of the selected object in all the models in the database. If there is more than one occurrence in any one model, the list will have more than one entry. The *Occurrences Tab* differs from the *Object occurrences Tab* in the *Navigation Bar* in that it displays all occurrences of a selected object, not just those in the current model. The *Object occurrences Tab* on the other hand shows all the object occurrences in the current model. If you select one of the occurrence entries and click on the Open Model Button, the model containing the occurrence will be opened in a new *Modelling Window* tab and the object occurrence selected. See Chapter 15 for more information on occurrences.

If no items are selected in the current model, the *Superior models Tab* shows any other models that have objects with assignments to the current model. The concept of assignments will be explained in more detail in Chapter 12.

## 9.4      Adding and Naming Objects

In Chapter 5 we had an introduction to creating a model where we added objects, named them and connected them together. We will now look at these operations in more detail.

### 9.4.1    Using the Symbols Bar

The *Symbols Bar,* on the far right-hand side of the *Modelling Window,* provides a palette of symbols for the objects available for use in the current model (see Fig. 9.4). The range of objects available is defined by the ARIS Method and may be reduced by the Method Filter in use. If you are using the ***Easy Filter*** there will probably be about 30 objects. If you have the ***Entire Method*** selected you may have more than 150 objects.

**Hint** – to find out which object a symbol on the *Symbols Bar* represents, hover your mouse over the symbol. A tooltip will appear giving the name of the object.

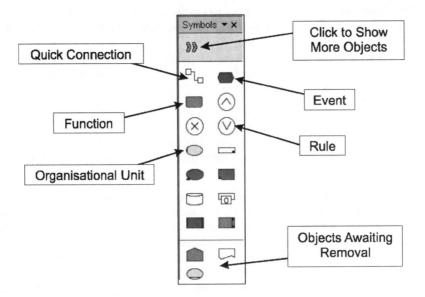

**Fig. 9.4** The Symbols Bar

You can alter the size of the symbol icons on the *Symbols Bar,* or additionally display the names of their objects by selecting the down arrow next to the *Symbols* label in the *Modelling Toolbar* title area and selecting Small icons, Large icons or Small icons with text.

The first item on the *Symbols Bar* is not in fact an object symbol, but the *Connection Button*; we will look at it shortly. The remaining symbols all represent objects we can place on the model. It is not in fact the entire set of objects available for use in the model, but a sub-set of those allowed by the Method Filter. This sub-set is initially set by ARIS, but you can configure the bar to include those symbols you use most frequently.

## Removing a Symbol

To remove a symbol from the bar, right-click on the symbol and select **Remove symbol**. The symbol is not deleted, but moved to a reserve list of symbols. If the symbol has already been used on the model it won't be removed, but placed at the bottom of the *Symbols Bar* underneath a dividing line (see Fig. 9.4). If, at a later date, all occurrences of the symbol are removed from the model, the symbol will also disappear from the *Symbols Bar*.

 **Hint** – when all the objects represented by a symbol marked for removal are deleted, the symbol may not disappear from the *Symbols Bar* until the next time the display of the bar is refreshed. This usually occurs when the model is reopened or its *Modelling Window* tab is reselected after viewing another model.

## Adding a Symbol

To view the symbols on the reserve list, click on the **Add symbols Button** at the top of the *Symbols Bar*. The *Add symbols Dialog Box* (Fig. 9.5) will now show the remainder of objects allowed by the Method Filter, but not currently shown on the *Symbols Bar*. You can select one or more of the symbols (use `<CTRL>+left-click` to select multiple symbols) and press the **Add symbols Button**. You can repeat this a number of times to choose the set of symbols you require. Once you have finished, press the **Close Button**. You should now see the new symbols added to the *Symbols Bar*. The order of symbols on the symbols bar is defined in the current Method Filter and can be set by the *ARIS System Administrator*.

The configuration of the *Symbols Bar* will appear the same in all models of the same type although the display of symbols for removal at the bottom of the bar may change depending on what symbols are in use in a particular model.

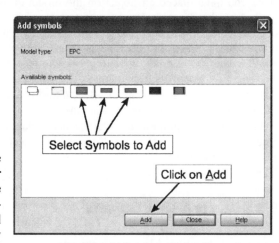

**Fig. 9.5** Add Symbols Dialog Box

### 9.4.2     Selecting and Placing an Object

To select an object for placing on a model, click on its symbol on the *Symbols Bar*. The symbol will be framed with a blue box. The mouse cursor (when it is over the *Modelling Window*) changes to a small rectangle with a cross above it. Click anywhere on the *Modelling Window* and an occurrence of the chosen object will be placed at the cursor location. The placed object is selected and the *Name* attribute text box is also selected so you can type a name to replace the default name. It is important to remember you have to select and click to place an object, you cannot drag and drop objects from the *Symbols Bar*.

### 9.4.3     Renaming an Object

You don't have to change the name of the object now; you can accept the default (press <Enter> or click elsewhere) and change it later. To change the name of an existing object, select the object and press the left mouse key again (not a double-click, but two single clicks), or Right-Click > Rename or press the <F2> key. The name text box will highlight and you can type in a new name. Depending on what model properties have been set (see Chapter 10), the text will either wrap inside the object or you can force line breaks by entering <Ctrl+Enter>.

### 9.4.4     Adding Multiple Objects

Once you have placed an object on the model drawing area you will notice the symbol on the *Symbols Bar* has reset (no longer has the blue box outline). To select another object, click the appropriate symbol and place the object as before. If you want to place multiple objects of the same type, click the symbol, place the mouse cursor at the first location where you wish to place the object, hold down the <Ctrl> key and click the mouse. The object will be placed at the mouse location, but the symbol will remain selected and you can continue to click and place additional objects as long as you hold the <Ctrl> key down.

When placing multiple objects the name box is not highlighted and all the objects are placed with the default name (the object type). You will need to manually rename them later.

## 9.5     Re-using Objects

As we have mentioned before, the power of ARIS is that it is not just a drawing tool, but a modelling tool where all the items are stored in an underlying database thus allowing detailed analysis and reporting. To make full use of this power we want to re-use objects representing key resources, for instance the departments, IT systems and data our organisation uses.

We can select existing objects for reuse in several ways:

- Using an existing object by name,
- Copy and paste an existing object,
- Drag and drop from the *Explorer Tree*.

## 9.5.1    Using an Existing Object by Name

If you enter the name of an object that already exists when placing or renaming an object, ARIS will detect this and display the *Select object Dialog Box* (see Fig. 9.6). The dialog box will display one or more objects of the same type that have the same name and ask you to chose if you wish to *Create or use an object with this name* (i.e. create a new object or give the existing object this name, even though it is not unique) or *Use an existing object* (in which case you select the object from the list). Although ARIS doesn't require you give objects unique names, it is desirable to do so.

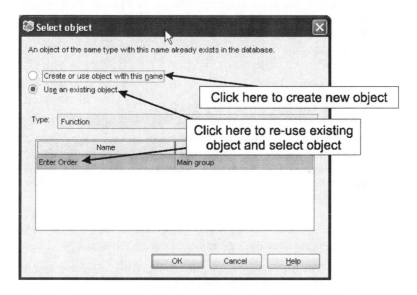

**Fig. 9.6** Select Object Dialog Box

 **Question** – I have accidentally created several objects with the same name and used them in different models. How can I correct this so I just have a single object?
**Answer** – don't worry, you can use the Consolidate... command to help you sort this out, but unfortunately it's outside the scope of this book.

If you think you already have an object you can re-use, but you are not sure of its exact name, you can just enter the first few letters (at least two) and search for likely objects by clicking on the Definition selection Button next to the name text box or by pressing the <Tab> key. Again the *Select object Dialog Box* (Fig. 9.6) will appear, but this time with list of objects with names having the same starting letters.

### 9.5.2    Copy and Paste an Existing Object

If you know the object you wish to re-use is in another model, you can open the model and simply cut and paste the object into your working model (Right-Click > Copy and Right-Click > Paste). If you use the Paste as command instead, make sure you select Occurrence copy; selecting Definition copy will create a new, duplicate, object with the same name, which is not what you want.

The appearance of the copied object will be based on how it appeared in the original model and the properties of the current model. As a result it may not look exactly the same as it did in the original model or the same as other objects of the same type in the current model. To keep the appearance the same as the current model set a default template in the model properties (see Chapter 10).

You can also copy and paste from the *Explorer Tree,* but it is easier to drag and drop, see below.

### 9.5.3    Drag and Drop from the Explorer Tree

If you know where an object is located in the ARIS group hierarchy you can drag and drop it from the *Explorer Tree*. Make sure the *Navigation Bar* is visible by clicking on the *Navigation Checkbox* and select the *Explorer tree Tab*. In the *Explorer Tree* click on the *Objects Checkbox* in the *Explorer Filter* area.

You should now be able to see the objects in the group hierarchy. When you have found the object you want to re-use, select it and, with the left mouse key pressed, drag it onto the *Modelling Window* and release the mouse.

 **Expert Tip** – to make it easy to find objects for reuse it is best to create 'library groups' (e.g. Departments, IT Systems) and move all objects of that type into the library.

## 9.6      Connecting Objects

We normally establish relationships between objects in ARIS by connecting the symbols representing them. The terms '*connection*' and '*relationship*' tend to be used interchangeably. To be strictly accurate, connections are those relationships made between objects by drawing them in ARIS Designer. There are other types of relationships (e.g. *implicit, explicit, assignment,* etc.), which we will come across later.

There are several ways of making connections depending on the particular style of editing you are using:

- Connection mode,
- Quick drawing of connections,
- Place and connect.

### 9.6.1    Connection Mode

The *connection mode* is used when we want to make many connections between objects, particularly when many of those objects are already placed on the model. If you need to place many new objects and connect them up, the *place and connect* mode (Section 9.6.4) is usually quicker.

First enable the *connection mode* by pressing the Connection mode Button on the *Designer Toolbar.* When activated the Connection mode Button will be framed and highlighted.

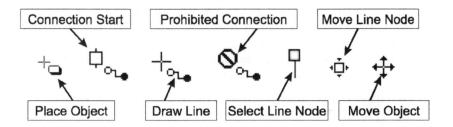

**Fig. 9.7** Designer Cursor Shapes

Now hover your mouse over an object. The cursor will change to a cross. If you move the cursor to the edge of the object you will see it changes to a small square with a jagged line attached (Fig. 9.8a) (the full set of cursor shapes is shown in Fig. 9.7). This indicates you are hovering over an attachment point. Left-click the mouse and as you move your cursor a connecting line appears (Fig. 9.8b). Move the cursor to the edge of a second object until you see the attachment cursor and click again to complete the connection (Fig. 9.8c). A connection line will now appear between the two objects.

If the connections points are in the same vertical or horizontal line, a single straight line will be seen. If they weren't lined up, a set of lines with right angles will be used (Fig. 9.8c). You can change the appearance of connection lines (see Chapter 10) or tidy them up (see Section 9.7.6). If you have the grid visible (press

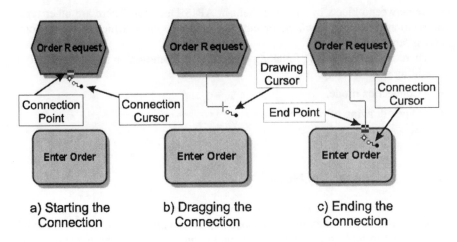

| a) Starting the Connection | b) Dragging the Connection | c) Ending the Connection |

**Fig. 9.8** Connecting Objects

the Toggle grid Button on the *Designer Toolbar*), the attachment points will snap to the grid, if not, you can attach anywhere.

The connection mode will stay enabled unless you deselect it, so you can continue to connect up objects as you wish. You can make multiple connections from the first selected object by holding down the <CTRL> key when you make the connection to the second object. A new connection from the first object will appear which you can connect to the third object. You can keep making connections to new objects until you release the <CTRL> key.

 **Hint** – if you are viewing a model or moving objects around you may find yourself accidentally making connections you  don't want. To avoid this turn off the *connection mode* by clicking the Connection mode Button so it isn't highlighted.

The disadvantage of the *connection mode* is it can be tricky to select an appropriate connection point, especially when using a zoomed out view and it is not always convenient to have the mode enabled for long periods. An alternative is to use *quick drawing of connections* (see Section 9.6.3).

### 9.6.2     Connection Types and Direction

The ARIS Method, and the Method Filter in use, will define the valid relationships (connection types) that exist between objects. If, when connecting objects, the *Prohibited Icon* (Fig. 9.7) appears instead of the connection icon, this indicates the current Method Filter does not allow a connection between those object types.

If a connection already exists between two objects, an error message may be displayed if you try to connect them again. However, it is possible to have different relationship types between the same two object types. In that case it is possible to make a second connection provided you chose a different relationship.

Relationships also have a direction and it makes a difference which way you draw the connection. Some object types will support connections between them in both directions, but with different relationships. Other object types will only allow connections in one direction.

This all sounds very confusing, but fortunately ARIS helps by displaying the available valid relationships when you connect objects. If there is only one valid relationship (in that direction), the connection will be made automatically. If there are several possibilities, the *Select relationship type Dialog Box* (Fig. 9.9) will show all the possible relationships (including any in the other direction) so you can chose the most appropriate.

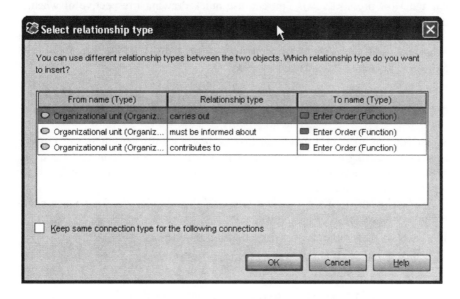

**Fig. 9.9** Select Relationship Type Dialog Box

 **Hint** – if you are making several connections of the same type between the same types of object, you can avoid having to repeatedly select the type by checking the *Keep the same connection type for the following connections Checkbox* at the bottom of the *Select relationship type Dialog Box* (Fig. 9.9).

Using the *connection mode* does mean you have to be aware of which direction to draw the connection. If you find this awkward, then it is easier to use the *quick drawing of connections* or *place and connect* modes which don't require you to know this (see below).

### 9.6.3    Quick Drawing of Connections

*Quick drawing of connections* allows a single connection to be quickly made between two objects without having to worry about selecting connection points or the connection direction. To use it:

1.  Click on the Quick drawing of connections Button on the *Symbols Bar*,
2.  Click in the centre of the first object,
3.  Click in the centre of the second object.

A connection will be automatically drawn between the two objects using the most direct route. *Quick drawing of connections* is no longer enabled so if you want to use it again you will need to select the Quick drawing of connections Button again (or press <F11>). You can use quick drawing irrespective of whether *connection mode* (Section 9.6.1) is enabled or not.

If there are several valid relationships available between the selected objects (in either direction) the *Select relationship type Dialog Box* (Fig. 9.9) will appear and allow you to choose the most appropriate.


### 9.6.4    Place and Connect

When you are creating a new model, or adding a significant amount of process flow to an existing model, there is a quick way to '*place and connect*' a sequence of objects without having to separately place them all and separately connect them up.

First make sure you are in *connection mode* by enabling the Connection mode Button on the *Designer Toolbar* and:

1.  Click on the symbol for the first object on the *Symbols Bar*,
2.  Click in the *Modelling Window* and place the first object,
3.  Enter a name in the text box,
4.  With the <u>first object still selected</u> click on the symbol on the *Symbols Bar* for the second object,
5.  Select the connection type from the pop-up window, if it appears (or do nothing to accept the default),
6.  Click in the *Modelling Window* and place the second object,
7.  Enter a name in the text box.

You will see the second object is placed and automatically connected to the first object (Fig. 9.10). The second object is now selected so you can enter a new name and, provided you keep an object selected in the *Modelling Window*, you can repeat this procedure a number of times to quickly create a process flow. If you want to place and connect to an object that is not the last object placed, just select a different object and carry on with step 4.

**Hint** – when you select an object in the *Modelling Window*, those object types that can be connected to it (as defined by the Method Filter) will be enabled on the *Symbols Bar*. Objects that don't have valid connection types will be greyed out.

The *place and connect* mode is probably the most useful for placing and connecting objects because it gives a visual indication of both the objects that can be connected and the valid connection types.

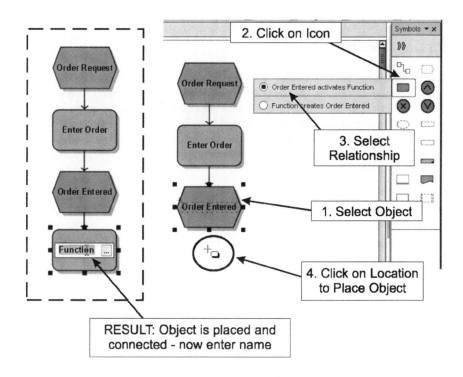

**Fig. 9.10** Place and Connect Objects

## 9.6.5 Place and Connect of Multiple Objects

You can combine the *place and connect* and *connecting to multiple objects* modes. When you come to place the second object (step 4 above), hold down the <CTRL> key. You can now place multiple copies of the second object. The only difference is the first object remains selected so you cannot rename the multiple objects as you place them; you will have to do this later.

**Expert Tip** – you can combine *place and connect* with *connecting to multiple objects* to quickly create a flow of functions and events and, at the same time, add resource objects (e.g. an *Organizational unit*) to the functions. Place and connect an event and function, select an *Organizational unit* and hold down the <CTRL> key when placing it. The function stays selected so you can select another event and continue the flow. When you have completed the flow all you have to do is rename the resource objects.

### 9.6.6    Nested Objects

When creating models representing hierarchical structures (e.g. *Organizational* charts, Value-added chain diagrams or Function trees, see Chapter 13), it is convenient to show objects on top of one another (or overlapping) to represent hierarchical or 'belonging to' relationships. To avoid having to make connections between these '*nested*' objects, and clutter up the model with lines, ARIS 7 allows automatic '*implicit relationships*' to be made between nested objects (Fig. 9.11).

To make a nested object relationship:

1.  Place the first object on the model,

2.  Place a second object on top of the first, or drag an existing object on top of the first (Fig. 9.11b)

3.  Select the required relationship from the *Create relationship Dialog Box* (Fig. 9.12).

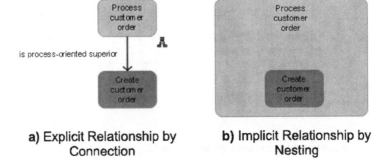

**a) Explicit Relationship by Connection**          **b) Implicit Relationship by Nesting**

**Fig. 9.11** Implicit Nested Object Relationship

If the second object disappears after you have placed it on top of the first, you will need to change the order of visibility of the objects:

1.  Select the visible nested object,

2.  Right-Click > Arrange > Send to back.

The second object should now be visible on top of the first (see Chapter 10 for more on arranging object order). When you place the second object on top of the first the *Create relationship Dialog Box* (Fig. 9.12) will show all the valid relationships between the two objects so that you can select the one you want. You don't necessarily have to select a hierarchical type relationship if other types are allowed, but this is normally the way nested relationships are used.

If you no longer want to be given the option to create an implicit relationship when you nest objects, you can turn this off by deselecting the *Continue creation of implicit connections Checkbox* at the bottom of the *Create relationship Dialog Box* (see Fig. 9.12).

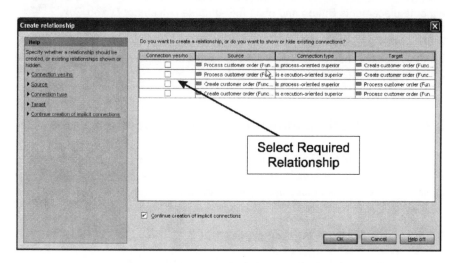

**Fig. 9.12** Create Relationship Dialog Box

## 9.6.7    Displaying Connection Types

Once you have made a connection it just appears as a line between the objects, so how can you tell which connection type it is? Ensure the *Properties Checkbox* is checked so the *Properties Bar* is visible 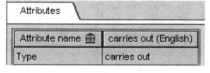 and select the *Attributes Tab*. Now select a connection and look at the *Type* attribute towards the top of the list. You will see it shows the type of connection (e.g. "*carries out*"). You cannot change the connection type by changing its attribute. If you want a different type of connection (assuming the method supports it) you will have to delete the connection and make a new one.

**Hint** – a quick way to identify the relationship type of a connection is
to hover your mouse over the connec-
tion. A tooltip will appear and show
the *Type* attribute. If the tooltip is
not visible, enable them at <u>V</u>iew >
<u>O</u>ptions...[*General/Objects*] and check
the *Show <u>t</u>ooltips* box.

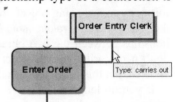

Any of the attributes of objects or connections can be displayed as text associated with the item on the actual model. We will look at how to do this in detail in
Chapter 14, but for the moment select a connection and click on the Edit
attribute placements Button and open the *Attribute placement Dialog Box*.
Click on the <u>A</u>dd... button at the top right corner of the dialog box and
select the *Type* attribute in the *Add attributes Dialog Box*. Press OK twice to close
the dialog boxes and you will now see the connection type displayed alongside the
connection you selected.

## 9.7        Selecting, Moving, Sizing and Deleting Items

To select one of the items in a model (e.g. an object or connection) simply click on
it. The eight boxes that appear around it indicate it has been selected. To deselect
all select objects, click in an empty space in the model.

### 9.7.1        Selecting Multiple Items

To select multiple items, click on an empty area of the model and drag the mouse
so as to draw an imaginary rectangle around the items. A rubber-band selection
area will appear and when you release the mouse button, all the items in the area
will be selected. You can also select multiple items by holding down the <Ctrl>
key and clicking on each of the items in turn.

### 9.7.2        Right-Click Item Selection

More advanced selection commands are available from the
<u>E</u>dit > <u>S</u>elect or the *Right-Click* > <u>S</u>elect Menu that appears
when you right-click on an item in the model area (see
Table 9.1).

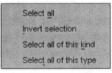

**Table 9.1** Right-Click Item Selection Options

| Selected item | Select Command Options | Meaning |
|---|---|---|
| Model (nothing selected) | Select all | Selects all items on the model (e.g. objects, connections, drawing objects). |
| | Invert selection | Selects all items not currently selected and deselects those already selected. |
| Item (e.g. Object or Connection) | Select all of this kind | Select all the same kind of items (e.g. all objects or all connections). |
| | Select all of this type | Select all items of the same type (e.g. all event objects or all activates connections). |

Note: if multiple items of different types are selected, the Select all of this kind command option will not appear.

### 9.7.3    Moving Objects

To move one or more objects, select them as described above. Click the mouse in the centre of the selected area (not on the small black boxes) and while continuing to hold down the mouse button, drag the cursor around the model. You will see an outline of objects as you move, and when you release the mouse the objects will appear in their new location. The lines representing the connections between the objects will automatically adjust, although how tidy the result is will depend on where you moved the objects to.

You can also use right-click drag and drop which will give the option (when you release the mouse key) of moving the objects or copying them.

### 9.7.4    Resizing Objects

You can resize an object, or group of objects, by selecting them and dragging the square black boxes at the edges of the selection area. Dragging a box in the middle of one of the sides will resize it in that direction (e.g. horizontal or vertical). Dragging one of the corner boxes will resize it in both directions at once. You cannot resize a connection; to alter the width of a connecting line, use the *Connection properties Dialog Box* (see Chapter 10).

If the grid is selected (also see Chapter 10), the resized object will snap to the nearest grid position. You can also use <CTRL + Key> combinations with dragging to select one or more sides to be resized or to override the grid (see Table 9.2).

**Table 9.2** Resizing Control Keys

| Key | Operation |
| --- | --- |
| Drag Side | Changes size of selected side of object, using grid settings. |
| Alt + Drag Side | Changes size of selected side of object, overriding grid settings. |
| Ctrl + Drag Side | Changes size of both opposite sides of an object to nearest grid setting. |
| Ctrl + Alt + Drag Side | Changes size of both opposite sides of an object, overriding grid settings. |

### 9.7.5 Moving Connections

The connections between the objects can also be selected by clicking on them. The lines will turn red and small boxes will appear at the ends of the lines (the connection points in Fig. 9.8) and at any corners. You can drag the connection points around the outline of the objects to which they are connected so the line connects in a different place. You can also drag the small boxes at corners of lines to alter the path the line takes.

**Hint** – you can move a connection from its current object to a new object by dragging the connection point off the current object and connecting it to a new object (provided the connection is allowed by the Method Filter).

**Warning** – for most models it is not wise to spend a lot of time manually moving objects and connections. Where available, it is better to use the Arrange > Layout command to bring up the *Layout preview Dialog Box* and automatically layout the model (see Chapter 10).

### 9.7.6 Aligning Connections

You may get some interesting results from experimenting with moving connections, but you can tidy up the lines by selecting one or more lines and Right-Click > Align Connection. ARIS will automatically redraw the line to be the best route between the objects.

### 9.7.7 Deleting Objects

To delete objects, select them and do one of the following:

* Edit > Delete,
* Right-Click > Delete,
* Select the Delete Button on the *Designer Toolbar*,
* Press the \<Delete\> key.

The object, and its connections to other objects, will be deleted from the model. The object itself is not deleted from the database, just the reference to it in this model. It will remain in the database until there are no longer any *occurrences* of it in any model and the Reorganize... database administration utility is run.

### 9.7.8 Undo and Redo

Once you have experimented with these operations for a while your model may end up as rather a mess and you may wish you could tidy it  up or revert back to the original layout. ARIS has multiple levels of *undo* and *redo* which enable you to revert back to any stage in editing operations since the last time the model was saved. Undo and Redo are  on the *Main Menu* under Edit and also can be selected from icons on the *Designer Toolbar*.

# Chapter 10    Model Appearance

In this chapter we look at how change the appearance of models, objects and connections. We look at how to align objects, the model layout facility and how to configure its operation.

## 10.1    Changing the Model Appearance

The appearance of models in the *Designer Module* is governed by a number of different elements:

- Zooming and Scaling (see Section 10.2),
- Model Appearance Properties (Section 10.3),
- Object Appearance Properties (Section 10.1),
- Connection Appearance Properties (Section 10.5),
- Model Layout (see Section 10.6),
- Object Alignment (see Section 10.6.2),
- Templates (see Section 10.7).

## 10.2    Zooming and Scaling

The *Modelling Window* shows a scaled view of the entire model. Depending on the size of the model and how it was last left, you may see everything in the model or just a portion of it. You can change the scale and position of the model view using the <u>V</u>iew commands and by using the *Model overview window*, as described below.

### 10.2.1    Model Overview Window

With very large models and high zoom factors it can be difficult to visualise where the visible area of a model is in relation to the whole model. However, this can easily be seen by using the *Model overview window Tab* in the *Navigation Bar*.

To make the *Navigation Bar* visible, click on the *Navigation Checkbox* at the top right of the *Designer Window* and select the *Model overview window Tab*. You can increase the size of the *Navigation Bar* by dragging on the window boundary.

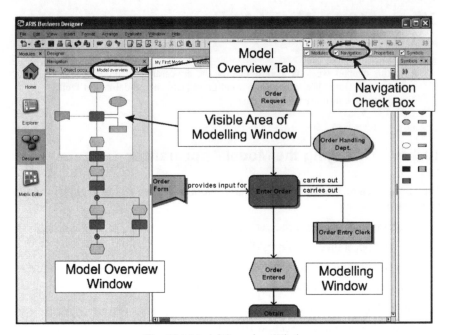

**Fig. 10.1** Model Overview Window

The *Model overview Window* (Fig. 10.1) shows a white shaded area representing the visible area of the model. As you scroll around the main model, or zoom in or out, the shaded area will also move or scale in synchronisation to give you a visual indication of the relationship between the visible area and the entire model. If you click on the white area on the *Model overview Window* and drag it around the window, the visible part of the model in the *Modelling Window* will also move to make that part of the model visible. This makes it very quick to locate a particular part of a zoomed model. This has the same effect as dragging the *Modelling Window* scroll bars, but is a much quicker, especially with very large models.

You can close the *Model Overview Window* at any time by un-checking the *Navigation Checkbox*.

## 10.2.2    View and Zoom Commands

The <u>V</u>iew sub-menu on the *Main Menu* has a set of commands for scaling the *Modelling Window*. The Zoom commands also have buttons on the *Designer Toolbar* (see Chapter 9) and, in addition, the *Size of appearance* button allows the scale of the screen to be set directly using the drop-down box, either by selecting one of the pre-set values or by entering a new value followed by <Enter>. The operation of the commands is shown in Table 10.1 along with their shortcut keys.

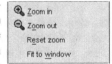

**Table 10.1** Model Scaling Commands

| Command | Shortcut | Action |
|---|---|---|
| <u>V</u>iew > <u>Z</u>oom In  | <+> | Increases scale of window area by 10% centred at the middle top of the window or on the selected object. |
| <u>V</u>iew > <u>Z</u>oom Out | <-> | Decreases scale of window area by 10% centred at the middle top of the window or on the selected object. |
| <u>V</u>iew > Original si<u>z</u>e | | Resizes the window to 100%. |
| <u>V</u>iew > Fit to <u>w</u>indow | | **Nothing selected** – rescales window so entire model fits in the visible area. |
| | | **Objects selected** – rescales window so selected objects fit in the visible area. |
| *Size of appearance Button* 110 % ▼ | | Shows the current scale factor of the model and allows selection of a pre-set value or over-typing of any value followed by <Enter>. |

**Hint** – if you have a mouse with a scroll wheel you can quickly zoom in and out of the *Modelling Window* by holding down the <CTRL> key and rotating the wheel. If you click on an object first, the zoom will be centred on the object.

## 10.3    Model Appearance Properties

The basic appearance of the model currently open in the *Designer Module* is defined by the settings in the *Format Dialog Box* of the model *Properties Dialog Box*. There are four sub-dialog boxes:

- **Representation** – model scale, colour, template, text appearance,
- **Connections** – rounding and bridge settings for connecting lines,
- **Print** – portrait / landscape, scale, black and white,
- **Grid** – use and width.

The appearance properties only apply to the model currently opened in the *Designer Module* unless you set the *Use as default* box. You can define the default settings to be applied to all new models using <u>V</u>iew > <u>O</u>ptions [*Model / For new models*] which has the same four sub-dialog boxes.

## 10.3.1    Representation

To set model appearance options in the *[Format / Representation] Dialog Box,* ensure no objects are selected, and do any of:

- Select the Properties Button on the *Designer Toolbar* and    (i)
  select *[Format / Representation]*,
- Format > Representation *[Format / Representation]* from *Main Menu,*
- Right-Click > Properties *[Format / Representation]*,
- Right-Click > Format > Representation *[Format / Representation]*.

Table 10.2 shows the options that can be set.

**Table 10.2** Model Properties – Format / Representation

| Command | Action |
|---------|--------|
| Scaling | Shows the current scale factor of the model and allows selection of a pre-set value or overtyping of any value followed by <Enter>. Same effect as using the *Size of appearance Button* on the *Designer Toolbar.* |
| Background color | Click on the box and select a colour from the palette to change the background colour from the default of white. Avoid very dark or bright colours. Alternatively set *Display wallpaper* (see below). |
| Text attributes in symbol | Provides four options for the display of the *Name* attribute text inside a symbol (see below). |
| Hide assignment icons | Selecting this option will cause the icons showing there are models assigned to objects to be hidden. This is useful for presentation purposes or in complex models with nested objects. |
| Remove colour behind text | Displays a white background to any text attributes displayed in an object (usually the *Name* attribute). Makes the text more readable against dark coloured objects. |
| Display wallpaper | Allows a pre-selected graphic to be used as a model background. **Note**: the graphic to use for wallpaper can be pre-selected using *Model Properties [Logo management {Wallpaper}]* in the *Administration Module.* |

| | |
|---|---|
| *Current template* | This allows a model template to be selected that will apply a pre-determined appearance to all existing and new objects, connections and displayed attributes (see Section 10.7). |
| *Use as default* | If checked, the saved properties will be used as the default for all new models created. This has the same effect as setting options using View > Options [*For new models / Representation*]. |

When you have changed options you can preview the effect on the current model by pressing the Preview Button (you may have to drag the dialog box out of the way to see the model underneath). If you are happy with the changes, press OK otherwise to revert to how things were before you opened the dialog box, press Reset; you can then try different options. To close the dialog box without making any changes, press Cancel.

### Text Attributes in Symbol

The *Text attributes in symbol* setting determines how lengthy text strings entered into the object's *Name* attribute will be displayed inside the object symbol (Fig. 10.2):

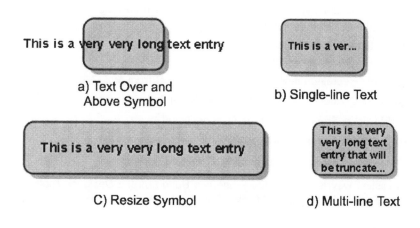

**Fig. 10.2** Text Attributes in Symbol Options

- **Text over and above the symbol** – displays all the text on a single line which may extend beyond the edges of the object (see Fig. 10.2a). You can force line breaks into the text by entering <Ctrl + Enter>.

- **Single-line text** – displays the text on a single line, but where text has to be omitted in order for it to fit in the box, it is replaced with three dots (...) (see Fig. 10.2b). Not recommended.

- **Resize symbol** – the symbol is automatically re-sized so all the text fits inside the symbol outline (see Fig. 10.2c). Not recommended because models with symbols of all different sizes look untidy.

- **Multi-line text** – wraps the text to fit on several lines, but where text has to be omitted in order for it to fit in the box, it is replaced with three dots (...) (see Fig. 10.2d).

*Multi-line text* is probably the most useful option, but there is a danger that objects can be misinterpreted when there is missing text. The *Text over and above the symbol* option is the safest because you see always see the entire name. You can decide yourself where the line breaks should be and it is good practice to try to choose short names.

### 10.3.2    Connections

To set the appearance of all connections in the *[Format / Connections] Dialog Box*, ensure no connections are selected and select any of following bewildering set of commands that achieve the same thing:

- Select the Properties Button on the *Designer Toolbar* and ⓘ
  select *[Format / Connections]*,

- Format > Representation [*Format / Connections*] from *Main Menu,*

- Format > Connections [*Format / Connections*] from *Main Menu,*

- Right-Click > Properties [*Format / Connections*],

- Right-Click > Format > Representation [*Format / Connections*],

- Right-Click > Format > Connections [*Format / Connections*].

The easiest way is to press the Properties Button on the *Designer Toolbar* and go to the [*Format / Connections*] Dialog Box. Table 10.3 shows the options that can be set.

**Table 10.3** Model Properties – Format / Connections

| Command | Action |
|---|---|
| *Bridge height:* | Sets the height of a curved bridge used to show where one connection crosses over another. |
| *Rounding intensity:* | Sets the radius of rounded corners of lines that change direction. Lines are at right angles if set to zero. |
| *New connections only right-angled* | When set (the default) the lines between two points will only be drawn at right angles (e.g. no diagonal lines). If unchecked the shortest connection between the two points will be drawn. |
| *Use as default* | If checked, the saved properties will be used as the default for all new models created. This has the same effect as setting options in **V**iew > **O**ptions [*For new models / Connections*]. |

The *[Format / Connections] Dialog Box* described above sets the properties for all connections in the model. In contrast, if you select a single connection and Right-Click > P<u>r</u>operties, the Connection properties Dialog Box will appear with a [Format / Connection appearance] Dialog Box allowing you to set properties (e.g. colour, line thickness, etc.) for just the selected connection (see Section 10.5).

## 10.3.3   Print

The *[Format / Print] Dialog Box* defines how this particular model will be printed (Table 10.4).

**Table 10.4** Model Properties – Format / Print

| Command | Action |
|---|---|
| *Print scale* | • Set print scale by selecting or entering a value in the % scale box, <br><br>• Press **Fit to page Button** to size model to fit on one page, <br><br>• Press the **Specify number of pages Button** and alter the sliders in the dialog box to select the number of pages the model should be printed on. |
| *Bla**c**k and white* | Prints model as a greyscale. |
| *Orientation* | Enables selection of Portrait or **L**andscape orientation. |
| *Use as default* | If checked, the saved properties will be used as the default for all new models created. This has the same effect as setting options in **V**iew > **O**ptions [*For new models / Print*]. |

### 10.3.4     Grid

The *[Format / Grid] Dialog Box* defines how grid will be displayed on this model (Table 10.5).

**Table 10.5** Model Properties – Format / Grid

| Command | Action |
|---|---|
| <u>U</u>se grid | Displays the grid as a matrix of dots as background to the model. The same effect can be achieved by pressing **Toggle grid Button** on the *Designer Toolbar*. |
| *Grid width* | • Sets the spacing of dots on the grid (2–100),<br>• Aligns objects by centring them on a grid point (Fig. 10.3a). |
| *Special grid model* | • Displays the grid as squares (minimum size 30),<br>• Aligns objects within the centre of the square (Fig. 10.3b). |
| U<u>s</u>e as default | If checked, the saved properties will be used as the default for all new models created. This has the same effect as setting options in <u>V</u>iew > <u>O</u>ptions [*For new models / Grid*]. |

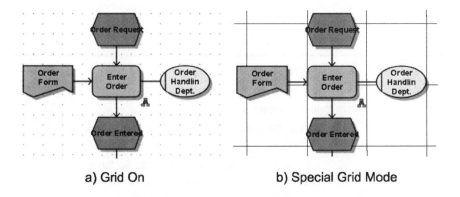

a) Grid On                          b) Special Grid Mode

**Fig. 10.3** Grid Modes

## 10.4      Object Appearance

The appearance of the symbols representing individual objects in a model can be changed by altering the settings in the *Object properties Dialog Box* (Fig. 10.4). You can make changes to the appearance of an individual object or select a number of objects and make changes to them all. To display the dialog box, select one or more objects and do any of:

- Select the Properties Button on the *Designer Toolbar* and  select [*Format / Object appearance*],

- <u>F</u>ormat > <u>R</u>epresentation [*Format / Object appearance*] from *Main Menu*,

- Right-Click > P<u>r</u>operties [*Format / Object appearance*],

- Right-Click > Format > <u>R</u>epresentation [*Format / Object appearance*].

Table 10.6 shows the options available.

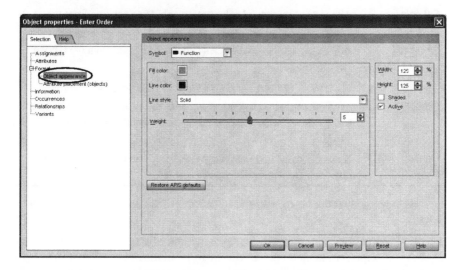

**Fig. 10.4** Object Appearance Dialog Box

**Table 10.6** Object Properties / Appearance

| Command | Action |
|---------|--------|
| *Symbol* | Many object types (e.g. functions) have alternative symbols that can be used to represent them, depending on the Method Filter in use. The alternative symbols available for the selected object are listed in the *Symbol* drop-down box. |
| <u>*Width*</u> | Shows the current symbol width as a % of its default and allows it to be changed. Can also be changed directly within a model by resizing |

*(Continued)*

**Table 10.6** (*Continued*)

| Command | Action |
|---|---|
|  | the object symbol (See Chapter 9). This may be constrained by the grid setting. |
| *Height* | Shows the current symbol height as a % of its default and allows it to be changed. Can also be changed directly within a model by resizing the object symbol (see Chapter 9). This may be constrained by the grid setting. |
| *Shaded* | Puts a shaded outline (shadow) around the symbol to give it a more three-dimensional appearance. |
| *Active* | If unchecked the symbol is displayed with a white fill colour and grey border. Can be used to show unused object in a reference design. May be used for configuring some *ARIS Controlling Platform* applications. |
| *Fill color* | Allows the background colour of a symbol to be chosen from the *Chose color Dialog Box*. |
| *Line color* | Allows the outline colour of a symbol to be chosen from the *Chose color Dialog Box*. |
| *Line style* | Allows the outline of the symbol to be *Solid, Dashed* or *Dotted*. |
| *Weight* | Shows the weight (i.e. thickness and intensity) of the symbol outline and it allows it to be changed by entering a value or dragging the slider. |
| *Restore ARIS defaults* | Resets the symbol appearance properties to those set by the Method Filter and any applied Template. |

A preview of what the object will look like can be seen by pressing the Preview Button.

 **Warning** – you should not alter the colour of an object symbol in order to represent something significant in modelling terms; for instance, to indicate those functions carried out by a particular department. The colour of the symbol is not stored as part of the object definition and cannot be easily reported on or analysed. Establish relationships to other objects instead.


## 10.5    Connection Appearance

The appearance of the lines used to connect object symbols together can be changed by altering the settings in the *Connection properties Dialog Box* (see Fig. 10.5). You can make changes to the appearance of an individual connection or select a number of connections and make changes to them all.

To display the dialog box, select one or more connections and do any of:

- Select the Properties Button on the *Designer Toolbar* and ⓘ
  select [*Format / Connection  appearance*],

- Eormat > Representation [*Format / Connection appearance*] from *Main Menu*,

- Right-Click > Properties [*Format / Connection appearance*],

- Right-Click > Format > Representation [*Format / Connection appearance*].

Table 10.7 shows the options available.

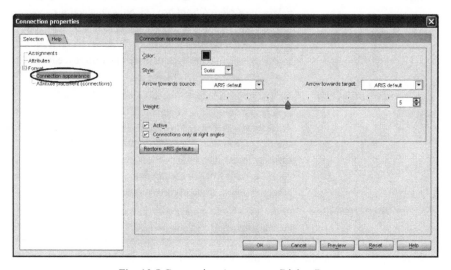

**Fig. 10.5** Connection Appearance Dialog Box

**Table 10.7** Connection Properties / Appearance

| Command | Action |
| --- | --- |
| Color | Allows the line colour of a connection to be chosen from the *Chose color Dialog Box*. |
| Style | Allows the connection line to be Solid, Dashed or Dotted. |
| Arrow towards source | Allows selection of different line ending styles (e.g. arrows) to be defined for the source object end of the connection. Selecting **ARIS default** will apply the style defined in the Method Filter. |
| Arrow towards target | Allows selection of different line ending styles (e.g. arrows) to be defined for the target object end of the |

**Table 10.7** (*Continued*)

| Command | Action |
|---|---|
|  | connection. Selecting **ARIS default** will apply the style defined in the Method Filter. |
| *Weight* | Shows the weight (i.e. thickness and intensity) of the line and allows it to be changed by entering a value or dragging the slide. |
| *Active* | Connections can be marked as inactive by removing the tick in the **Active Checkbox**. Inactive connections appear 'greyed-out', but this is often difficult to distinguish from the normal connection appearance. Whether a connection is shown as active or inactive makes no difference to the relationships shown for the objects. |
| *Connections only right-angled* | To enable the selected connection to run diagonally rather than at right angles, uncheck the **Connection(s) only at Right Angles** box. This is different from the similar setting in the model *Properties* dialog box [*Model Appearance*] Tab, which sets the option for all new connections. You will not see any immediate difference, but diagonal lines will be used when the object is moved. |
| *Restore ARIS defaults* | Resets the symbol appearance properties to those set by the Method Filter and any applied Template. |

A preview of what the connection will look like can be seen by pressing the Preview Button.

# 10.6     Model Layout

The layout of objects and connections in a model can be defined manually by the user or, for many models, automatically by ARIS. In addition, there are a number of helpful tools and commands.

### 10.6.1     The Model Grid

#### *Setting and Using the Grid*

By clicking on the Toggle grid Button on the *Designer Toolbar*, a drawing grid will be superimposed behind the model. The grid mode and width of the grid can be set in the model properties *Right-Click > Properties [Format / Grid] Dialog Box* as we described in Section 10.3.4.

The grid is indicated by a matrix of dots and can be used to align objects and connections, thus making drawing easier and improving the appearance of your model. The spacing of the dots can be set by altering the *Grid Width* slider to values between 2 and 100.

The grid settings can be enabled as the default for new models by setting similar options in the *View* > *Options... [Model / For new models / Grid] Dialog Box*.

## Snapping Objects to the Grid

New objects created in the model while the grid is turned on will automatically be aligned so as to be centred on a grid point, as will objects moved within the model. The edges of the object will not necessarily line up with the grid dots because there is no direct relationship between the size of an object and the grid setting. If you resize an object by dragging the edges of the object, it will snap to a size that allows the object to be centred on the next grid point in the direction you are dragging.

If you select the *Special grid mode* field in the *Grid Dialog Box* (Section 10.3.4) the grid will be display as a matrix of squares (minimum size 30) with the centre of the square at a grid point. Any objects you create, move or size will now be aligned so as to fit into the centre of a square or group of squares.

## Snapping Connections to the Grid

With the grid turned on, any connections made between objects will have connection points at grid points and any right angles in the lines will have their corners at grid points. Moving existing connections will also cause them to snap to grid points. With very large grid settings this can lead to limited connection points and strange routing of lines.

## Aligning to the Grid

Objects or connections created or moved when the grid is not turned on will not be aligned to the grid. They will still remain unaligned even when the grid is turned on. To align existing objects or connections to the grid:

1.  Ensure the grid is turned on (grid dots should appear superimposed on the model),

2.  Select the items you wish to align,

3.  Arrange > Align to Grid from the *Main Menu* or *Right-Click Menu*.

The objects and connections will now move onto the grid. The spacing between the objects will be adjusted so they fit the grid and this may not always result in an even spacing.

If you just select an object and align it to the grid, the object will now be on the grid, but its connections will still be off-grid. To correct this, select a connection and Arrange > Align to Grid. The line's connection points and corners will now move onto the grid. The Right-Click > Align connection command will also move connection line corners onto the grid, but it won't move connection points.

### 10.6.2    Aligning Objects

If you want to line up objects so they are all in the same row or column, they are equally spaced, or the same size, you can do this quickly by using the align commands. There are twelve commands available. Select the objects you wish to align and do any of:

- Click on the down arrow next to the Align Button on
  the *Designer Toolbar* and select the alignment option,

- Ar̲range > A̲lign from the *Main Menu*,

- Right-Click > A̲lign.

A pop-up menu will appear with the options shown in Fig. 10.6. If you are doing a lot of alignment work you can move the pop-up menu onto the *Modelling Window* so it is always visible. Click on the down arrow next to the Align Button and click on the double line above the first entry and drag it onto the Modelling Window. The pop-up *Arrange Menu* will detach and stay visible (Fig. 10.6). You can close it by clicking on the Close Button (**x**).

Note: if the grid is turned on, but some of the objects being used as the basis for alignment are not on the grid then, after alignment, none of the objects may be on the grid. For instance using Align to b̲ottom to an object not on the grid will align all selected objects up to it and hence they will be off-grid. This can be corrected by selecting all the objects and using Ar̲range > Align̲ to Grid.

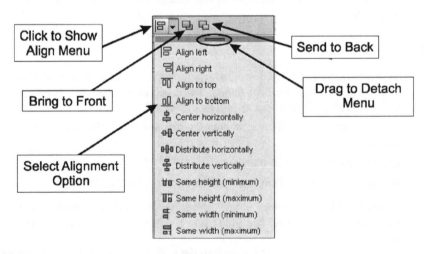

**Fig. 10.6** Arrange Menu

## 10.6.3      Arrange Object Order

It is possible to move objects so they overlap each other. This can be useful for presentation purposes and it also possible to make *implicit relationships* between nested objects (See Chapter 9). without having to connect them up. To control the order in which objects overlap each other, select one or more of the overlapping objects and select Arrange from the *Main Menu* or *Right-Click Menu*.

You will be given four options for setting the display order of the objects:

*   Bring to front,
*   Send to back,
*   One level forward,
*   One level backward.

By using these commands on various objects you can control they way in which they overlap each other. The Bring to Front and Send to Back commands can be issued more quickly using the buttons on the *Designer Toolbar*.

## 10.6.4      Grouping

If you have carefully laid out part of your model, manually selected the route of connecting lines and set the order in which objects overlap, you will be annoyed if the automatically layout facility subsequently undoes all this good work. You may also want to manually move some of the objects and connections while still retaining the layout they have in relation to each other. You can preserve this layout by *grouping* the items together. Select all the objects you wish to group and Arrange > Group or Right-Click > Group.

The group can now be selected and moved as a single entity. The internal structure and connections of the group will remain unchanged, but the connections to objects external to the group will alter as they are moved. You can still make connections from objects internal to the group to objects outside the group.

If the automatic model layout is used, the group will be treated as a single entity and the end result of the entire model will not necessarily look the same as without the grouping.

To ungroup a selection, Arrange > Ungroup or Right-Click > Ungroup.

## 10.6.5      Automatic Model Layout

Trying to manually lay out a model neatly can be a time-consuming process so ARIS provides an automated model layout facility.

## Layout Preview Dialog Box

To automatically layout a model, make sure no objects are selected and

- Arrange > Layout... or  Right-Click > Arrange > Layout....

The *Layout preview Dialog Box* will be launched (Fig. 10.7).

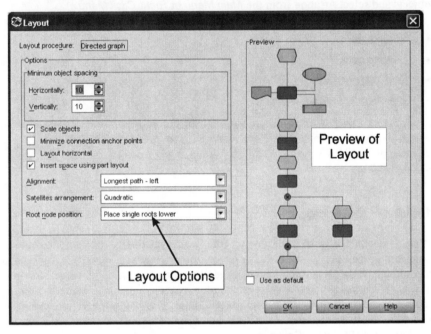

**Fig. 10.7** Layout Preview Dialog Box

On the left-hand side of the *Layout preview Dialog Box* are a set of layout options and on the right-hand side a preview of what the model will look like using those options. If you click OK, the model will be changed to that layout.

At the top of the options area, the *Layout procedure* field shows what type of layout algorithm is being used (e.g. *Directed graph* for an EPC).

Beneath it the *Minimum object spacing* fields define how close objects can be in the horizontal and vertical planes. You can alter these fields to spread out the layout of the model. If the grid is switched on the values are the minimum spacing and the actual value will be at the next grid position (see Section 10.6.1). Table 10.8 shows other layout options for an EPC.

**Table 10.8** Automatic Model Layout Options

| Command | Action |
| --- | --- |
| *Scale objects* | Allows the size of objects to be automatically increased if there are a large number of connection points that need to be accommodated. Normally used with rules (e.g. *XOR*). |
| *Minimise connection anchor points* | Reduces the number of connection points and may place them on top of one another. Not recommended. |
| *Horizontal layout* | Lays out the process flow from left to right rather than top to bottom. Not recommended. |
| *Insert space using part layout* | When selecting part of a model for partial layout (see below), ensures objects don't overlap the existing model by introducing appropriate spaces. |
| *Alignment* | • **Centred** – main process flow is in the centre with branches to left and right, <br> • **Longest path centred** – similar to Centred, <br> • **Longest path left** – main process flow is on the left with branches to the right. Always displays something at the top left of the model, <br> • **Longest path right left** – main process flow is on the right with branches to the left. |
| *Satellites arrangement* | • **Horizontally** – displays resource objects (e.g. *Organizational unit*) in a horizontal line out from the connected function, <br> • **Vertically** – displays resource objects (e.g. *Organizational unit*) in a vertical line out from the connected function, <br> • **Quadratic** – displays resource objects (e.g. *Organizational unit*) in a square block. |
| *Root node position* | • **Arrange roots above** – displays all incoming root nodes (events) at the top of the model, <br> • **Place single roots lower** – displays incoming events as close as possible to the point where they join the model, <br> • **Place roots with components lower** – optimises display to minimise distance between incoming events and all connected objects. |
| *Use as default* | If checked, the saved layout options will be used as the default for all new models using this *Layout procedure*. This has the same effect as setting options in View > Options [*Layout*]. |

Other model types may have different or additional layout options depending on the layout algorithm they use.

The most common of these other options is:

- **Change to vertical layout** – specifies the level of hierarchy after which objects are placed vertically rather than horizontally.

The result of the model layout will depend on how your model has been connected and on various ARIS set-up options (e.g. if the grid is on). If the Layout produces unexpected results, you can return the model to its previous state using the Undo command described above.

Very large or complex models may lead to layouts with overlapping objects or other layout artefacts. If this occurs try changing the *Alignment* and *Root node position* settings.

### Recommended Layout Settings

Recommended settings are:

- *Scale objects* – **on** (checked),
- *Minimise connection anchor points* – **off** (not checked),
- *Horizontal layout* – **off** (not checked),
- *Alignment* – **Longest path centred**,
- *Satellites arrangement* – **Quadratic**,
- *Root node position* – **Place single roots lower**.

If you are using *ARIS Web Publisher* it is best to use Longest path left to ensure web pages have some of the model visible at the top left.

### Default Layout Options

If you want the layout options defined above to be used with all models of that type (e.g. all EPCs), click the *Use as default Checkbox* and click OK.

Alternatively you can set up the default layout options for all model types from the *View > Options [Layout] Dialog Box*. At the top of the box the *Layout procedure* field allows you to select the type of layout algorithm you want to define (e.g. *Directed graph* for an EPC). The lists of options below will change to those relevant to the selected algorithm and you can set appropriate values.

If you know the model type you want to set the layout for, but not which layout procedure it uses, click on the Select... Button. The *Layout procedure Dialog Box* will provide a list of model types and their associated layout procedure from which you can select the one for which you wish to set the defaults.

### 10.6.6 Part Layout

The part layout facility allows you to select just a part of the model and use the automatic layout algorithm to lay out that segment. The effect depends very much on the nature of the model and the relation of the part to the whole. Select one or more objects and Arrange > Part layout or Right-Click > Arrange > Part layout.

The *Insert space using part layout* option in the *View > Options... [Model / Layout] Dialog Box* allows you to select whether part layout should open a space in the model for the new layout, or layout the objects where they are located even if they overlay other objects.

### 10.6.7 Insert and Remove Space

Often when you are working on a model, you need to add additional objects and connect them into the existing process flow. Once you have placed and connected the objects, you can use the model layout to produce a new layout. However, there is often no room in which to put the objects while you are connecting them up, or maybe you don't wish to use the model layout facility. In these situations you end up manually moving parts of the model around the window, trying to make space for the new objects. Instead you can use the Insert and remove space command to add vertical or horizontal space:

- Arrange > Insert and remove space or
  Right-Click > Insert and remove space
- Choose Vertically or Horizontally.

The mouse cursor will change to a crosshair and a vertical or horizontal dashed line will appear where the space insertion or deletion will start. Move the mouse and click again to complete the action (see Fig. 10.8 and Table 10.9).

The terms horizontal and vertical can be slightly confusing in this context, but the icon on the menu makes it clear:

- Vertically – expands or contracts the model left to right,
- Horizontally – expands or contracts the model up and down.

**Table 10.9** Insert and Remove Space Actions

| Required Effect | Action |
| --- | --- |
| *Add Vertical Space* | Move mouse to the right and click. |
| *Remove Vertical Space* | Move mouse to the left and click. |
| *Add Horizontal Space* | Move mouse down and click. |
| *Remove Horizontal Space* | Move mouse up and click. |

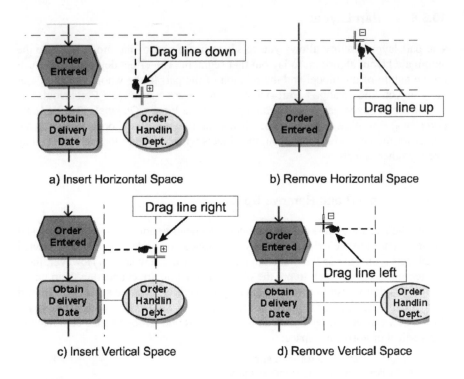

a) Insert Horizontal Space            b) Remove Horizontal Space

c) Insert Vertical Space              d) Remove Vertical Space

**Fig. 10.8** Insert and Remove Space

## 10.7        Templates

### 10.7.1        Introduction

If you frequently wish to change the appearance of one or more object or connection types in a model, or the model itself, you can define *ARIS Templates*. You can apply a chosen, pre-defined, template to objects, to the entire model or set it as a default for all newly created models.

### 10.7.2        Creating a Template

A template is defined using the *Template Wizard* in *Administration Module* and will typically be defined by an *ARIS System Administrator* so as to apply a common '*look and feel*' to specific types of model. Table 10.10 shows what can defined using a template, but detailed description of how to create templates is beyond the scope of this book.

**Table 10.10** ARIS Template Wizard

| Dialog Box | Settings |
| --- | --- |
| Symbol Appearance | Fill color, Line color, Line style, Line weight, Scaling, Shadow. |
| Place symbol attributes | Placement, Font format, Alignment, With attribute name, As icon. |
| Select connection appearance | Line color, Line style, Line weight, Arrow towards source, Arrow towards target. |
| Place connection attributes | Placement, Font format, Alignment, With attribute name, As icon. |
| Select model background | Model background. |

### 10.7.3    Applying a Template to a Model

To apply a pre-defined template to a model:

- Format > Apply template…,
- Right-Click > Format > Apply template….

Now select the template from the list. If you have one or more objects or connections selected, the template will be applied to those items. If you have nothing selected, the template will be applied to the whole model. Templates only affect those objects and connections for which settings have been defined and several templates can be applied in an additive manner to create an overall desired effect. The template only affects the objects and connections selected at the time the template is applied, any new objects will adopt the style of the current model template (see below).

### 10.7.4    Setting the Current Model Template

If you wish a template to be applied to a model all the while, so all new objects and connections will take on that style:

1. Ensure nothing in the model is selected,
2. Right-Click > Properties [Representation],
3. Click on the Change… Button adjacent to the *Current template* field,
4. Select the required template from the *Select template Dialog Box*.

This template will now be applied to the model and will also affect all new objects and connections.

If you want this template to apply to all models of the same type, tick the *Use as default Checkbox*. This has the same effect as setting the same options in <u>V</u>iew > <u>O</u>ptions [*For new models / Representation*].

# Chapter 11    Objects and Relationships

In this chapter we look at the range of additional objects we can use in the EPC and how these enable a process model to be put into context with the resources needed to deliver it and the environment in which it operates.

## 11.1    Introduction

Chapter 7 described the concept of the *Event-driven process chain* and how function, event and rule objects can be used to represent complex process flows. The real power of ARIS is realised when, in addition, we start to model the relationships between the process and the business environment in which it operates.

By adding a fourth category of objects, which we have loosely termed '*resources*', (the correct ARIS term is '*non-structurally relevant objects*') to the EPC we can now model the relationships between the process and:

- Organisation,
- Systems,
- Data,
- Knowledge,
- Information Carriers,
- Products,
- Objectives and Measures,
- General Resource.

There are over 150 object symbols available in the EPC for modelling the above items, albeit some are alternatives for the same object. No single process model will use them all and, normally, we restrict the available objects using a Method Filter, both to aid usability and to enforce modelling standards. In the rest of this chapter we will look at how resources are allocated to functions in the EPC, their relationships and how these relationships can be viewed and used.

## 11.2    Types and Instances

Some resource objects come in two forms, the standard object and the '*type*' object (e.g. *Application system* and *Application system type*). The *type* object represents a general type of item while the standard form represents a specific instance of it. For example, "Personal Computer" is a type of application system, while "Dell Latitude Cpi, serial 0001" is a specific instance of an application system (computer). The same applies to organisational objects and some data objects.

We use the form of object most appropriate for the viewpoint we are modelling. If we are modelling a generic sales handling process we might use an *Application system type* to represent a typical call handling system. Later, we may wish to use the generic model as the starting point for modelling a very specific sales department using particular systems and resources. In that case we would work through the model, replacing the generalised *Application system type* objects with the more specific *Application system* objects.

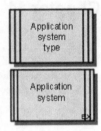

You can use either form of object in the standard EPC model and there is also a version of the EPC, the *EPC (instance)* model, aimed at modelling those specific instances of processes. These different forms and models can be confusing, so normally we just model at the *type* level using the standard EPC. The main thing is to be consistent.

## 11.3    Making Resource Allocations

### 11.3.1    Connecting Objects

We normally establish relationships between objects in a model by connecting their symbols together. The terms '*connection*' and '*relationship*' tend to be used interchangeably although there are other types of relationships not shown by connections.

Allocating a resource to a function is straightforward. Open the EPC model describing your process flow, select the appropriate resource object from the *Symbols Bar,* place it in the model and connect it to the function object. For a reminder on how to make connections, see Chapter 9. The type of relationship the connection represents will depend on the object selected and the Method Filter currently in use.

As we saw in Chapter 9, with some resource objects it is possible to make the connection in either direction; from the resource to the function or from the function to the resource. The direction of the connection will define a different type of relationship between the resource and the function, for instance an input or an output. Other resources only have a valid connection in a single direction.

If you attempt to connect two objects for which there is only one valid relationship, it will normally be made straightaway (although this depends on which connection mode you are using; see Chapter 9).

Other resources may have several possible relationship types, depending on the Method Filter in use. In this case you will be asked to select the required relationship from a list or the *Select relationship type Dialog Box* (Fig. 11.1). In this case, it is also possible to make several connections between the object

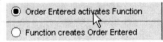

and the same function, each using a different relationship. The only restriction is each type of relationship between any pair of objects may only be used once. Whether this actually makes sense will depend on the objects and the process you are modelling.

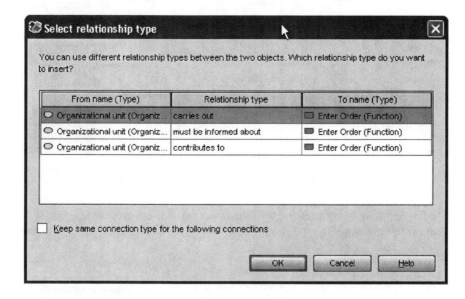

**Fig. 11.1** Select Relationship Type Dialog Box

A function may have connections to many objects and because these relationships are stored in the underlying database, it does not matter in which model they are made. Once a connection is defined, it is always available for reporting and analysis. This means we don't have to use a single model containing all the connections we require, but we can structure our models so each one contains a manageable amount of information pertinent to the viewpoint we are interested in. Typically we store functional relationships in a separate *Function allocation diagram* (see Chapter 12).

The full definition of all the possible relationships between all types of object is defined by the ARIS Method, which also defines which relationships are visible in which models. It is important to note that a relationship between two objects valid in one model type, say an EPC, may not be valid in another model type, say an *Access diagram*, even though both of those objects can be used in both models. To find out which relationships are valid, consult the ARIS Method Manual (Help > Methods Manual from the *Main Menu*) or experiment with connecting different objects in different models. Of course, when experimenting you must use the **Entire Method** filter, otherwise you may find the filter has restricted some possible relationships. Fig. 11.2 shows an example of some connections to commonly used resource objects.

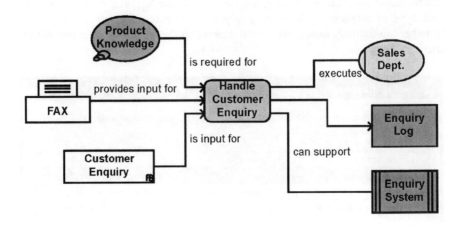

**Fig. 11.2** Typical ARIS Objects and Relationships

Once you have made a connection, you can look at the type of relationship you have made by inspecting its *Type* attribute in the *Attributes Window* (see Chapter 14).

 **Hint** – a quick way to identify the relationship type of a connection is to hover your mouse over the connection. A tooltip will appear and show the *Type* attribute. If the tooltip is not visible, enable them at V̲iew > O̲ptions...[*General / Objects*] and check the *Show t̲ooltips* box.

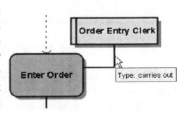

Although many of the resource objects have several connection types, they don't always define the type of relationship you want, or may not describe it in exactly the way you would like. For instance, the concept of 'process ownership' is a useful way of managing a process, but ARIS has no "owns" relationship between the *Organizational unit type* and functions. The nearest equivalent is probably "*is technically responsible for*".

 **Expert Tip** – you can rename a connection type using the *Administration Module* or you can refine what a connection means for your application by entering a description into the *Connection role* attribute.

It is also possible to make '*implicit relationships*' between objects by nesting them (see Chapter 9).

# 11.4 Resource Objects

We will now look at each of the main categories of resource object, identify the most useful objects, their main relationships and what they are used for.

Some categories, for instance organisation resources, have a large number of objects. They are all available in the EPC, but it is recommended you use a Method Filter to drastically limit the number of objects used in your application. Otherwise you may find different people start to use them in different ways and consistency becomes compromised. Using the full range of objects of a particular type is more applicable in the specific models describing those resources (e.g. the *Organizational chart*) where you can establish hierarchies and classifications.

## 11.4.1 Organisation

### Objects

Organisational objects represent the people who perform the process tasks represented by ARIS functions. We can represent specific people, departments, roles or teams, depending on the context and detail of the model.

Table 11.1 shows a limited set of organisational objects that cover most situations and can be simulated in *ARIS Simulation* (the *Organizational unit type* object cannot be used for simulation). The symbols are mostly yellow, but the visible distinction between them is difficult to spot, which is another good reason for limiting the range of object types used.

 **Hint** – to identify a specific symbol on the *Symbols Bar*, hover your mouse over the symbol and a tooltip will appear showing the object name. If the tooltip is not visible, enable them at View > Options... [*General / Objects*] and check the *Show tooltips* box.

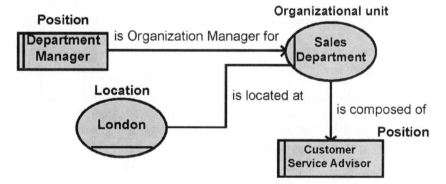

**Fig. 11.3** Organisation Objects Inter-relationships

**Table 11.1** Organisational Objects

| Symbol | Object | Use |
|---|---|---|
| Organizational unit | Organizational unit (Yellow) | The business department performing a task (e.g. "Sales Department"). |
| Position | Position (Yellow) | Roles performed by individual people (departments may be composed of positions, e.g. "Customer Service Advisor", or a position may have a specific responsibility for the department, e.g. a Department Manager). |
| External person EXT | External Person (Outline) | A person external to the company (e.g. "Customer"). |
| Location | Location (Yellow) | The physical location where the task is done (e.g. "London Stock Exchange"). |

The relationship between these organisational objects is shown in Fig. 11.3 (modelled in an *Organizational chart*). In practice, you can represent all types of people resource with an *Organizational unit* object whether it represents a single person or several, but the use of the *Position* and *External person* objects is useful in making those distinctions clear. Strictly speaking, *Location* is not actually an organisation object, but is grouped with them because location is usually inextricably linked with a company's organisation.

There are other organisational objects we have not shown and the relationships between the organisational objects themselves are varied and complex. These are mostly useful when modelling the organisational structure of a business in an *Organizational chart* model. When used in an EPC, it is best to severely restrict the objects available (Fig. 11.4), otherwise people interpret them in different ways. For instance, the difference between a *Position* and a *Person type* (not shown) is very subtle.

## Relationships

There are several relationships that can be made by connecting organisation objects to a function. Location has a single *"is executed at"* relationship, but the others have many relationships and it is best to limit these to a basic set such as:

- *"carries out"* – does the work,
- *"contributes to"* – collaborates with others to do the work,
- *"must be informed about"* – needs to be told when the work is done,
- *"is technically responsible for"* – 'owns' that part of the process.

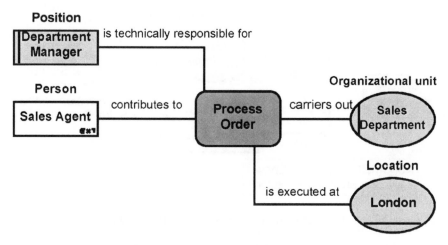

**Fig. 11.4** Organisational Relationships

These are shown in Fig. 11.4. The *"carries out"* relationship tends to mean a person or department uniquely performing the role; *"contributes to"* means one of several people or departments collaborating to do the job. If you attach more than one organisational object with a *"carries out"* relationship, it means any one of them can do the job, but only one is needed. You may attach several organisational objects to a function to represent all the people or departments with a role to play, as shown in Fig. 11.4.

### *Hierarchical Organisational Relationships*

The granularity at which you model the organisation doing the work will depend on the level of detail at which you are modelling. In Fig. 11.4 we have said the **Sales Department** does the work. If we are working at a more detailed level, we might wish to model the exact role undertaking the work (e.g. "Customer Service Advisor"). We would then use an *Organizational chart* model to show **Customer Service Advisors** were *Positions* in the **Sales Department** (Fig. 11.5).

People are often tempted to show, in the same EPC, both the **Sales Department** and the **Customer Service Advisor** as carrying out the function (Fig. 11.5). This enables them to see both levels of detail at the same time. Strictly speaking this is not correct, because you are mixing two levels of hierarchical detail in the same model. However, it is clearly useful, especially if you don't model any lower levels of detail.

The question of whether to stick rigidly to a hierarchical approach or to put a lot of information in one model to get a more concise representation is one you will be continually faced with. If you are just putting together one or two models for a specific purpose, and you have no intention of developing the models further or re-using them, you may feel you can get away with a certain amount of poetic licence. If, however, you are modelling a complex project or wish to share your

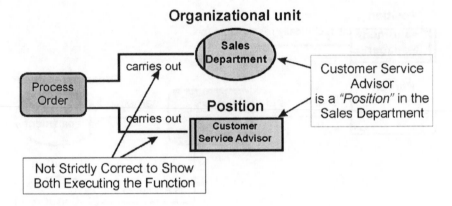

**Fig. 11.5** Hierarchical Organisational Relationships

models with others, you must stick to an agreed methodical approach. It may be obvious to you that a **Customer Service Advisor** is part of the **Sales Department**, but it won't be to others. The advantage of using the ARIS Method is it creates a common, well-understood approach. If you depart from it, it loses its value.

### 11.4.2    Application Systems

#### *Objects*

Application Systems resources represent the computer and software applications used to support the business. They can range from large-scale corporate mainframe computers down to a humble desktop calculator. There are many application systems objects that can be used to define how a hierarchy of systems, sub-systems and software modules support a business. Most are best used in the *Application system* models with only a limited number normally used in the EPC (see Table 11.2).

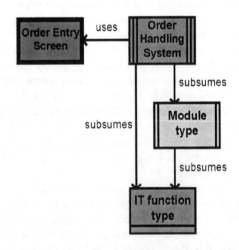

**Fig. 11.6** Hierarchical Organisational Relationships

Fig. 11.6 shows the relationships between these system objects (modelled in an *Application system type Diagram*). For the majority of EPCs only the *Application system type* and *Screen* are used. The *Module type* and *IT function type* would only be used when modelling at a very detailed level.

**Table 11.2** Application System Objects

| Symbol | Object | Use |
|---|---|---|
| Application system type | Application system type (Blue) | A software system running on a computer used to support the carrying out of a function (e.g. "Sale Department System"). |
| Module type | Module type (Yellow) | A recognisable part of a system performing a specific detailed operation (e.g. "Order Entry Module"). |
| IT function type | IT function type (Blue) | The lowest level of Application System operation. Only used at very detailed levels of modelling. |
| Screen | Screen (Green) | The design of a particular display screen format (GUI) used by a system to support functions requiring user input or displaying information to users. |
| List | List (Outline) | The design of a particular printed list or form used by a system to support functions providing printed user output. |

## Relationships

Fig. 11.7 shows the allocation of an *Application system type* and *Screen* object to a function. The *Application system type* object only has one type of relationship with the function: "*supports*". In ARIS, systems are not thought of as carrying out a task or function, but as supporting a task.

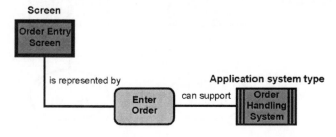

**Fig. 11.7** Application Systems Objects Inter-relationships

The *Screen* object represents the design of the *Graphical User Interface* (GUI) the system uses to interact with a person entering or viewing data. Its relationship is fairly obvious and simply says the **Enter Order** task "*is represented by*" the **Order Entry Screen**. It can be quite useful to model the screens used at different points in the process, especially as you can link graphic files containing a screen shot of the display to the *Screen* object using the *Link* attribute (see Chapter 14). For representing the design of printed output data, you can use the *List* object.

It is important to note that the *Screen* and *List* objects represent the design of the presentation of the input and output data, not the data itself. The actual data is modelled using information and data objects (Section 11.4.3).

**Hint** – if you are modelling a process automatically carried out by a computer system (e.g. a workflow system), you can denote this by replacing the function symbol with a *System function actual* symbol. The object is also a function and the only difference is the appearance of the symbol. The function will still be shown as "*supported by*" the system rather than carrying it out.

You can either pick the *System function actual* from the *Symbols Bar*, or change an existing function symbol from the *Properties > [Format / Object appearance] Dialog Box*.

### 11.4.3    Data

#### *Objects*

If you were modelling a manufacturing process, the conversion of raw materials into a product would be a key aspect of the model. In the IT world, data is our raw material and we would expect all the functions in our model to have a relationship with data objects.

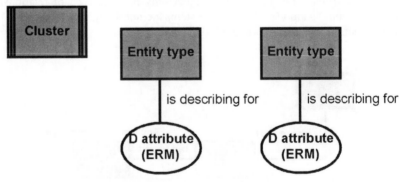

**Fig. 11.8** Data Object Inter-relationships

In practice, it is surprising how many people produce complex IT process models without any thought for their raw material (the data). We can't emphasise enough how important it is to include data in your models.

We can model data 'formally', using recognised data modelling standards (e.g. *Entity Relationship Modelling (eERM)*) or less formally using the language your business uses. The *Technical term* object is used for modelling information from a business perspective and the *Cluster, Entity type* and *Attribute* objects for more formal data modelling. These are shown in Table 11.3.

**Table 11.3** Data Objects

| Symbol | Object | Use |
|---|---|---|
| Technical term | Technical term (Outline) | A piece of business information. |
| Entity type | Entity type (Blue) | A real-world entity (e.g. customer or employee) described by data attributes. |
| Cluster | Cluster (Red) | A collection of related Entity Types (e.g. people, comprising customers and employees). |
| D attribute (ERM) | D attribute (ERM) (Outline) | A specific piece of data describing some aspect of a real-world entity represented by an Entity Type (e.g. customer name). |

### Formal Data Modelling

Many people will be familiar with formal data modelling using entity–relationship models and entry–attribute models. Fig. 11.8 summarises the key relationships between the three formal data objects (modelled in an *eERM* model). You will notice there is no physical connection between the *Cluster* and the *Entity types*. The *Cluster* is just a collection of related entities and there is no direct link in the model between them.

The use of *Entity* and *Attribute* objects is best when a formal data model of the business or the systems has already been modelled. If you do not have a formal model, but still wish to model the information used by your process, use the *Technical term* object. You can also use the *Class diagram* to model data using objected-oriented (OO) approaches.

### Informal Information Modelling

*Technical terms* are much more flexible than the formal data objects. The *Technical terms model* (Fig. 11.9) can be used to arrange the *Technical terms* in a hierarchy, or to map synonyms to show how different parts of the business use different terms for the same piece of information.

A particularly useful aspect of the *Technical terms model* is it can be used to model how a hierarchy of *Technical terms* maps to the *Cluster*, *Entity* and *Attribute* objects of the formal data model. Thus in the requirements capture phase of the project you can informally model business information using *Technical terms*. Later, in the design phase, you can map them to the formal data objects as a precursor for systems implementation.

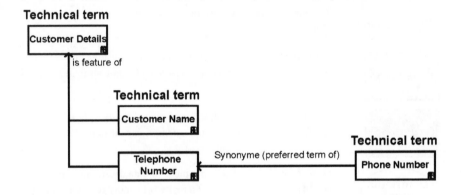

**Fig. 11.9** Technical Terms Objects Inter-relationships

### Relationships

There are several types of relationship between data objects and functions, and connections can be made in either direction. Connecting from an object to a function represents an input, while making the connection in the other direction represents an output (see Fig. 11.10a). The most useful relationships are shown in Table 11.4.

**Table 11.4** Data Object Relationship Types

| Connection Direction | Relationship | |
|---|---|---|
| **Input Connection** (from data object to function) | is input for | (Read) |
| **Output Connection** (from function to data object) | has output of | (Creates) |
| | changes | (Updates) |
| | deletes | (Deletes) |
| | archives | |

People often use the term 'CRUD' to describe whether a process '*Creates*', '*Reads*', '*Updates*' or '*Deletes*' an item of data. Table 11.4 shows the ARIS relationships corresponding to each of the CRUD terms.

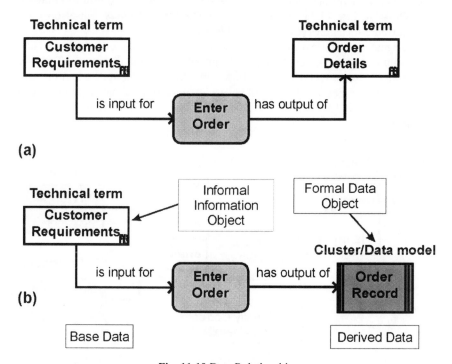

**Fig. 11.10** Data Relationships

When making allocations of data resources to functions you can mix both informal and formal object types as shown in Fig. 11.10b. For instance, you can represent the structure of a paper order form used as an input to a task using a *Technical term*. The output of the task, a computer record of the order details, can be shown as a formal data *Entity type*. This neatly shows the transformation of informally structured information into formally structured data. This also highlights the concept that in IT-based businesses, each step of the process (the function) is in fact a '*transformation*' of input information into output information (sometimes described as '*base data*' into '*derived data*'). If you are not sure which to use, use the *Technical term* as shown in Fig. 11.10a.

### Hierarchical Data Relationships

Because we can structure both informal information and formal data in a hierarchical manner, we can choose what level of granularity we wish to use depending on the level of detail of our model. When we looked at organisation objects in Section 11.4.1 we saw that sometimes we might want to know not only that the **Sales Department** carried out the function, but also that it was specifically the **Customer Service Advisor**. We suggested that although you could connect both objects to the function, it was not strictly correct to mix levels of hierarchy on the same model. Exactly the same situation arises with data. It is useful to know that **Enter Order** in Fig. 11.11 not only changes **Customer Details**, but also exactly which attribute it changes (**Customer Address**).

Once again we can use a single data object in the EPC and model the hierarchical relationship between objects in an eERM attribute allocation diagram or Technical *terms model*. Alternatively, you can show both objects being updated on the same model as shown in Fig. 11.11. We will have a lot more to say about modelling hierarchically in Chapter 13, but whichever way you choose, the important thing is to be consistent.

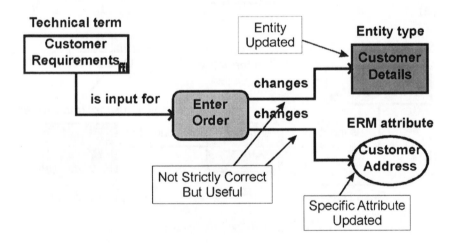

**Fig. 11.11** Hierarchical Data Relationships

## 11.4.4      Information Carriers

### *Objects*

The ARIS concept of data and information is that it is always stored somewhere, either in an electronic medium (e.g. a file or magnetic tape) or in non-electronic media (e.g. a FAX or card file). These are represented in ARIS by the *Information carrier*. There is only one *Information carrier* object (see Table 11.5), but there are a variety of alternative symbols (Fig. 11.12) representing different types of data storage media. Some of these are clearly physical data stores (e.g. FAX, file), while other are more abstract, for instance, data imparted via a telephone call or through someone's expertise.

**Table 11.5** Information Carriers

| Symbol | Object | Use |
|---|---|---|
| 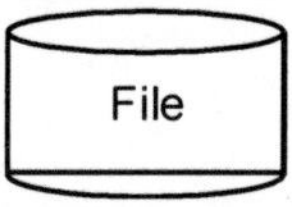 File | Information Carrier (Outline) | The storage medium in which data is carried. |

**Fig. 11.12** Information Carriers

## *Relationships*

Fig. 11.13 shows the relationships of an *Information carrier* to a function. Connections between *Information carriers* and functions can be made in both directions. The connection from the *Information carrier* to the function represents an input and the relationship is "*provides input for* " and, in the other direction, "*creates output to*".

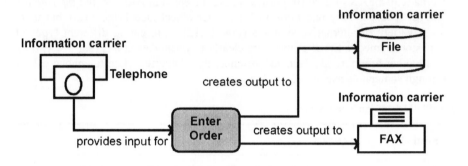

**Fig. 11.13** Information Carrier Relationships

## *Modelling Structured and Unstructured Information*

If you compare Fig. 11.13 (*Information carriers*) with Fig. 11.10 (*Data*) you will notice their relationships look very similar. Data objects (e.g. *Entity type*) and *Information carriers* represent the data or information used by a function, and they both have similar input and output relationships to the function. Both types of object can have *Technical terms models* or data models assigned to them, allowing more detailed descriptions of the format of the data or information. So why do we need both types of object?

The data objects represent, in an abstract way, the data itself, while the *Information carriers* define where the data is physically stored. This definition makes sense for *Information carrier* symbols such as *File* and *FAX*, but doesn't seem so appropriate when using the *Telephone* and *Expertise* symbols. An alternative way of thinking is the *Information carriers* define how the data is delivered or '*carried*' to and from the function.

The distinction between the object types can be made clear by explicitly showing the relationship between them. A connection can be made between a data object, such as an *Entity type*, and an *Information carrier* creating a "*lies on*" relationship. We can now see in Fig. 11.14 the function **Enter Order** receives information by **Telephone**, refers to **Pricing Information** from a **Price List** document and creates a formal data record, an *Entity type* **Order Record** which is stored in a *File* in the **Order Database**.

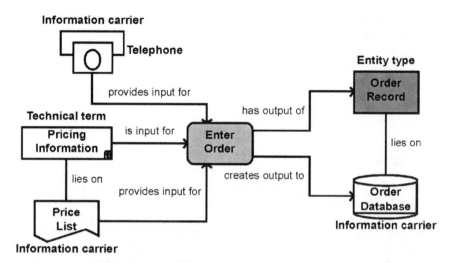

**Fig. 11.14** Modelling Structured and Unstructured Data

We could, of course, show *Entity types* for the **Price List** and **Telephone** and show those *Entity types* lying on their respective *Information carriers*. However, it is unlikely that the price list will be very formally defined (in data modelling terms) so it is better represented by a *Technical terms* object. It is even less likely that a telephone call will conform to a structured data format, so we only show the **Telephone** as an information carrier.

It is not necessary to use all of these different object types all the while, but it can be useful to make these distinctions when modelling processes where data is particularly important.

**Table 11.6** Modelling Structured and Unstructured Information

| Objects and Connections | Meaning |
|---|---|
| ⌷ Telephone — Information carrier | Very informal and unstructured information delivered via Information Carrier. |
| Pricing Information (Technical term) — lies on → Price List (Information carrier) | Well-understood (but not formally defined) business information stored or delivered via Information carrier. |
| Order Record (Entity type) — lies on → Order Database (Information carrier) | Data stored in an Information carrier (usually computer-system related) for which there are formal data models |

We recommend the conventions shown in Table 11.6. The connection between the data objects and *Information carriers* can be made in other models, but by making these '*secondary relationships*' in the EPC it makes explicit their exact role in relationship to the function.

### 11.4.5    Knowledge

#### *Objects*

Previously, we saw that data could be thought of as a more formally defined form of information. Similarly, both information and data can be thought of as progressively more formal representations of knowledge. Knowledge is everything we know that is relevant to the process. It may be held in people's heads, written in documents or stored in a system as data. In process modelling we are mostly interested in the more formal representations of information and data, and we would not normally try to model all of the knowledge related to a process. However, where a particular piece of knowledge is key to a process step, it makes sense to model it. This is particularly valuable in making explicit the 'corporate knowledge' essential to running a business, which so often is not written down. There are two knowledge objects, as shown in Table 11.7.

**Table 11.7** Knowledge Objects

| Symbol | Object | Use |
|---|---|---|
| Knowledge category | Knowledge category (Purple) | A particular area of knowledge the business has (when used in an EPC, it represents knowledge a person undertaking a task must have). |
| Documented knowledge | Documented knowledge (Purple) | Business knowledge specifically written down (e.g. operating procedures). |

The use of knowledge objects can be interpreted fairly liberally and *Documented knowledge* is usually a sub-division of a *Knowledge category*. *Knowledge maps* and *Knowledge structure diagrams* are very useful models for representing all aspects of business knowledge. However, in order for them to be meaningful in an EPC we have to be more specific about how knowledge objects are used.

#### *Knowledge Category*

The *Knowledge category* object is best used to represent specific key and exceptional knowledge an individual person must have in order to carry out a task.

It would not be sensible to model all the knowledge required to undertake each task; it would be tedious and would clutter the models. Normally, we assign to a task, a person from a specific team or a person who has a specific role and assume membership of the team, or the role, defines their skills. We can model these skills using the knowledge objects in a *Knowledge map*. Sometimes, however, a task requires very specific knowledge (e.g. how to operate a piece of equipment) not everyone who might normally be allocated to the task may have. By modelling this using a *Knowledge category* we can draw special attention to this require- ment. This may in turn cause us to reflect on whether we need to define a new type of role with the appropriate skill.

### Documented Knowledge

*Documented knowledge* is useful to represent written knowledge necessary to do the task, for instance a written operating procedure.

The example shown in Fig. 11.14 requires, in order to complete the **Order Entry** task, information has to be read from a **Price List**. In that example the **Price List** was modelled as a *Document*, not as *Documented knowledge*. So when should you use a *Document Information carrier* and when should you use a *Documented knowledge* object?

There are two tests we can apply to find the answer:

- Is the information transformed into the output?

- Is the structure of the information important?

We mentioned earlier the idea that a function '*transforms*' inputs into outputs. In an IT environment it takes '*base data*' and transforms it into '*derived data*'. In the order entry example, the base data is the customer order details given over the telephone and the derived data is the **Order Record**. If there is a written procedure describing how to go about taking a customer order, although it is clearly impor- tant knowledge needed to do the task, the information in the procedure is not itself transformed into the **Order Record**; it is not 'base data'. Furthermore, we are not particularly interested in how the information in the procedure is structured. Thus, the written procedure would be modelled as *Documented knowledge*.

Now let us use the same test to consider the **Price List** document. Is the infor- mation transformed into the output? Well sort of. The product price is definitely an input to the order. Is the structure of the price list important? Well maybe. If the product range were complex it would make sense to model it in a formal struc- tured way.

We can see this example is not clear-cut one way or another, but on balance it is best modelled as data stored in an *Information carrier*. In doubtful cases, ask yourself: "when implementing the process are you likely to want to store the data in a database?" If the answer is yes, it is best to model it as data rather than knowledge.

We can summarise the use of knowledge, information and data objects as:

- **Knowledge** – unstructured, but required to do the function,
- **Information** – unstructured, transformed by the function,
- **Data** – structured, transformed by the function.

### Relationships

Fig. 11.15 shows the relationships between a function and the knowledge objects. The connections can be made in either direction. The connection from the object to the function has the "*is required for*" relationship described above. In addition, it is perfectly sensible to talk of tasks creating knowledge, particularly documented knowledge, so the connections can be made the other way around to show a function "*creates*" knowledge. There is also a further relationship representing a function "*has knowledge of* " a *Knowledge category* but this is not such a useful relationship.

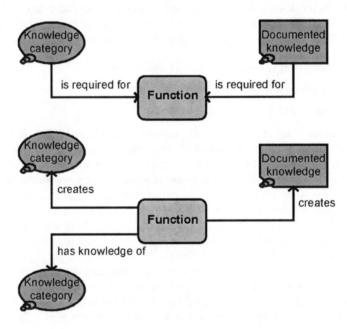

**Fig. 11.15** Knowledge Relationships

## 11.4.6    Resource

### Objects

Although we have loosely termed all the objects we have discussed in this chapter as representing resource, there are in fact two specific physical resource objects as shown in Table 11.8.

**Table 11.8** Physical Resource Objects

| Symbol | Object | Use |
|---|---|---|
| **Operating resource** | Operating resource | Specific resource that must be available to undertake a task and can only be used by one function at a time (e.g. a machine). |
| **General resource** | General resource | Other non-specific resources, typically consumables that can be used or created by functions. |

Most tasks use physical resources of some form so, just as with knowledge, we only normally model resource we wish to draw particular attention to or, later wish to simulate.

## 11.4.7    Relationships

Fig. 11.16 shows the function allocations for the resource objects. There is only a single relationship for the *Operating resource* object which shows it "*is an operating resource of*" the function. The object is usually taken to represent a fixed resource, such as a piece of machinery (e.g. a photocopier), which must be present in order to do the task and can only be used by one task at a time.

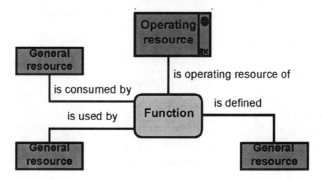

**Fig. 11.16** Physical Resource Relationships

The *General resource* has more relationships available and is usually used, particularly for simulation, to represent consumable resource (e.g. the paper in the photocopier). Connecting the *General resource* to the function defines that the function makes use of the resource.

The *"is consumed by"* relationship defines that the function consumes some of the resource such that the quantity of available resource is less after the function is complete. The *"is used by"* relationship shows the function uses the resource, but does not actually deplete the quantity available.

Connecting the function to the *General resource* has a single *"produces"* relationship which represents the function creating new resource. All of these *General resource* connections have *Quantity* attributes that can be used to define a numeric value for the creating and consumption of the resource. These can be used by *ARIS Simulation* where the real value of the resource becomes apparent. The availability of machinery and consumables can be dynamically modelled to see the effect on the process of bottlenecks and shortages

## 11.4.8    Business Environment

### *Objects*

The objects described so far are the most useful for modelling processes in the EPC. There are many more objects available and shows a few of those that are particularly useful for showing how a process interacts with the business environment. Fig. 11.17 shows the basic relationships for these objects.

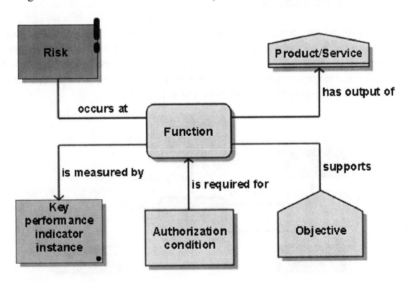

**Fig. 11.17** Business Environment Relationships

**Table 11.9** Additional Objects

| Symbol | Object | Use |
|---|---|---|
| Objective | Objective | A business objective met as a result of carrying out the process. |
| Product/ Service | Product/Service, | A product or service created by a process. |
| Risk | Risk | The danger that a process or a particular step in a process will not achieve its objective. |
| Key performance indicator instance | Key performance indicator instance | A key measurement to indicate if a process or a step in a process is achieving its objective. |
| Authorization condition | Authorization condition | Authorisation required before the *Organizational unit* can complete the task. |

## Objective

The *Objective* object represents the goal or purpose of a process or process step. A hierarchy of business *Objectives* can be modelled in the *Objectives diagram* or Balanced Scorecard *BSC Cause-and-effect diagram*. These *Objectives* can be added to the EPC to show which process step "*supports*" their achievement. This is particularly powerful in linking a Balanced Scorecard to real operating processes.

## Product/Service

The *Product/Service* object (also available with alternative symbols for *Service* and *Information Service*) can be arranged in a hierarchy of products and product options in the *Product/Service tree model*. These objects can be used in an EPC to show which processes deliver these products. It is also possible to connect the *Product/Service* object to the function in the other direction to represent a product "*is used by*" or "*consumed by*" the task (e.g. assembling an 'IT solution' from a number of products).

### Risk

The *Risk* object is intended to be used in conjunction with the *Business controls diagram* and *ARIS Audit Manager* as part of a formal risk assessment to meet the needs of Basel II or Sarbanes–Oxley financial compliance legislation. However, the *Risk* object can usefully be used by anyone to indicate a risk "*occurs*" at a particular process step.

### KPI Instance

The *KPI instance* object is used to indicate a step in a process step where a key measurement is made to indicate process performance. The object has attributes for actual, target and planned values which can be used in conjunction with *ARIS Balanced Scorecard* to automatically update the *BSC Cause-and-effect diagram* which in turn can be used to automatically update a performance dashboard.

### Authorization Condition

The *Authorization condition* can be used to show an *Organizational unit* cannot carry out a function until the correct authorisation is obtained. Authorisation will typically be provided in document form, so the authorisation could be modelled as *Documented knowledge*. However, the use of the *Authorization condition* object is useful to draw attention to specific authorisation points in a process (e.g. 'Quality Gates').

## 11.5    Putting it All Together

All the most important objects that can be allocated to a function in an EPC have now been introduced. By putting them all together, as shown in Fig. 11.18, the process flows we defined in the previous chapter can be extended to represent how the available resources implement a process and how it interacts with its environment.

The model in Fig. 11.18 is just by way of an example; it would be a rare occasion when you would need to use all of these objects. Just because they are available, don't feel obliged to use them all. Just use those pertinent to the viewpoint and level of detail at which you are modelling. However, the example does illustrate how much information can be modelled when the need arises.

If we break the diagram down into its constituent parts, we can see it answers the key questions we wish to know about a process – who, what, where, how, why and when.

We can see this precisely defines the function, the resources it uses and its relationship to its environment. All of this information is stored in the ARIS database and is available for analysis, reporting and, where appropriate, simulation.

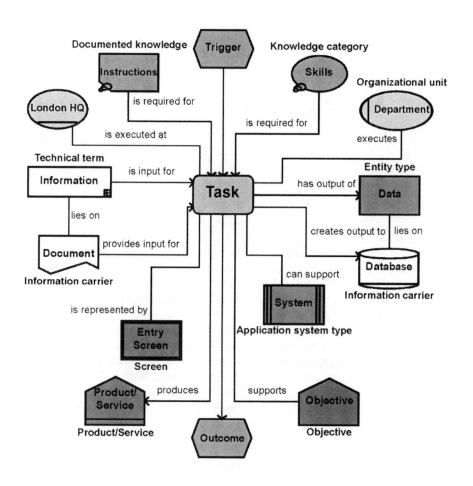

**Fig. 11.18** Putting it All Together

## 11.5.1 The Function as a Transformation

While we would rarely use all the objects shown in Fig. 11.18, it is important for any particular project to define the minimum set of objects and relationships that will capture the information required. By defining the set of objects modellers should use, you can enforce standards and ensure consistency of approach and meaning. A valuable way to help people understand what is required is to re-enforce the concept of a function as a '*transformation*'. That is to say, it takes an input and transforms it into an output. People undertake this transformation using resource and possibly supported by systems. To do the transformation, people need knowledge and possibly procedures.

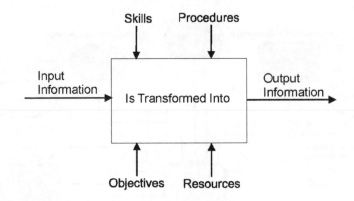

**Fig. 11.19** Process Transformation Template

This concept is summarised in Fig. 11.19. As each step in the process is modelled, use this template as a check-list to decide if all the required information has been gathered. It can also be used to check if the function has been correctly identified. For instance, if you can't identify the input and output for a function, you should question whether it really is a function.

One exception to this is a function making a decision, where it is not immediately obvious it has an input and an output. It can be argued that the change in the process flow is the output, but in addition, the result of the decision might be documented somewhere, so there may be a physical output as well.

A good starting point for setting standards for a modelling project is to provide modellers with a simplified version of Fig. 11.18 using just those resource objects relevant to the level of detail at which you wish people to model.

### 11.5.2    Using Libraries of Resource Objects

The simple examples so far just contain one function and its resource allocations. Of course in a real EPC there would be many functions and it is very likely the same resources would be used by several functions. For instance, the same *Organizational unit* might carry out many functions or the same *Application system type* may support many functions.

When creating resource objects and connecting them to functions it is very important not to create many duplicate objects with the same name. The power of using ARIS relationships is it enables us to ask questions such as: "tell me all the tasks supported by this system" or "tell me all the data accessed by this organisation". It is only possible to carry out this analysis if each time we refer to a resource we ensure it is an *occurrence* of the same object.

A good way to manage your resource objects is to create a library of objects by placing them all in a single group. We looked at re-using objects in Chapter 9 and it is important to make use of these techniques to create and use libraries of resource objects.

# 11.6     Viewing Relationships

We can view connections and their relationships in several ways:

- Graphical representation,
- Attribute placement,
- The Attributes Window,
- ARIS Reports,
- The Function Allocation Diagram (FAD).

## 11.6.1     Graphical Representation

Simply by connecting two objects together, a relationship is established between the objects. This can be viewed in the *Designer Module* and its meaning is often clear from the connection and context. We can also establish relationship by nesting objects (e.g. showing a *Position* inside an *Organizational unit*). This graphical representation is very clear and how to create nested relationships was described in Chapter 9.

## 11.6.2     The Type Attribute

The type of the relationship between two objects is defined by the *Type* attribute of the connection. You can view this, but not change it, from the *Attributes Dialog Box* (Right-Click > <u>A</u>ttributes) or *Attributes Tab* on the *Properties Bar*.

To display the *Attributes Tab*, ensure the *Properties Checkbox* is checked so the *Properties Bar* is visible and select the *Attributes Tab*. Now select a connection and look at the *Type* attribute towards the top of the list. You will see it shows the type of connection (e.g. *"carries out"*). You cannot change the

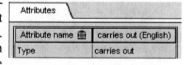

connection type by changing its attribute. If you want a different type of connection (assuming the method supports it) you will have to delete the connection and make a new one.

**Hint** – a quick way to identify the relationship type of a connection is to hover your mouse over the connection. A tooltip will appear and show the *Type* attribute. If the tooltip is not visible, enable them at <u>V</u>iew > <u>O</u>ptions... [*General / Objects*] and check the *Show <u>t</u>ooltips* box.

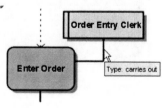

### 11.6.3     Attribute Placement

By making the value of the *Type* attribute of a connection visible in the EPC, we
make explicit the exact relationship the connection represents. All of the examples
given so far in this chapter show the attribute placement in addition to the graphical
representation. Attributes can be made visible on all connections or just on those
that are important or might not be obvious. We will describe attribute placements
in Chapter 14. You can also create an ARIS '*Template*' (see Chapter 10) defining
a standard set of attribute visibility. This can be applied to a model to automatically set the chosen attributes to be visible.

### 11.6.4     Relationships Display

The *Relationships Tab* on the *Properties Bar* is the most useful way of viewing relationships, and in fact the relationships between any objects.

Ensure the *Properties Checkbox* is checked so the *Properties*  ☑ Properties
*Bar* is visible and select the *Relationships Tab*. Select an object
and the *Relationships Tab* will show all the relationships an object has with any
other object in the database, not just those objects in the current model.

You can also display relationships from the *Explorer Module*. Ensure the *Objects
Checkbox* is ticked on *Explorer Checkboxes* and select the object in the *Explorer
Tree*. Right-Click > Properties [Relationships] and the *Object properties Dialog Box*
will show the same display as the *Relationships Tab*.

| Relationship type | Name ▲ |
|---|---|
| is activated by | Trigger |
| creates | Outcome |
| has input of | Information |
| has output of | Data |
| has output of | Product/Service |
| gets input from | Document |
| is carried out by | Department |
| is represented by | Entry Screen |
| supports | Objective |
| is supported by | System |
| is carried out at | London HQ |
| requires | Instruction |
| creates | Instructions |
| creates | Skills |
| has | Risk |

**Fig. 11.20** Relationships Tab

Fig. 11.20 shows the result for the function in the example shown in Fig. 11.18. You can see every relationship between the function and all other objects is listed. To read the display correctly, think of the object you selected and read the list from left to right. For instance, starting at the top row:

- **Task** *(Function)*     *"is activated by"*     *(Event)* **Trigger**,

- **Task** *(Function)*     *"creates"*     *(Objective)* **Outcome**,

- **Task** *(Function)*     *"has input of"*     *(Technical term)* **Information**, etc.


### 11.6.5    ARIS Reports

All the information in the database about ARIS objects, their attributes and connections can be extracted and displayed by '*ARIS Reports*'. Reports can be created in the *Administration Module* using the '*Script Wizard*' or the '*Script Editor*'. Using Java Script we can effectively write a computer program and thus we can perform far more elaborate analysis than is available through the relationship displays. For instance, it is possible to identify all the implicit relationships between unconnected objects sharing connections to a common object. ARIS provides a comprehensive set of report scripts to cater for the most commonly used reporting tasks.


## 11.7    Function Allocation Diagrams

By now you may be thinking, all this detail may be very useful, but it is producing very complex diagrams. You are absolutely right, but there is a solution. Instead of putting the function allocations in the EPC, they can be put in their own diagram: the Function allocation diagram (FAD). The FAD can be 'assigned' to the function object in the EPC showing it provides additional information about the function and its relationship to other objects. This allows the EPC to remain uncluttered and makes the process flow more visible. Creating *Function allocation diagrams* and assigning models to objects is covered in the next chapter.

# Chapter 12    Model Assignments and the Function Allocation Diagram

In this chapter we introduce the concept of model assignments. We look at how they are created and viewed, and how they are used to create model structure. We describe how an EPC may be kept 'lean' by assigning a Function Allocation Diagram to its functions and the special operations applicable to assigned FADs.

## 12.1    Model Assignments

One of the main strengths of ARIS is that we can create many different model diagrams within the same database. These models can be used to partition the overall business model into manageable chunks or to provide different viewpoints. We can locate these models in different ARIS groups so as to provide structure to the database. However, we need to be able to link the models together to provide an overall structure to the design and provide an easy way to navigate between them. This linking is provided by making an 'assignment' between an object and a model.

An assignment has four roles, it:

- Provides a relationship between an object and a model,
- Establishes a hierarchical structure for the models in the database,
- May provide an implicit relationship between an object and the objects in the assigned model (e.g. in a *Function tree* or *ERM model*),
- Provides a quick way of navigating between models.

Below, we will look at how model assignments are created and used. Assigning a *Function allocation diagram (FAD)* to functions in an EPC is one of the most common uses of model assignment, so we will also look at the specific assignment operations that can be used with a FAD.

### 12.1.1    The Relationship Between an Object and a Model

An assignment is a relationship, like those between two objects, but in this case between a model and an object. The assignment indicates the assigned model or models provide more information about that object. This may be further detail about what the object represents (e.g. a sub-process for a function) or information about the relationships between the object and other objects (e.g. in a *Function allocation diagram*).

Which models can be linked to which objects is defined by the ARIS Method and is subject to any restrictions imposed by the current Method Filter. The Method may not allow any model assignments at all for some objects, but normally several types of model can be assigned. Usually, once one model of a particular type has been assigned to an object, no more models of that type can be assigned. The exception is many EPCs can be assigned to a function object.

Sometimes assigning a model to an object will also make an implicit relationship between the object itself and the objects in the assigned model. For instance, in Chapter 11 we introduced the concept of a data object called a *Cluster* comprised of a collection of *Entity types*. If you assign an *ERM* model to the *Cluster* and place the *Entity type* objects in the *ERM* model, this will automatically create the relationship the *Cluster* "*consists of*" *Entity types*.

## 12.2    Creating Model Assignments

There are four ways a model can be assigned to an object:

- Create a new model and assign it to an object,
- Assign an existing model to an object,
- Drag and drop assignment of an existing model,
- Use the Assignments > Hide command
  (only for assigning FADs in *ARIS Toolset*).

### 12.2.1    Create and Assign a Model

Because assigned models provide additional information about the objects we have already modelled, we often wish to create a new model and assign it to an existing object in one operation. To do this, select the object (e.g. a function) you wish to make the assignment to in the *Explorer Module* or *Designer Module* and:

1. Right-Click > Properties [*Assignments*]  or  Right-Click > Assignments...,

2. Select New....

Or
Right-Click > New > Assignments.

The *Assignment Wizard, Select model type Dialog Box* (Fig. 12.1) will provide a list of models which can be assigned to the object. Select a model type (e.g. an EPC) and press Next. You will now need to select the group in which to put the model from the *Select model/group Dialog Box* and press Finish. The *Assignments Dialog Box* should now show there is an assigned model of type EPC. The name of the model will be the same as the object to which it was assigned so it is always wise to make sure the object has a suitable name before making the assignment.

**Warning** – you can independently change the names of an object and its assigned model. If you do change one, they do not automatically update in synchronisation.

The available model types for the selected object are defined by the ARIS Method and may be restricted by the Method Filter in use. The list is also limited by which models you have already assigned to the object.

 **Question** – why can't I see the model type I want to assign to my object in the *Assignment Wizard Select model type Dialog Box*; I know it is allowed in the Method Filter?
**Answer** – typically you can only assign one instance of each model type to an object. Look in the *Assignments Dialog Box* and check if there is already a model of that type listed. If there is, you will not be able to assign a second model of that type (except for EPCs, mentioned above). If there isn't a model of that type listed, models of that type are not allowed by the ARIS Method or the current Method Filter.

You can now press OK (or Cancel, as the assignment has already be made) to close the *Assignments Dialog Box*. If you made the assignment in the *Designer Module,* or you subsequently open a model containing the object to which you made the assignment, you will see the object now has the *Assignment Icon* at its bottom right-hand corner.

When you create some types of assigned model (e.g. *Function tree* or *FAD*) the object originally selected will automatically be placed into the assigned model for you. This is because these models are intended to allow additional relationships to be defined for the object. Other model types (e.g. the EPC) are a decomposition of

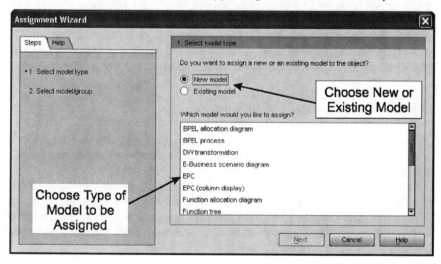

**Fig. 12.1** Assignment Wizard

the detail of the original object so it would make no sense to have the object in the model.

## 12.2.2    Assigning an Existing Model

Sometimes you may wish to assign a model you have already created to an object. Follow the same procedure as before; select the object in the *Explorer Module* or *Designer Module*:

1.    Right-Click > Properties [*Assignments*]  or  Right-Click > Assignments...,

2.    Select New....

This time tick the *Existing model Checkbox* in the *Select model type Dialog Box* (Fig. 12.1). Carry on as before selecting the model type, but in the *Select model/group Dialog Box*, instead of choosing the group where you want to save the new model, choose an existing model. Only existing models of the type you have chosen will be displayed for you to select from. If you try to assign a model you have already assigned, the dialog box will just close.

 **Hint** – when assigning an existing model to an object, don't forget to tick the *Existing model Checkbox* in *Select model type Dialog Box*, otherwise you may create a new model by mistake. If you do, use the *Explorer Module* to delete the unwanted model. The assignment link will be deleted automatically.

The only difference between making an assignment to a new model or to an existing model is likely to be the name of the assigned model. Making an assignment to a new model will always name the assigned model to be the same as the selected object. When assigning to an existing model, the model will have already been named. It makes no difference to the operation of ARIS what the assigned model is called. However, you may find it easier to manage your models if the name of the assigned model is meaningful in relation to the object to which it is assigned. This is particularly true of FADs assigned to functions.

## 12.2.3    Drag and Drop Assignments

If you need to make a number of assignments of existing models to objects, a quick way to do this is to drag and drop from the *Explorer Tree* in the *Designer Module Navigation Bar*.

First make sure the *Navigation Bar* is visible by clicking on the *Navigation Checkbox*. Select the *Explorer tree Tab* and make sure the *Models Checkbox* is ticked. Navigate the *Explorer Tree* to find the model you want to assign. Select it with the left mouse key and drag it onto the *Modelling Window* over the symbol of the object to which you wish to assign it.

When you release the mouse key the *Create assignment Dialog Box* will ask you if you want to *Create assignment* or *Open model*.

Selecting Open Model will just open the model in the *Designer Module* and no assignment will be made. Selecting **Create assignment** will assign the chosen model to the object. If the assignment is not allowed, one of the following will happen:

- If the Method Filter does not allow that type of object to be assigned to the object type you will see the error message: "Unable to create assignment. This model type cannot be assigned to this object type",

- If you try and assign a model you have already assigned, nothing will happen,

- If you have already assigned a different model of that type (except for EPCs), you will see the error message: "Unable to create assignment. An assignment for this model type already exists".

> **Question** – why, when I drag a model onto an object, does it just open the model and not make the assignment?
> **Answer** – you must make sure you save the model containing the objects you are trying to assign models to before you drag and drop the model.

Using drag and drop this way is a very quick method for making large numbers of model assignments, but it is very easy to make mistakes, so be careful. We will see below how to view assignments and delete those we don't want.

### 12.2.4    Hide Assignments

One of the most frequent model assignment tasks is to assign a *Function allocation diagram* (FAD) to a function in an EPC. To make this easier and quicker, there is a shortcut method for doing this using the Assignment > Hide command. Unfortunately, this is currently only available in *ARIS Toolset*. However, because it is so useful, and probably will find its way into *ARIS Business Architect* in the future, we have described it in Section 12.8.

## 12.3    Viewing and Opening Model Assignments

The *Designer Module* provides a visual indication that an object has a model assigned to it by displaying the *Assignment Icon* at the bottom right-hand corner of the object. The icon only tells you one or more models are assigned, not what sort of models. Now we have assigned models to objects, how  can we see which assignments we have made and open the assigned models?

There are several ways:

- The *Assignments Dialog Box*,
- The *Assignment Icon* in the *Designer Module*,
- The *Assignments Tab* in the *Properties Bar*.

### 12.3.1    The Assignments Dialog Box

To view the models assigned to an object:

1.  Select the object in the *Designer Module* or the *Explorer Module*,
2.  Right-Click > Properties [*Assignments*] or Right-Click > Assignments....

The *Assignments Dialog Box* will now show a list of any assigned models. To open one of them:

1.  Select a model from the *Assignments Dialog Box*,
2.  Select Open and press OK.

The assigned model will open in a new *Modelling Window* tab in the *Designer Module*.

### 12.3.2    The Assignment Icon

When using the *Designer Module* there is a quicker way to open an assigned model. Hover your mouse over the assignment icon and you will notice the cursor changes to a shape similar to the icon. Double-click on the *Assignment Icon* and the model will open. If there is more than one model assigned to the object, the *Assigned model Dialog Box* will give you a choice (Fig. 12.2). This is a very useful way to quickly navigate through models. However, when there is a lot of detail on the model, and you are viewing it at a large scale, it can be difficult to accurately click the icon. In this situation it is better to use the *Assignments Tab* in the *Properties Bar* (see below).

**Warning** – often people expect if you double-click on the object, the assigned model will open. However, in the *Designer Module*, double-clicking on the object opens the *Properties [Format / Object appearance] Dialog Box*.

**Expert tip** – you can choose whether or not to display the *Assignment Icon* for objects with assigned models. To turn the icons off, go to the *Model Properties [Format / Representation] Dialog Box* and tick the *Hide assignments icons Checkbox*. This can be useful on complex models or those with nested objects.

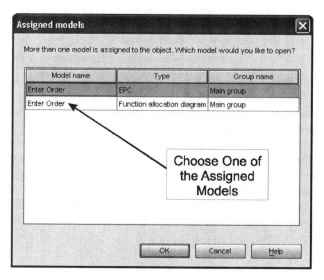

**Fig. 12.2** Assigned Model Dialog Box

### 12.3.3 The Assignments Tab

Double-clicking on the *Assignment Icon* is a quick way to open assigned models, but if you want to quickly see which models are assigned, or if there are multiple assigned models and you want to quickly choose which to open, using the *Assignments Tab* on the *Properties Bar* is the best approach (Fig. 12.3).

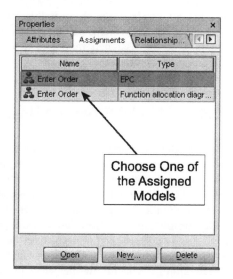

Ensure the *Properties Checkbox* is ticked and select the *Assignments Tab* on the *Properties Bar*. If you now select an object, the *Assignments Tab* will display any models assigned to that object.

If you select one of the listed models, some or all of the buttons at the bottom of the *Assignments Tab* become active:

**Fig. 12.3** Properties Dialog Box, Assignments Tab

- Open – opens the model in the *Designer Module,*
- New... – opens the *Assignment Wizard* (Fig. 12.1),
- Delete – deletes the assignment relationship from the object to that model.

Because the *Assignments Tab* can be left open all the while you can quickly go around the model, selecting objects and viewing their assignments. This is much quicker than using the *Assignments Dialog Box* (Section 12.3.1) which would have to be opened separately for each object.

You can also execute the Open and Delete assignment commands from the *Right-Click Menu*. In addition, as well as being able to view the model's properties and attributes, the *Right-Click Menu* allows you to go straight to the model's location in the *Explorer Module* by selecting Go to > Occurrence in Explorer. This will open up the group structure and highlight the selected assigned model in the *Navigation Bar Explorer Tree* (it will automatically open the *Navigation Bar* if it is not already open).

## 12.4    Deleting Assignments

You can delete the assignment relationship between an object and a model by selecting an assigned model in the *Assignments Dialog Box* or *Assignments Tab* and pressing the Delete Button. This will remove the entry in the assignments list and, if this was the only model assigned to the object, it will also remove the *Assignment Icon* from the object in the *Designer Module.*

Deleting the assignment will not delete the model; it remains in the ARIS group structure. If the assigned model is deleted, any assignment relationships will automatically be deleted.

## 12.5    Model Structure Using Assignments

Using model assignments we can now link models together in a way that represents the structure of the information we are modelling. Users of the model can navigate through the information in an intuitive way. For instance, if we are viewing an EPC and we notice a function has assigned models (signified by the *Assignment Icon* in the *Designer Module*), then if we check and see it is an EPC, we can be reasonably sure it will represent a sub-process description. Similarly, if we see there is a model assigned to a *Technical term*, we can expect it will be a *Technical terms Model* describing the detailed definition of the *Technical term.*

Therefore, if you follow the ARIS principles and assign models in a sensible way, users will easily be able to navigate around your model structure. It is then much easier to navigate from one model to another, rather than to have to search through the group structure trying to guess from the model's names what they are used for.

We recommend you try to ensure all the models in your database are fully linked together. Sometimes this can be difficult to achieve because the restrictions of the ARIS Method do not always allow you to assign the model you want to a particular object. This may influence which models and objects you choose to use.

Having a fully linked model structure becomes essential if you intend to publish your models using *ARIS Web Publisher*. The Java enabled versions of published models do have an Explorer-like component enabling users to navigate the ARIS group structure. However, because the 'hyperlink' concept is so ubiquitous on the Internet, users will expect to be able to navigate by clicking from one model to the next. This means if you intend to publish on the Web it will influence the way you build and link your models in ARIS.

 **Expert Tip** – a useful strategy to adopt, certainly if you are using *ARIS Web Publisher*, but equally valuable in ARIS itself, is to create an 'overview model'. Make sure the overview model is the only model in the **Main Group** place all other models in groups underneath the **Main Group** and link them to the overview model. Anyone opening the database or viewing it on the Internet will now immediately know where to start.

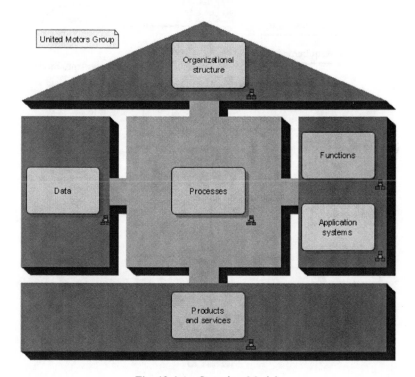

**Fig. 12.4** An Overview Model

The overview model (or 'meta-model') provides an introduction to what the database contains and all other models can be reached through assignments from objects in the model. Fig. 12.4 shows an example overview model ("start model") from the **Demo70** database where each object in the model represents the business areas modelled and each object has models assigned to it that allow the users to navigate through the model structure. Alternatively you can use other standard models such as the *Value added chain Diagram* for the overview model.

## 12.6    The Lean EPC

In the previous chapter we looked at how objects could be allocated to functions to represent the resources used by a process and the environment in which it operates. Using an EPC with function allocations (an *'extended'* EPC) enables us to precisely define the process in as much detail as required. However, the process diagrams may now become very complicated and could span many pages of printed output.

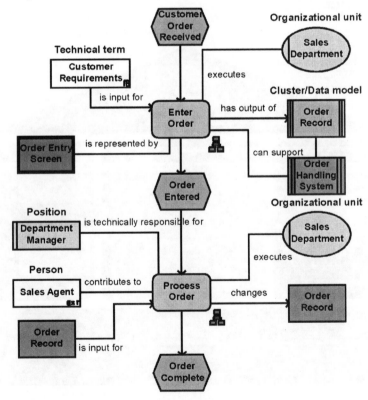

**Fig. 12.5** An EPC with Function Allocations

Fig. 12.5 shows a simple example of an EPC with function allocations. Imagine what a large process would look like where every function has as many connected objects. However, we don't need to define all these relationships in a single model. Because all the objects and relationships are stored in the underlying database, they can be defined in any suitable model and still be available for inspection at any time. So instead of having all those connections in the EPC, we can use a model designed just for this purpose: the *Function allocation diagram (FAD)*. We can assign a FAD to each function in the EPC and thus keep the EPC as a much simpler 'lean' EPC that just describes the process flow.

## 12.7     Function Allocation Diagrams

The *Function allocation diagram (FAD)* is very similar in appearance to the EPC. The FAD has nearly all the same objects available as the EPC, and has the same connections between the function and the other objects (Fig. 12.6). The only exceptions are the FAD has no *Rule* objects and, although an *Event* object can be placed in the model, it is not possible to link functions to events. These items aren't needed because we don't model the process flow in the FAD. For each function in an EPC, we create a separate FAD model showing just the object relationships for that function. We then assign the FADs to the functions and remove the function allocations (i.e. the connections to the resource objects) from the EPC.

We have the choice whether to make the functional allocations in the EPC first, and transfer them to the FAD, or to create them in the FAD in the first place. It is largely a matter of personal preference, but ARIS provides some additional facilities specifically for creating FAD assignments allowing us to be flexible in making the choice. In general, it is better to model the relationships in the EPC, where

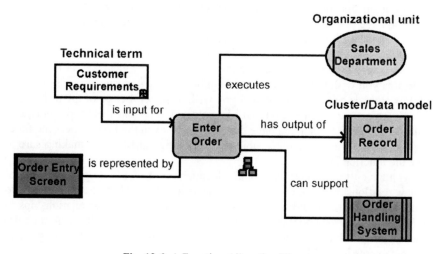

**Fig. 12.6** A Function Allocation Diagram

you can see them in context of the process flow, but then to transfer them to the FAD to keep the EPC 'lean'.

There are essentially four ways to create and assign a FAD to functions in the EPC:

- Create and assign a new FAD,
- Assign an existing FAD,
- Drag and drop a FAD assignment,
- Use the Assignments > Hide command in the EPC (*ARIS Toolset* Only).

We looked at the first three of these methods earlier in the chapter, so we will only need to briefly review them in the special context of the FAD. The last method, Assignments > Hide, is special to the FAD.

### 12.7.1    Create and Assign a New FAD

To create a new FAD and assign it to an object in the *Designer Module*:

1.  Select a function,
2.  Right-Click  > New > Assignments,
3.  Ensure the *New model* box is ticked,
4.  Select the "*Function allocation diagram*" from the drop-down list,
5.  Press Next,
6.  Choose the group where you wish to save the model,
7.  Press Finish.

If you have already defined function allocations in the EPC (e.g. made connections from the functions to resource objects), you can now transfer them to the FAD you have just created. A quick way is to copy the function and its connected resource objects from the EPC and paste them into the FAD. There is already a copy of the function in the FAD, placed there automatically when the model assignment was created, but you can delete this. Click the left mouse key at one corner of the area you wish to copy, and drag the mouse to the opposite corner so a selection box 'rubber-bands' over the area you wish to select. Let go of the mouse and multiple objects and connections will be selected. You can then copy and paste them into the FAD. When you have done this, and saved the FAD, delete the function allocations (i.e. the resource objects) in the original EPC, but making sure to leave the function intact.

If you haven't made any functional allocations in the EPC, or you wish to create new relationships, you can add new objects into the FAD and connect them to the function just as we did before in the EPC. If you inspect the relationships in the FAD (use the *Relationships Tab* in the *Properties Bar*) you will see all the relationships to the objects in the FAD, and also the relationships to the trigger and outcome events in the EPC.

To create a FAD for another function in the EPC you follow the same approach, but be careful about duplicating resource objects. If you want to add a new relationship in the FAD to a common resource you have used elsewhere (e.g. "Sales Department"), it is important to use an occurrence of the same object. Only this way will you be able to perform subsequent analysis to identify, for instance, all the functions the "Sales Department" carries out. So don't create a new object and give it the same name, but re-use the resource object from the original EPC or another FAD (see Chapter 9).

### Multiple Relationship Definitions

By following the instructions above you will now have two models: an EPC and a FAD. Both contain the same function, and we were careful to tell you to delete the original function allocations after transferring them to the FAD. Does this matter? Yes it does. If we kept the definition in both, and later decided to makes changes to the function allocations, we have to remember to make the changes in both the EPC and the FAD.

**Warning** – the relationships stored in the ARIS database are the sum total of the relationships defined in all models in the database. Avoid duplicating the same connection in multiple models, otherwise this will make future changes more difficult to track and implement as models become out of step.

**Question** – I have deleted a connection between a function and an object in the FAD, but when I view relationships it is still shown. Why is that?

**Answer** – it is probably because there is still a copy of the connection in the associated EPC. The relationship will not actually be deleted until you remove every occurrence of the connection from every model in which it appears.

## 12.7.2    Assigning an Existing FAD Model

Normally we create a new FAD and assign to an object in one operation, however we can also assign an existing FAD to a function in an EPC. To make the assignment, follow the instructions given in Section 12.2.2.

**Warning** – it only makes sense to assign a FAD to a function that is an occurrence of the same object as the function already used in the FAD. The whole point of the FAD is it shows the relationships between the function in the EPC and other resource objects. Hence, there is no point at all in assigning a FAD to a function which is a different object to the one in the FAD.

## 12.8      Show/Hide Assignments

This book is aimed at users of *ARIS Business Architect* and *ARIS Business Designer*. However, in this section we are going to make an exception and discuss the hide and show assignments commands of the *ARIS Toolset* because they are so useful for easily and quickly creating FADs. We expect these commands will very soon find their way into a future release of *Business Architect* and *Business Designer* and, while their operation may not be exactly the same as the *ARIS Toolset* commands described here, we think it us useful to explain their principles.

### 12.8.1      Hide Assignments

We suggested in Section 12.7 that the best way to model the relationships between a function and resource objects, is to model the objects and connections in an EPC, copy them to a *Function allocation diagram* and remove them from the EPC. This is a rather laborious process, but if you have already modelled the relationships in the EPC you can create the FADs automatically with *ARIS Toolset* by 'hiding assignments':

1. Select a function,
2. Right-Click > Assignments,
3. Select Hide.

The result is dramatic. All the objects connected to the function disappear! But, before you get too worried, notice an *Assignment Icon* has also appeared. Open the assigned model (double-click on the *Assignment Icon*) and you will see the assigned model is a FAD containing all the function allocations from the EPC (Fig. 12.7). Even better, you don't have to create each one individually, you can select all the functions in the model and hide all the assignments in one go:

1. Select any single function,
2. Right-Click > Select,
3. Choose Select All Objects of the 'function' Type

All the functions in the model will be selected and, with your mouse over the selected area, Right-Click > Assignments > Hide as before. Now all the connected objects will disappear and a complete set of FADs will have been created for all the functions. The FADs will automatically be put in the same group as the EPC, but you can move them elsewhere using the *Explorer Module*.

**Warning** – if the same resource object occurs in several places in an EPC, use a separate occurrence of the object to connect to each function (Fig. 12.8). Do not be tempted to use a single object and make multiple connections to each function. Assignments > Hide works through the model a function at a time, and once the object has been hidden for the first object it won't be transferred into the FADs for the other objects.

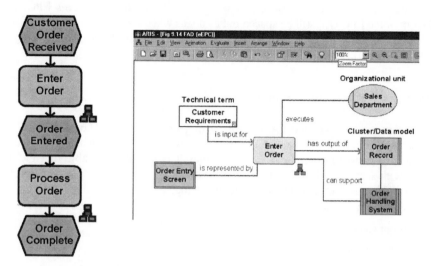

**Fig. 12.7** Hide Assignment to Create a FAD

If you have two functions in a model with the same name (not recommended, but not invalid), if you try Assignments > Hide on both of them you will get an error message. This is because ARIS will try to create FADs with the same name as the object, and it is not valid to have two models of the same type and with the same name in the same group.

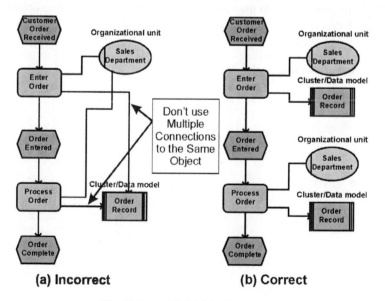

**Fig. 12.8** Avoid Multiple Connections

Once we have hidden all the assignments we will be left with a '*lean*' EPC. The layout of the EPC will still be spaced out as it was when we had the resource objects visible, but we can make this more compact by using the layout facility (Right-Click > Layout).

### 12.8.2    Show Assignments

Now that we have created FADs, either using Assignments > Hide or any of the other methods described earlier, the lean EPC we are left with makes the process flow simpler to follow. However, sometimes it is useful to be able to view the EPC with some or all of the function allocations visible. We can show the previously hidden assignments by doing the following:

1.  Select a function,

2.  Right-Click > Assignments,

3.  Select Show.

The function allocations defined in the FAD will now be made visible in the EPC. We can perform this operation on a single function or on all functions by selecting them all as described above. The result will appear rather a mess at first, but we can easily tidy it up by using the layout facility (Right-Click > Layout). In complex models it is best to use Assignments > Show on just those parts of the model in which you have a special interest.

 **Warning** – the Assignments > Show operation will only work if the function object in the FAD is an occurrence of the function object in the EPC. If you manually assign the wrong FAD to the function, or the FAD is empty, the error message "Unable to find objects or relationships to show" will be displayed when you use Assignments > Show.

# Chapter 13    Modelling your Business Structure

In this chapter we discuss the need for structure in modelling and describe horizontal and vertical structuring. We look at simple ways of linking models together in a horizontal structure and more advanced techniques for vertical structuring. We also introduce some additional models that support the management and visualisation of vertical hierarchies.

## 13.1    The Need for Structure

One of the most powerful aspects of ARIS is the wide variety of models it provides for giving different viewpoints of a business. The definition of objects and their connections is always stored in the underlying database, so the relationships between business entities can be defined in any appropriate model. These relationships can be visualised and analysed in other models and reports. Thus, it is possible to partition a business model into different individual models to aid model creation, management and use.

In order to make best use of this capability we need to consider a structured approach to modelling and have an understanding of techniques for linking models together. As suggested in earlier chapters, the linking of models becomes increasingly important when the final results are to be published on the Web. People viewing your models on the Web will expect to be able to navigate your model structure via hyperlinks, and hence it is important to have a fully linked model structure.

## 13.2    Horizontal and Vertical Structures

We can structure our models horizontally by segmenting models into manageable chunks which link together, or we can segment them vertically in a hierarchical structure that decomposes each model into increasing levels of detail. In small projects we might only use simple horizontal structures, while in large complex projects we would probably use both horizontal and vertical structures.

Fig. 13.1 shows models structured both horizontally and vertically. The top layer of the structure (Fig. 13.1a) shows a high-level process modelled in a single EPC. For convenience it is shown horizontally, but the principle is the same when models are laid out vertically. There are four functions in the process and it is natural for us to want to model them in further detail. The second layer of the model (Fig. 13.1b) shows how two of these functions have been decomposed into two separate EPCs containing further detail. We now have a vertical structure represented by the decomposition of the high-level process into more detailed models.

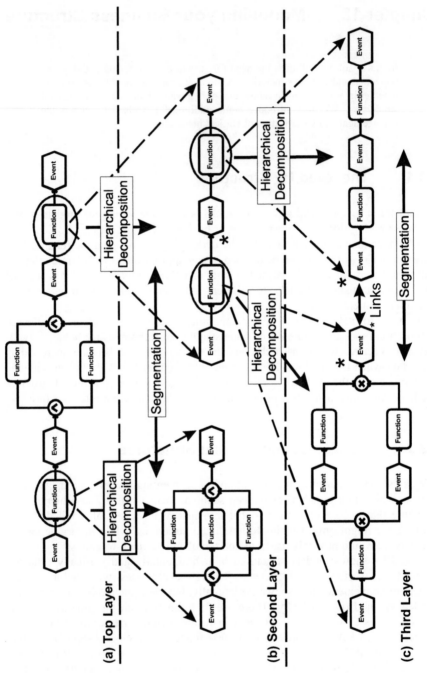

**Fig. 13.1** Horizontal and Vertical Structure

However, the two EPCs at the second level do not stand in isolation to one another. They each represent different segments of the entire process modelled at that level of detail. So there is also a horizontal structure at layer two, represented by the decomposed models (there is no horizontal structure at layer 1 because there is only one model).

We can see the horizontal segmentation structure more clearly if we move down and look at layer 3 (Fig. 13.1c). Again, two of the functions at layer 2 are decomposed into more detail in separate EPCs in layer 3. This time, the functions are adjacent to each other in the process flow. The functions are of course separated by an event (marked with a star). When we decompose these functions at layer 3, the more detailed sub-processes must also be adjacent to one another. In fact, the event that is the outcome of the sub-process representing the first function must be the triggering event for the sub-process that is the decomposition of the second function. They are in fact the same event (marked with stars).

If we create our model structure correctly, all of the segmented EPCs at any decomposition layer should link together in a complete and consistent way. Each layer should also decompose consistently into the layer below. Ideally, therefore, the entire horizontal and vertical structure should fit together in a complete and consistent manner.

In practice, this is not always easy to do. We may not want to model all the processes in a given layer, so our models may not completely connect up. There are also some theoretical constraints to how consistent vertical decomposition can be (see Section 13.5.1). However, the ideal of a fully connected and consistent model is always something to have as a goal.

Based on what we have just said, you may think you should always start modelling by first designing and creating this structure, and then neatly fitting all your models into it. If you are able to do this, go right ahead. In practice this is rarely achievable, few people can correctly visualise the entire structure of their models before they start modelling. More likely the structure will emerge as a result of detailed modelling. By all means think about structure before you start, and create a rough outline, but don't spend too long working on this. Decide at which level in the hierarchy the most important aspects of the project will be represented, and start detailed modelling at this level. Once you have produced a couple of detailed models you should start to get a feel for the emerging structure. Re-visit your rough model structure and adjust it as necessary. The whole process of modelling and creating the structure will proceed in an iterative manner. Sometimes you will have to adjust the structure and sometimes you will need to alter your models to fit the structure. But just like assembling mechanical components, don't try to force them together.

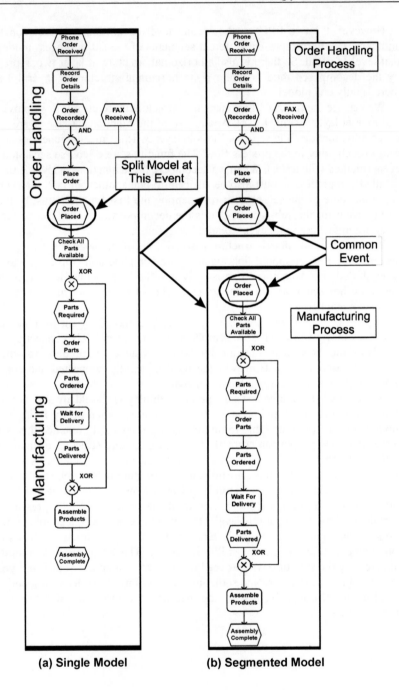

**(a) Single Model**          **(b) Segmented Model**

**Fig. 13.2** Horizontal Segmentation

## 13.3 Horizontal Structure

### 13.3.1 Segmentation

Horizontal segmentation is the easiest form of model structure to both understand and visualise. Instead of creating a single large EPC describing our whole process, we split it up into a number of linked models. For example, Fig. 13.2a shows a process similar to the examples in Chapter 7. The top part of the process deals with taking and processing an order. The bottom part of the process deals with manufacturing the order. These are different elements of the business; they would be done by different departments, and follow one after the other. Therefore, it seems quite natural to split this process up into two separate models as shown in Fig. 13.2b. Each model now describes one key element of the end-to-end process.

You may wonder why we have called it 'horizontal segmentation' when in fact we have split the model vertically: the top of the model from the bottom. We should make it clear that when we refer to horizontal segmentation, we mean horizontal in terms of layers of a hierarchical structure (Fig. 13.1), not the direction in which the model is laid out (EPCs may be laid out vertically or horizontally). That is to say, we are segmenting models that are modelled at the same level of detail. In simple projects you may only be modelling at one level of detail, but in a more complex project you may have a hierarchical decomposition, where each layer of the hierarchy is itself segmented.

The example shown is quite straightforward in that it easily segments. You will find that some models, for instance those with complex interactions and loops, do not segment so easily. Don't spend too much time trying to work out how to segment your models before you start serious modelling. It is better to model using one large EPC and segment it later. You will often find a natural structure emerges.

### 13.3.2 Linking Models Using Events

Although we have split the original model in Fig. 13.2a into two separate segments, we still want to indicate that the two models in Fig. 13.2b are part of an overall end-to-end process and they are directly linked to one another. The way we do this is to use a common event that is the outcome of the first process and the trigger for the second process. In Fig. 13.2a the boundary between the two halves of the process is an event called **Order Placed**. When we split the model we leave the **Order Placed** event at the end of the "Order Handling" process, but we also include it as the start of the "Manufacturing" process.

 **Warning** – when linking models together using events, the event that is the trigger for the second model must be an *occurrence copy* of the event that is the outcome event of the first model (see Chapter 15 for more information on occurrence copies).

By using the same event to link the models we can navigate between models by looking for occurrences of the event. For instance, if you were to select the **Order Placed** event in the "Order Handling" process (Fig. 13.2b) and look at the *Occurrences Tab* on the *Properties Bar* you will see the display shown in Fig. 13.3. You can clearly see the event occurs in both the "Order Handling" process and the "Manufacturing" process which gives us a clue that the event is linking the models together. If you select the **Manufacturing Process** entry and Right-Click > Open, ARIS will open the "Manufacturing Process" model with the object selected and positioned in the centre of the *Modelling Window*.

 **Warning** – do not be tempted to copy an event occurring in the middle of a process flow in one model and re-use it in another model. The name may be the same as the one you want for the second model, but in reality it should be a completely different object. If you do this you are effectively linking the two models together. Instead use different events and give them slightly different names.

Using this approach we can easily navigate between linked segmented models, but it is important to use an *occurrence* of the same object. If you have two different objects, using the same name, there is no link between the models and you cannot navigate using occurrences.

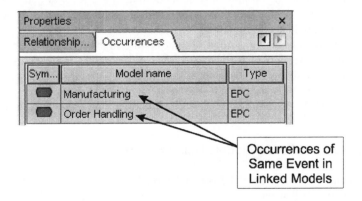

**Fig. 13.3** Linked Event Occurrences

### 13.3.3    Using the Process Interface Object

Readers who have used other modelling or drawing tools, or perhaps have used Microsoft PowerPoint for drawing processes, will be familiar with the concept of an 'off-page connector'. The connector is a symbol indicating the drawing of the process model continues on a separate sheet.

There is an equivalent symbol available in ARIS called the
'*Process interface*'. However, in ARIS we create more than
just drawings, we create models represented in the underlying database.

So, in addition to using a linking event, we can also use the *Process interface*
object to represent the process the event links to as shown in Fig. 13.4. This gives
a more visual indication of the connecting models in the horizontal structure and
avoids the need to look at the occurrences of the linking event.

We recommend using different *Process interface* objects at the end of one
process and the start of the next (unlike the linking events which are occurrences
of the same object) and typically give them names something like "TO: Manufacturing Process" and "FROM: Order Handling Process".

You can take this approach a step further and assign the linked model to the
*Process interface* (see Chapter 12 for more on model assignments). Navigating to
the linked model is now just a matter of opening the model assigned to the *Process interface*. This is a useful approach, but can initially seem confusing because
normally, as we shall see later in the chapter, an EPC assigned to a function
(which is what the *Process interface* object really is) represents a decomposition
of the function. This is clearly not the case here. Coupled with the fact that the
EPCs now appear to end with a function, the use of the *Process interface* seems to
conflict with the normal use of the function in an EPC.

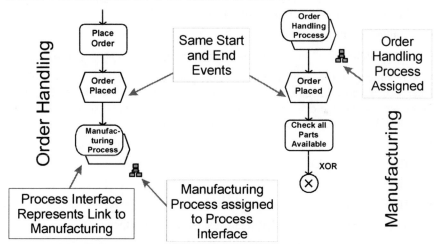

**Fig. 13.4** Linking Models with the Process Interface

 **Expert Tip** – if you use the *Process interface* to connect models, your
models will fail the `StructureRules.sem` *Semantic Check* if the
"Each path must begin and end with an event" rule is chosen. Instead
choose the "`Each path must start and end with an event
or a process interface`" rule.

### 13.3.4    Rules for Horizontally Segmenting Models

Let us recap the rules for linking horizontally segment Models:

- Get the model right first and segment later,
- Link models using events,
- Make an occurrence copy of the linking event,
- Don't make copies of other events,
- Attach separate *Process interface* objects at the end and start of connecting models,
- Assigned the linked model to the *Process interface*.

### 13.3.5    Segmenting Existing Models

Segmenting existing models is straightforward, provided the models lend themselves to a segmented structure. Some models will exhibit a natural structure while others will be highly interconnected and are best left as they are. When deciding whether to segment a model, look for areas of the process with:

- Limited connections to other parts of the process,
- Connections through events (not rules),
- Limited use of loops,
- A common distinct theme (e.g. order processing, manufacturing, etc.).

Sometimes you may have to re-model the process in a slightly different way in order that it can be segmented. Look back at the example model in Fig. 13.2. There seem to be two distinct parts of the model, the left-hand side and the right-hand side. Let us apply the above tests to this model:

- There are limited connections (four) between the two segments,
- Three of the connections are made via rules,
- There is a single loop,
- The right-hand side has a common theme (order validation),
- It is not clear whether the left-hand side has a distinct theme.

Based on our criteria above, it doesn't look an ideal example for segmentation, but as an exercise, let us have a go at it anyway.

First we need to make sure we can isolate the two parts of the process so they are only connected by events. The version of the model in Fig. 13.5 has been altered slightly so, instead of a branch after the **Order Recorded** event, the model is split after the **Record Order Details** function. This enables an extra event (**Confirmation Required**) to be added that becomes the link between the two models. You can compare the models in Fig. 13.2 and Fig. 13.5 to convince yourself they are logically the same.

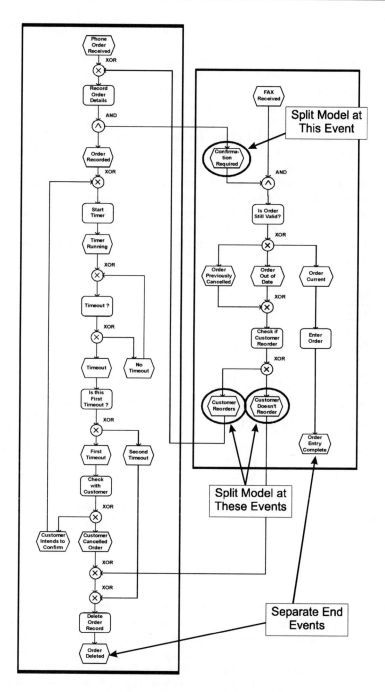

**Fig. 13.5** Segmenting an Existing Model

Similarly, we have remodelled the outcome of the **Check if Customer Reorder** decision to create a **Customer Doesn't Reorder** event which links the models.

Both the left-hand side and right-hand side processes combine when complete at the **Order Entry Complete** event. This gives us a problem. We can't easily add a new linking event after the **Enter Order** function and find a way of joining it to the **Order Entry Complete** event. We would have to add an extra function to join the two paths and still finish the model with an event. We don't want to do that, so we have created separate end events for each process segment and not bothered to join them. Finally, the loop is still present, but it has a convenient linking event, so we will leave it in place.

As we can see from Fig. 13.5 the process can now be segmented into two halves with three events (shown circled) linking the two parts of the process. To break them apart, first break the connection between the linking event and one half of the process (Fig. 13.6a). Now make an occurrence copy of the linking event and connect the copy to the process segment whose connection you have just deleted (Fig. 13.6b).

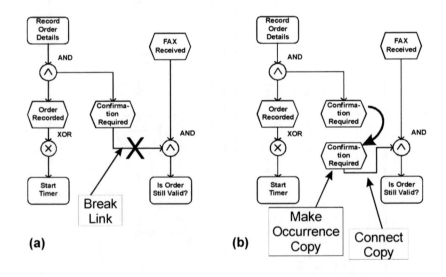

**Fig. 13.6** Breaking the Links

Once you have done this for the three events, the process will be in two isolated segments. You can now create a new EPC and copy one of the segments into it. Once you have saved it, delete the segment from the original EPC. You will now have two EPCs, each with one with a segment of the original process linked through three common events. You can now add *Process interfaces* to the linking events in the two segmented models and assigned the linked model to them. It is a good idea to make a copy of the original EPC (or backup your database) before you follow this procedure, just in case you make a mistake.

**Warning** – while segmenting a model by breaking it apart at the common events, do not use the auto layout facility. Because the links between parts of the model are now broken, auto layout will interpret the model in a very different way. Once the models have been saved in separate EPCs, then you can run auto layout.

This example was a little contrived because we wanted to show how to segment an example model we already had, rather than create a model especially for the purpose. If you feel the end result is two models that don't look as though they should be separate models, then maybe you are right. This is a good lesson. If you try to segment your own models (or design them in a segmented way in the first place) and feel you are making artificial boundaries, stop and check if the approach is sensible. The point of segmentation is to make the models easier to understand, visualise and manage. If the segmentation is too contrived, the benefit will be lost.

### Segmenting Complex Models

Although the example above may have been rather contrived, it was fairly straightforward. When trying to segment complex models, it is very easy to get lost while breaking apart the model at the common events.

A neat trick to help manage complex model segmentation is to temporarily reconnect the disconnected parts back together using the *Process interface* object. Follow the approach described above to break apart the model at the common events, create an occurrence copy of the event and connect each copy of the event to one half of the segmented model (Fig. 13.7a). Now we connect those two occurrences of the common event together using the *Process interface* (Fig. 13.7b).

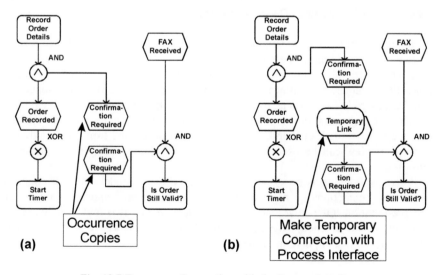

**Fig. 13.7** Temporary Connection with the Process Interface

The *Process interface* is a function with a different symbol so it is valid to use it to connect two events. Work through the model, segmenting the common events, confident in the knowledge you can go back and find those you have already done by looking for the Process interface. Using this approach you can also use automatic model layout because the connection integrity of the model has been maintained. It will look slightly different from the original model layout because of the additional *Process interface* objects.

When you have completed the segmentation exercise and have checked it is correct, delete all the *Process interface* objects. The model will now fall apart into the two segments.

### 13.3.6    Combining Segmented Models

Often we want to combine previously segmented models, either because we no longer want them segmented, or because we want a temporary view of what the entire process looks like. We can re-combine the models manually by copying and pasting all the models into a single EPC, and reconnecting them using the reverse of the process described in the previous section.

However, there is a much easier way. Provided we have correctly linked our models using common events, we can get ARIS to automatically combine them by using the *Model Generation* command (*ARIS Business Architect* only).

## 13.4    Vertical Structure

### 13.4.1    Hierarchical Decomposition

A commonly used design technique is to start by creating a high-level concept and to continue by adding successive levels of detail. This works well because few people can work at a detailed level and still maintain an overall view of how everything fits together. Sometimes the conceptual view will be discarded once the detailed design has been done, but more frequently it is retained to aid understanding and support future development. On other occasions, the design may initially be done at a detailed level and a conceptual view abstracted from the detail. The conceptual view can be used for verification and validation, or for explanatory purposes.

Process modelling is no exception. Detailed process models may be complex with many interactions, so high-level conceptual views are required to aid design and presentation. Of course, we are not limited to just two levels of hierarchy (conceptual and detailed). We can create as many levels as we wish, each one being a further decomposition of the one above.

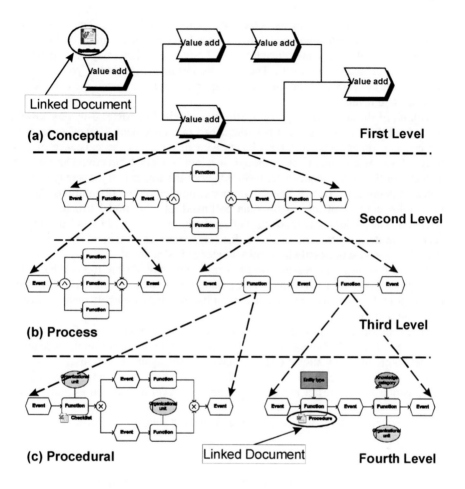

**Fig. 13.8** A Three-Layer Model Hierarchy

There are various views about how many levels there should be. Some people are adamant there should be only three. Others think no more than seven (see example in Chapter 4). In practice, the answer is somewhere in between. Typically, we can divide the hierarchy of levels into three layers:

- **Conceptual** – a business viewpoint,
- **Process** – the structure of how the business operates,
- **Procedural** – the detail of specific tasks.

Each of these layers may be subdivided into several levels. The conceptual layer may have one or two levels, the process layer may have three or four, and maybe there will be just one procedural level. So in total there may be somewhere between three and seven levels. There are no definite rules, but if you have too many levels the clarity of the hierarchical approach may be lost in the complexity of layers and levels.

Not all of these layers may necessarily be modelled in ARIS. The very lowest procedural definitions are often best described in a document. However, because we can link documents to ARIS objects we can represent the existence of this lowest level of documents even though it is not modelled directly. The same is also true of the highest conceptual level. Many of the conceptual ideas may be described in documents, requirements definitions and pictorial representations. Again, these other sources of information can be linked into the model structure. Thus, ARIS becomes a complete repository of all the information and knowledge representing the design. We can also take this further and use a *Knowledge structure diagram* to represent exactly how our knowledge is structured.

Fig. 13.8 shows a representation of such a hierarchy. At the top, we have the conceptual layer modelled using a *Value-added chain diagram* (described in Section 13.6.1). Documents and graphics might be included to support such a conceptual representation.

In the middle is the process layer. This layer contains two levels of a hierarchical process model. At the bottom is the procedural layer. In this example, a detailed model (with function allocations) is shown which again decomposes from the process models above. We have shown documents attached to some of the objects representing a further, but not directly modelled, level of procedures and checklists.

The overall model structure has three layers and four levels (layer two is split into two levels).

### 13.4.2    Creating Hierarchy Through Model Assignments

We establish a model hierarchy in ARIS using model assignments. We described how to assign models to objects in Chapter 12, but we mostly concentrated on assigning *Function allocation diagrams* (FADs) to functions to provide an alternative place to model additional relationship information.

The FADs did not represent a decomposition of the functions, but additional information about the function. In that respect, the assignment of FADs is an exception. Most model assignments in ARIS are made to models that provide additional detail (decomposition) about the particular object, as shown in Table 13.1.

The creation of a hierarchical structure using most of the models shown is fairly straightforward. The most complex form of hierarchical modelling is process decomposition created via a hierarchy of assigned EPCs, and it is this topic we are now going to discuss in more detail.

**Table 13.1** Hierarchical Models Assigned to Objects

| Object | Assigned Model | Hierarchical Representation |
|---|---|---|
| **Function** | EPC | Decomposition of the function into a more detailed sub-process. |
| **Event** | Event diagram | Decomposition of the event into more detailed sub-events. |
| **Rule** | Rule diagram | Decomposition of the rule into a more complex rule structure. |
| **Application system type** | Application system type diagram | Decomposition of the system into sub-systems, modules and functions. |
| **Organizational unit** | Organizational chart | The organisational hierarchy of the business. |
| **Technical term** | Technical terms model | Decomposition of the Technical term into its information structure. |
| **Entity type** | eERM attribute allocation diagram | Single-level definition of the Attributes comprising an Entity. |
| **Knowledge category** | Knowledge structure diagram | The structure of business knowledge. |
| **Information carrier** | None | Although a Technical terms or eERM model can be assigned to show the structure of carried data. |
| **Product/Service** | Product/Service tree | The structure of the business' products and services. |
| **Authorization condition** | Authorization hierarchy | The structure of authorisation in the business. |
| **Objective** | Objective diagram | The structure of the business objectives and critical factors. |

## 13.4.3    Decomposing Functions with EPCs

Fig. 13.9a shows a typical high-level process model we might wish to decompose. It has a single trigger from the outside world, called **Process Trigger**, and a single outcome, **Process Complete**. There are four functions: **Function A**, **Function B**, etc. Lets us first look at how we would decompose **Function A** into a detailed sub-process, as shown in Fig. 13.1b. First we assign a new EPC model to **Function A** to hold the decomposed detail. To make the assignment, we can use one of the techniques described in Chapter 12.

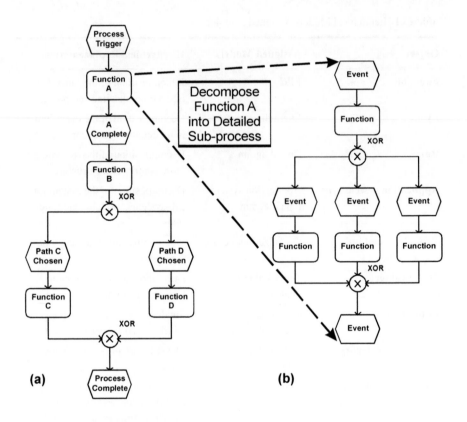

**Fig. 13.9** Decomposing a High-Level EPC

For instance, use the Right-Click > New > Assignments command. The result will be a new, empty EPC called "Function A".

In this model we now start creating a more detailed process flow. As always we will start with an event, but what is the event called? In the high-level EPC, *Function A* was triggered by the event called *Process Trigger*. Our "Function A" model still represents the same function (albeit in more detail), so it must be triggered by the same event. Following the same logic, the outcome event of the "Function A" model must be the same as at the high-level (e.g. *A Complete*). So we start modelling a decomposed sub-process by copying the trigger and outcome events from the high-level model to the sub-process model. These events become a kind of template into which we insert the rest of the detailed process.

It is important to make an *occurrence copy* of those events, not create new ones with the same name. The decomposition of *Function A* now looks like Fig. 13.10.

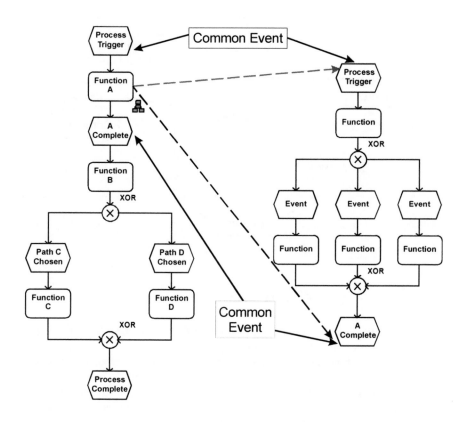

**Fig. 13.10** "Function A" Decomposed

Now let us perform the same operation on **Function B** in Fig. 13.9a. Again we create an assignment to a new EPC called "Function B" and copy the events from the high-level process into it. This time, because **Function B** takes a decision, there are two outcome events, **Path C Chosen** and **Path D Chosen**, which are combined by an **XOR** rule. Our detailed model must also have those two outcome events and the process must represent an **XOR** of those outcomes, so we copy the **XOR** rule and its connected events as shown in Fig. 13.11.

For a quick way to do this: in the high-level model select the entire area from **A Complete** down to **Path D Chosen** and copy and paste it into the "Function B" EPC. This will also copy the **Function B** object, but we can now delete this to just leave the events and the **XOR** rule. We now fill in the detail of the "Function B" sub-process between the trigger and outcome events.

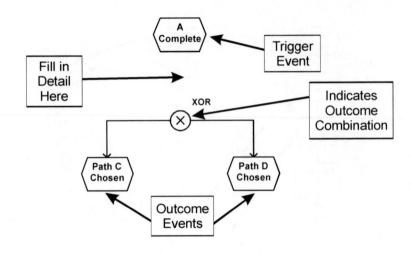

**Fig. 13.11** "Function B" Template

We can now repeat the operation for **Function C** and **Function D**. The end result will be a set of four models as shown in Fig. 13.12.

You can see each model is related to the next through the common events linking the models together in exactly the same way as described for segmented models in Section 13.3.1. In fact, whenever we create a set of hierarchical models in this way, we automatically produce horizontal segmentation at the same time as vertical decomposition. As mentioned before, provided we correctly link our models using common events, we can use the *Model Generation* command (not covered in this book) to connect the four detailed models together to show the complete 'end-to-end' process at that level of the hierarchy.

You will notice the "Function C" and "Function D" sub-process models look slightly strange because they have an **XOR** rule with only one branch. If you look at the high-level model, you will see **Function C** and **Function D** share the same outcome event, **Process Completed**, connected via the **XOR**. This means both the sub-process models must have **Process Completed** as their outcome event. If later we want to use *Model Generation* to connect all the four sub-processes together, and have a single **Process Completed** outcome event, we must include the **XOR** rule in both the sub-process models. Moreover, both sub-process models must have an occurrence of the same rule object, so the model generator will recognise that both sub-processes are connected via the same rule to the same outcome event. This strange artefact of hierarchical modelling only occurs when we combine branches at the last event in the process, and when we wish to use Model Generation. If you are not interested in *Model Generation*, you don't need to put the **XOR** in the sub-processes.

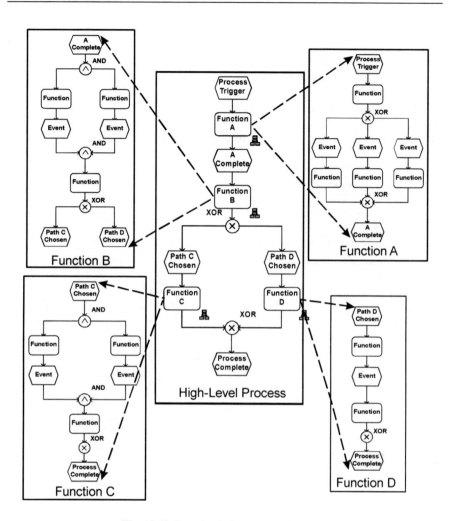

**Fig. 13.12** Completely Decomposed Model

### 13.4.4    Sub-process with Complex Triggers and Outcomes

We discussed above how to handle multiple triggers and outcomes, and the need to ensure consistent linking of sub-processes. This is fairly straightforward with simple examples, but we need to consider some of the more complex situations that occur in practice. Look again at **Function B** in our example and the template for its sub-process (Fig. 13.11). At the high-level, **Function B** has two outcome events split by an **XOR**. When we created the sub-process we copied the events and the **XOR** into the model to ensure the outcome of the sub-process was the same as the high-level function.

If we fill in some detail for the sub-process, it may look similar to Fig. 13.12. This looks quite straightforward; the sub-process shows additional process steps before the last function that makes the decision. But imagine as we do more design work on the process we find it is more complex, and in fact looks more like the process shown in Fig. 13.13a.

The *XOR* from the top-level model has disappeared. The two outcomes, although still logically an exclusive OR, no longer result from a decision at the last part of the sub-process, but arise from separate branches of the sub-process.

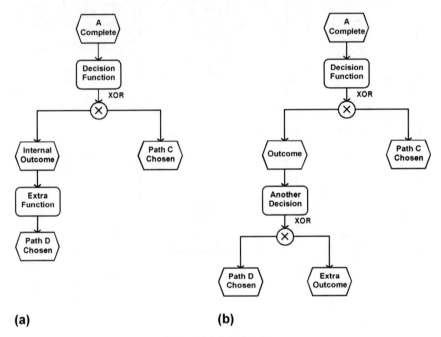

**(a)**                                    **(b)**

**Fig. 13.13** Multiple XOR Outcomes

 **Warning** – only use the rule copied from the high-level model when it is connected to the copied high-level events in exactly the same way as in the high-level model. Once you change the way events are connected in the lower-level model, delete the rule and, if necessary, create new rules where they are needed.

In fact, copying the rule from the high-level model is not important in this case. It is different from the rule connecting the **Process Complete** event. In that case we wanted to ensure the ARIS *Model Generator* could spot both sub-processes joined to the single outcome event for the whole process. In this case, the **XOR** rule does not affect the sub-process linking, only the logic of the overall model. What is important is using the same events to ensure the sub-process models link together. The reason for copying the rule (and its connections) is as a reminder that the outcome of the sub-process must be some sort of **XOR** of the events. You could just as easily copy the events and use a new **XOR** to temporarily connect them. This is actually probably safer.

However, the question we now have to ask is "are the high-level representation and the sub-process representation logically consistent?" In this example, we think you will agree they are. The outcome is an **XOR** and at the high level we are not interested in how those two alternatives arise.

Let us now make the example slightly more complicated. Imagine that instead of two outcomes from **Function B** combined with an **XOR**, there are now three. Two arise from a decision at one function in the sub-process, while the third arises from a separate part of the sub-process (Fig. 13.13b). How would this compare with a high-level model with three outcome events combined by an **XOR**? Again, logical consistency is maintained. If we wanted, we could use two connected **XOR** operators at the high level, but this doesn't add much value.

Let us change the **XOR** defining the two outcomes from the same decision function to an **OR** (Fig. 13.14a). Now our high-level model is no longer consistent. The high-level model tells us there are three outcomes, only one of which can actually occur. We can see from the detailed model that this is not correct. Both of the two related outcomes (**Path D Chosen** and **Extra Outcome**) may occur, but not at the same time as the **Path C Chosen** outcome. Does it help if we change the **XOR** rule in the high-level model to an **OR**? – well it's better, but still not correct because it implies that any combination of the three outcomes may be valid, which we know is not correct. The only way to accurately represent this in the high-level model is to use an **XOR** followed by an **OR** (Fig. 13.14b).

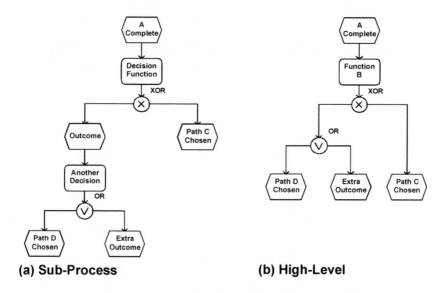

**(a) Sub-Process**                                    **(b) High-Level**

**Fig. 13.14** Multiple Outcome with Different Rule Types

Using this representation at the high-level looks rather strange, but it is logically correct. Exactly the same issue arises with complex trigger combinations. Of course, you may decide you are happy to use just a single *OR* at the high-level and rely on people looking at the detailed sub-process models to see the true logic. Provided you use an *OR* (which keeps open the logic of the outcomes) rather than an *XOR* (which is definitely wrong) this is a reasonable approach. However, consider a fourth example where the relationship between the two events on the same function (*Path D Chosen* and *Extra Outcome*) is an *AND*. How is this represented at the high-level? You could just about argue that an *OR* still represents all possible outcomes, but it misses the essential fact that two of the outcomes always occur together. The only correct way is to use an *XOR* followed by an *AND*.

### 13.4.5    Assignment Relationships

If we inspect the relationships of one of the functions in the high-level model, for instance *Function A*, we will see a display similar to Fig. 13.15.

As well as the relationships to the connected events, *Function A* is also shown as being the "*is process-oriented superior*" for all the functions in the sub-process. This type of relationship is an '*assignment relationship*'. It is not made by directly connecting the high-level functions to the functions in the sub-process, as we would if we were making a relationship between an *Organizational unit* and a function. The relationship is automatically created by the operation of assigning the sub-process model to the high-level function and putting functions in the sub-process. The assignment relationships allow us to trace, not just how the process decomposes into more detailed processes, but also the function hierarchy. The

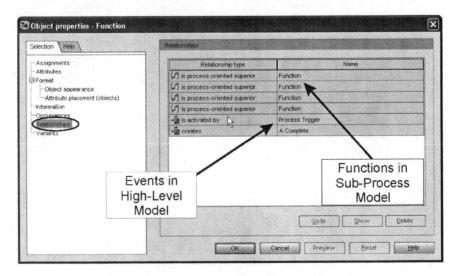

**Fig. 13.15** Function Relationships in Hierarchical Models

function hierarchy shows how each function is comprised of a set of more detailed functions. We can visualise this hierarchy in a *Function tree* model which can be automatically generated from a hierarchical set of EPCs using the ARIS *Model Generation* command.

# 13.5   Benefits and Drawbacks to Hierarchical Modelling

We have now described the basics of hierarchical modelling. It has some key benefits:

- Partitions the overall design into a sensible and manageable structure,
- Reduces the size of individual models,
- Provides a framework for managing variability,
- Allows end-to-end processes and other views to be generated.

However, not everything about hierarchical modelling is straightforward. There are a number of complexities and issues arising from using this approach:

- Model consistency,
- Managing complex triggers and outcomes,
- Theoretical limitations to hierarchical modelling,
- Synchronising event and function decomposition.

## 13.5.1   Theoretical Issues with Hierarchical Modelling

The problem of modelling complex triggers and outcomes, described above, highlights a characteristic of hierarchical decomposition. Each lower level of the hierarchy adds extra detail which increases our understanding of the overall process design. Hence the high-level models must be abstractions or simplifications of the detail at lower levels. This theoretical characteristic of hierarchical models has several ramifications:

- The interaction between high-level functions will not be entirely consistent with the actual interactions at the detailed level,
- It may not be possible to neatly segment the lower levels of the model into the simple functional areas used at high-levels,
- There is no absolute definition of what constitutes a level in the hierarchy,
- The amount of detail in a level may not be consistent,
- There is no single, unique way to decompose a high-level model into detailed sub-process models.

Because, by their very nature, the lower levels of the design have extra detail, we may find the interconnections between functional areas are far more complex than shown at the high-levels. We have already seen a simple example of this when we looked at complex triggers and outcomes in Section 13.4.4. In this example, we tried to reflect that structure back up to the high-level model. However, when the interactions are even more complex there comes a point where you cannot do this. At this point, you just have to accept that the top-level model is a simplification. For the same reason, the neat boundaries you may have drawn around the functional areas of your business will tend to blur when you get down to detailed end-to-end processes.

Although we have spent a lot of time talking about layers and levels, we have not given a precise definition of what these are. The reason is that there is no precise definition. It is up to you to define what are suitable levels of detail for your modelling project. You will need to decide whether to partition your models based on levels of complexity or levels of importance. You will also find it very difficult to be consistent about this. Quite often you will find yourself mixing very simple, but highly significant, functions on the same level as highly complex functions. Your only guide here is whether it looks sensible and aids clarity.

Finally, it is not possible to define a high-level model of a business and expect it can be implemented, unambiguously, without any further definition or explanation. This mistake is often made. People expect to be able to define a high-level model, have somebody decompose it into a fully complete design and implement it to achieve exactly what the person specifying the concept wanted. This cannot be done. It is not because the designers are not doing what is wanted, but because it is theoretically impossible. "But", we hear you ask, "isn't this the way software is designed – top-down?" Yes, it is, but the reason that software (or other engineering projects) can be done in this way is that they usually work within '*architectural frameworks*'.

Each time you go down a level in a hierarchical design you add more detail. By definition, that detail was not present in the higher layer, so the higher layer cannot precisely define how that detail is implemented. To make those decisions, further questions have to be asked or assumptions made. The same is true in software engineering. If the high-level model defines a task called "save file to disk", lower levels of the model have to determine how this is done. There are many ways that information can be written to computer disk drives, and there are many ways that the user interface controlling this operation may be presented to the user. However, if this operation is done within the Microsoft Windows environment, the method and the user-interface will largely be defined. The Microsoft Windows environment is an architectural framework, and by using it much of the extra detail required at the lower levels in the design is specified for you.

In the process world, architectural frameworks are not so common, but increasingly they are starting to appear. They may be provided by the particular applications systems you may use or by business sector reference models. Perhaps the most extensive commercially available systems-based process framework is provided by SAP R/3. It is no coincidence that a major use of ARIS is in the design and configuration of R3 systems. Frameworks not based on systems include "eTOM" (for telecommunications), "SCOR" (for supply chain management) and "ITIL" (for IT service management).

For the most part, designers will have to make their own decisions and assumptions as the design progresses. For this reason, there is no unique way of decomposing a high-level model, and many low-level solutions will achieve the same result. If a number of solutions can achieve the same result, why does it matter which is chosen? It matters because the high-level definition is rarely complete or sufficiently well-defined. Quite often the non-functional requirements (e.g. performance, ease of maintenance, cost, etc.) have not been well described. As a result, the final design may well work, but be hopelessly inefficient or impossible to maintain.

So, hierarchical modelling is not simply about defining a high-level model and assuming everything will automatically flow from it. Rigorous requirements capture, design, verification and validation techniques have to be used at every level coupled with the use of appropriate architectural frameworks.

## 13.6    Modelling at the Conceptual Layer

We showed above (Section 13.4) how to create a vertical model structure based on a hierarchy of assigned EPCs and how such a hierarchy typically consists of three layers, the top one of which is the 'conceptual' layer. We need some way of representing this conceptual layer that is not as detailed as a full EPC model, but which still allows a consistent decomposition from it. There are two models we might use at the conceptual layer: the *Value-added chain diagram* or an EPC used in a restricted 'high-level' sense.

### 13.6.1    The Value Added Chain Diagram

Fig. 13.16 (a simplified version of the **DEMO70 Company Overview** model) shows a typical example of a *Value-added chain diagram* (VACD). Although they look unfamiliar, the main objects in the VACD are functions, but with different symbols. You can copy and paste these functions back and forth between the VACD and an EPC. The symbol will change depending on which model they are in. The big difference when using the functions in a VACD is that they are connected together without any intervening events or rules. The VACD represents a high-level view of the functions that add value to a business and the approximate order in which they proceed. The relationship between adjacent functions is normally "*is predecessor of*". Because we are not modelling a detailed process flow, we don't need events or rules to describe exactly how the functions relate to one another.

In addition to the flow of the process we can, in the same model, also represent some of the high-level hierarchy associated with these functions. There is a second relationship that can be used between functions, defined as "*is process–oriented*

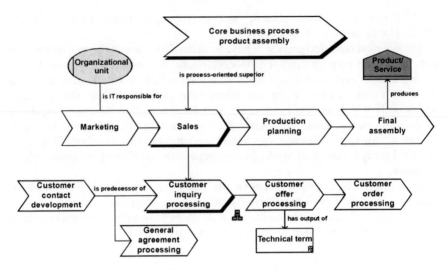

**Fig. 13.16** The Value Added Chain Diagram

*superior*". We came across this relationship in Section 13.4.5. In that case it was an automatically created '*assignment relationship*', but in the VACD we can manually make this relationship by making a connection between the functions.

We can see examples of this relationship in Fig. 13.16 between **Core business process product assembly**, **Sales** and **Customer inquiry processing**. By using these flow and hierarchical relationships we can quickly represent the top-level structure of our business and how it operates. We can then assign EPCs representing more detailed models of those key operations to the VACD functions in the normal way.

We can also use some organisation, data and product objects in the VACD. These are used to indicate the organisation carrying out the business operations, key items of data and the products they produce.

The VACD is a form of conceptual version of the EPC and is useful when you don't want the full detail the EPC can model.

### 13.6.2    The EPC as a High-level Model

You don't have to use a VACD as your high-level model; you can use an EPC and it is not compulsory to use the full level of detail the EPC provides.

Fig. 13.17 shows a conceptual model similar to that shown in the previous section, but modelled using an EPC. You can see we are still able to connect the functions together using the "is predecessor of" relationship (dotted line), provided the Method Filter in use allows this. Your ARIS System Administrator may use a Method Filter to prevent direct function to function connections in order to enforce the EPC modelling standards. If this is the case, you will not be able to create a high-level EPC.

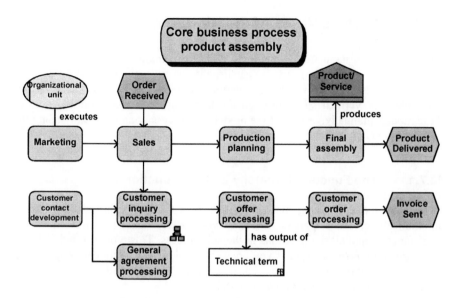

**Fig. 13.17** The EPC as a High-level Model

We are not able to make an "*is process–oriented superior*" relationship in the EPC (hierarchical representations are done by model assignment), but this is a minor inconvenience compared with the benefit of having events. We can now use events to represent the important external triggers for our business and, perhaps more importantly, the key business outcomes. We also have access to the full range of resource objects available in the EPC, but these should be used very sparingly in high-level models.

The EPC used this way can be very valuable as a high-level model, provided it is underpinned by a detailed set of EPCs conforming to the standard ARIS Method. What you should not do, under any circumstances, is use this type of approach (without all the events and rules) for modelling detailed processes. We can't stress enough that it is the inclusion of events and rules that provides ARIS models with the degree of rigour to ensure effective process design.

 **Expert Tip** – to support the use of models such as the EPC for different purposes, you can define new models types based on a common underlying model (e.g. the EPC). So for instance you can define Level 1, Level 2 and Level 3 models, all based on an EPC, but with different subsets of objects and relationships to suite their specific use.

 **Expert Tip** – the ARIS *Structuring model* provides a single generic object to which any of the models allowed by the Method Filter can be assigned. This can be use to create overview or conceptual models for use at the top level of a hierarchy.

## 13.7     Vertical Views of the Hierarchy

Although we can navigate the hierarchy both horizontally and vertically, it takes considerable mental effort to try to visualise the structure of a complex set of hierarchical models. Instead, we can use various ARIS model types to view various horizontal and vertical slices through the hierarchy. We may produce some of these models manually, as part of the modelling process or automatically using the ARIS *Model Generation* command.

### 13.7.1     The Function Hierarchy and the Function Tree

As we saw above the assignment of an EPC to a function in a high-level model automatically creates a "*process-oriented superior*" relationship between the high-level function and all the functions in the sub-process. This type of relationship is an '*assignment relationship*'. If you create multiple levels of model assignments, a hierarchy of these relationships will be created. We can model and view these relationships using the *Function tree* model.

The *Function tree* shows a static view of the function hierarchy, as opposed to the hierarchy of assigned EPCs that shows a dynamic view. That is to say, it just shows how a function is broken down into sub-functions (tasks or business function areas) without any consideration of process flow. Fig. 13.18 shows an example of a *Function tree* with four levels of hierarchy.

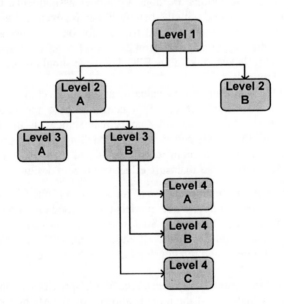

**Fig. 13.18** The Function Tree Model

Where the **Level 3 B** function decomposes to three **Level 4** functions, the model automatically changes from a horizontal layout to a vertical layout. This option helps produce easy-to-read diagrams. The level at which the layout orientation changes can be set by setting the value in the *Change to Vertical Layout* box (the default is 2) in the *Layout preview Dialog Box* (Right-Click > Arrange > Layout). When you connect functions together in the *Function tree* you will be given a choice of one of three relationship types:

- "*is process-oriented superior*",
- "*is execution-oriented superior*",
- "*is object-oriented superior*".

'*Process-oriented*' means the functions are all associated with the same process, albeit at different levels of detail. This relationship is created automatically between functions in a hierarchy of assigned EPCs. '*Execution-oriented*' means the functions all do the same type of task, for instance "planning" or "data entry". '*Object-oriented*' means all the functions are associated with processing the same thing (typically a data object).

### 13.7.2 Decomposing Events with the Event Diagram

Previously (Section 13.4.3), we said that decomposed sub-processes have the same trigger and outcome events as the high-level model. However, if we can decompose the function into more levels of detail, can we not also decompose the events? Well the answer of course is that we can. Consider the simple example in Fig. 13.19a. The process is triggered by a customer order being received. In reality, the order might be received by telephone, FAX or email. In the high-level process we are not interested in this distinction, but when we come to model the **Enter Order** function in more detail (Fig. 13.19b) we can see the sub-process starts differently depending on how the order was received. Therefore, in the detailed model we now need to have three different trigger events.

As it stands, although we know the three new trigger events are intended to represent a decomposition of the original **Order Received** event, we have not explicitly modelled it. So how do we do that? We made the hierarchical association between the function in the high-level process and its detailed sub-process model through a model assignment. We do the same for the event. It wouldn't make sense to assign the sub-process model to the event (the event doesn't decompose into a process), so instead we assign an *Event diagram* to the event.

We assign the *Event diagram* to the event in the high-level model using the same approach as described for assigning EPCs to functions (see Chapter 12). If you try this, you will notice there is a more limited choice of model types that can be assigned to events (which also depends on the Method Filter in use).

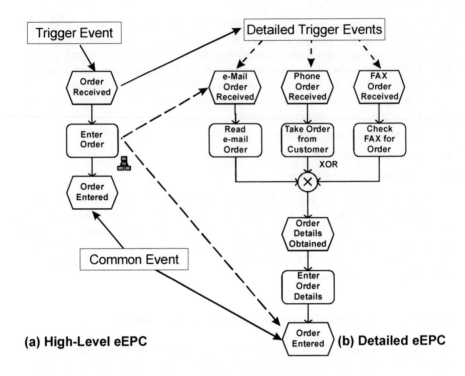

**(a) High-Level eEPC**                                    **(b) Detailed eEPC**

**Fig. 13.19** Hierarchical Events

An empty *Event diagram* will now be created and in it you can put the three trigger events (***FAX Order Received***, etc.), as shown in Fig. 13.20a.

If you now inspect the relationship properties of the original event in the *Relationships Tab* of the *Properties Bar* you will see the three new events are shown as "*subordinate events*". These relationships are '*assignment relationships*'. Just as described with decomposed functions (Section 13.4.3), they are not made by directly connecting the high-level event to the sub-events, but by the operation of assigning the *Event diagram*.

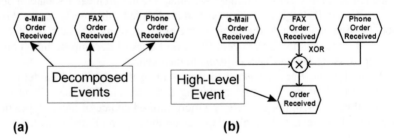

**(a)**                                                    **(b)**

**Fig. 13.20** Event Diagram

If you wish to make the relationship between the original event and the subordinate events clearer, you can place a copy of the original high-level event into the *Event diagram*. You can then manually connect it to the decomposed event objects using the *"has subordinate event"* relationship.

## 13.7.3    Model Linking with Decomposed Events

We have now seen how we can create events in the sub-processes that are more relevant to the level of detail being modelled. We have also seen how these detailed events can be shown to be hierarchically related to the more generic event at the higher level. The example shown in Fig. 13.20 decomposed a trigger event, but exactly the same can be done with any event in the high-level process. Originally, the events in the high-level process were copied down into the decomposed models to link the sub-processes together. Therefore, if we choose to decompose a high-level event linking two functions together, the models that are the decomposition of the functions must both use the same decomposed events as their outcome and triggers respectively.

We also have to make sure the decomposition makes sense in both of the linked sub-processes. For instance, if the **A Complete** event (Fig. 13.20) is decomposed into three events, it means the "Function A" sub-process must have three outcomes when modelled at that level of detail. It also means the "Function B" sub-process must have the same three events as triggers when modelled at that level of detail. In that way, the "Function A" and "Function B" sub-processes will be consistent at their level in the hierarchy. It can take quite a bit of mental effort to get your mind around modelling event hierarchies, if you don't really need hierarchical events, don't bother with them; remember one of our basic rules:

**"Keep it simple – clever models often confuse."**

# Chapter 14    ARIS Properties and Attributes

In this chapter we look in more detail at ARIS Properties and Attributes. We look at the Properties Dialog Box and the information it displays, the ARIS Attributes Window, Attributes Tab and show how to view, edit and use Attributes.

## 14.1    Introduction

In the previous chapters we have made a number of references to *ARIS Attributes* and *ARIS Properties*. Use of these facilities is fundamental to using ARIS, so in this chapter we will look at them in more detail.

## 14.2    ARIS Properties

ARIS Properties consist of all the information, directly accessible by the user, the ARIS Database stores about objects, models, groups, users and databases. This information includes ARIS Attributes which we look at later, plus further information about the use of an item, its appearance, its relationships to other items, its configuration, administration, etc.

The *Properties Dialog Box* is the key to viewing and entering information related to ARIS items. Table 14.1 shows those items with properties and from where they can be viewed. Some properties can also be view from the *Properties Bar* in the *Designer Module* (Section 14.2.3).

**Table 14.1** ARIS Items with Properties

| ARIS Item | Module | Properties Dialog Box Display | |
|-----------|--------|-------------------------------|---|
| **Server** | Explorer | Proxy and SSL settings | |
| **Database** | Explorer | General (read only) | |
| | Administration | General | Logo management |
| | | Header and footer | Method filter |
| | | Identifier | Page layout |
| **User,** | Administration | Change password | User group association |
| **User Group** | | Identifier | Function privileges |
| | | Method filter | Access privileges |
| **Font** | Administration | Font format | |
| **Group** | Explorer | Access privileges | Attributes |

*(Continued)*

**Table 14.1** (*Continued*)

| ARIS Item | Module | Properties Dialog Box Display | |
|---|---|---|---|
| **Model** | Explorer<br>Designer | Attributes[2]<br>Information<br>Format[1]<br>  - Representation[1]<br>  - Connections[1]<br>  - Print[1]<br>  - Grid[1] | Superior models[2]<br>Variants |
| **Object** | Explorer<br>Designer | Assignments[2]<br>Information<br>Relationships[2]<br>Format[1]<br>  - Object appearance[1]<br>  - Attribute placements (objects)[1] | Attributes[2]<br>Occurrences[2]<br>Variants |
| **Connection** | Designer | Attributes[2]<br>Format<br>  - Connection appearance<br>  - Attribute placements (connections) | |
| **Free-form Text** | Designer | Attributes[2]<br>Format<br>  - Free-form texts | |
| **Model Attributes** | Designer | Attributes<br>Format[1]<br>  - Model attributes | |
| **Graphic Object** | Designer | Graphics objects | |

**Note 1:** Available in the *Designer Module* only.

**Note 2:** Also available in *Designer Module Properties Bar*.

### 14.2.1    Properties Dialog Box

To display the *Properties Dialog Box*, select an item (e.g. an object) in the *Explorer Module* or the *Designer Module* and do any of the following:

- Select <u>E</u>dit > P<u>r</u>operties from the *Main Menu,*
- Right-Click and select P<u>r</u>operties from the pop-up menu,
- Press <ALT><ENTER>,
- Click on the *Properties Button* on the *Toolbar,*
- Double-Click on an object in the *Explorer Module* or *Designer Module*.

   The *Properties Dialog Box* (Fig. 14.1) provides a variety of sub-dialog boxes providing different information depending on the type of item selected (e.g.

model, object, and connection). While some dialog boxes are specific to particular items, others are common to many items. For this reason, if you select items of different types (e.g. events and functions, or objects and connections), the *Properties* dialog box will display a sub-set of properties relevant to both (e.g. *Object appearance, Connection appearance, Attribute placement (objects), Attribute placement (connections)*).

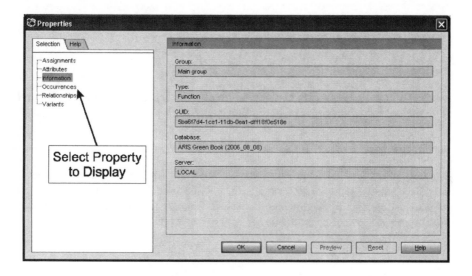

**Fig. 14.1** Properties Dialog Box

Section 14.2.2 provides a summary of the main *Properties Dialog Boxes*. Some of the properties can be changed (e.g. object size, attribute value) while others provide a read-only display of properties defined in other ways (e.g. the relationship between objects defined by connecting them together in the *Designer Module*).

Object properties can be displayed in the *Explorer Module* or the *Designer Module*, but the *Format* and *Attribute placement Dialog Boxes* are only relevant within the *Designer Module*.

To display the properties of a model, select it in the *Explorer Module* and issue one of the *Properties Dialog Box* commands above. For a model already open in the *Designer Module*, ensure no objects are selected and do one of the above.

 **Hint** – the *Properties Bar* in the *Designer Module* displays tabs equivalent to the *Occurrences, Relationships, Assignments* and *Attributes Object Property Dialog Boxes*. This enables you view these object properties quickly and directly without having to bring up the *Properties Dialog Box*.

**Hint** – to quickly identify the type of relationship represented by a connection between two objects, select the connection and look at the *Type* attribute in the *Attributes Tab* or the *Properties Bar*.

## 14.2.2    Properties Sub-Dialog Boxes

The *Properties Dialog Box* has a number of different sub-dialog boxes, some or all of which are visible depending on the item selected.

### Access Privileges

Available in the *Explorer Module*, applies to *Groups* and defines which *Users* and *User groups* have access to *Groups* within a database.

### Assignments

Applies to *Objects*. This is one of the most important property displays for objects because it allows you to view and define which models are assigned to which objects. We looked at assignments in detail in Chapter 12. Object assignments can also be viewed in the *Assignments Tab* of the *Properties Bar*.

### Attributes

The *Attributes Dialog Box* is available for most items. It shows similar information to that shown in the *Attributes Window* (Section 14.3.1), but is reduced in both size and function (see Fig. 14.6). Attributes can only be shown for a single item, and it is most useful for quickly entering individual attribute values.

### Attribute Placements

Available from the Object properties Dialog Box and Connection properties Dialog Box from within the *Designer Module*, it allows the values of attributes to be made visible on the model. This is described in more detail in Section 14.1.

### Change Password

Available in the *Administration Module*, allows the *Password* associated with a *User* to be changed. The *Password* of the *Logged-in user* can also be changed by selecting the database and issuing the Right-Click > Change password... command.

### Connection Appearance

For *Connections* selected in the *Designer Module,* the *Connection properties Dialog Box* allows you to change the appearance (*Color,* *Style,* *Weight,* *Arrow direction,* *Connection style*) of the line representing a connection between two objects. The use of the *Connection properties Dialog Box* to change the appearance of connections is described in more detail in Chapter 10. You can quickly display the *Connection appearance Dialog Box* by double-clicking on a connection in the *Designer Module.*

Connection appearance can also be changed by applying a template to the model (see Chapter 10).

### Font

Available in the *Administration Module,* applies to *Font formats* and allows the *Font, Font style* and *Size* to be changed and new fonts created.

### Format

For the current model open in the *Designer Module,* allows various print, display, connection appearance and grid options for the model to be set in the *Representation, Connections, Print* and *Grid Dialog Boxes.* These only apply to the current model, but similar settings can be set as a default for all new models using *View* > *Options* [For new models] from the *Main Menu.* You can quickly display the *Representation Dialog Box* by double-clicking in the *Designer Module Modelling Window* with no items selected.

For a selected object, provides *Object appearance* and *Attribute placements (objects) Dialog Boxes* (see above and below).

The use of the *Format Dialog Box* to change the appearance of a models and objects is described in more detail in Chapter 10.

### Free-form Text

Available in the *Designer Module,* allows the *Contents* of a *Free-form text* field to be changed, its *Font format* selected and its *Alignment* set (see Section 14.4.5). The *As comment* field can also be set to display the *Free-form text* field inside a note icon. You can quickly display the *Free-form text Dialog Box* by double-clicking on free-form text in the *Designer Module.*

### Function Privileges

Available in the *Administration Module,* applies to *Users* and *User Groups* and defines what special operations *Users* can carry out.

### General

Available in the *Explorer Module*, applies to *Databases* and shows the current *Database name*, the *Server name*, the selected *Method filter* and *Logged-in user*.

### Graphic Objects

Applies to inserted graphic drawing objects in the *Designer Module* and allows the *Line colour*, *Line style*, *Weight*, object *Fill color*, *Rounding* and *Shading* to be defined.

### Header & Footer

Available in the *Administration Module,* applies to databases and defines the language, content and font styles for headers and footers displayed on model printouts.

### Identifier

Available in the *Administration Module* and allows identifiers to be defined and enabled to provide a unique reference for ARIS items created within the database. Applies to *Users* and *User groups* and allows the identifier to be set for modelling changes made by *Users* that can be used for administrative purposes.

### Information

Applies to *Models* and *Objects* and provides general read-only information including *Group, Type, Database, and Server*. It also displays the *Global Unique Identifier (GUID)* for the selected item. The GUID is a completely unique identifier for all the main ARIS items.

### Method Filter

Available in the *Administration Module*, allows the *ARIS System Administrator* to assign the *Method Filter* the selected *User* will use when they log in to the database.

### Model Attributes

Available in the *Designer Module*, allows the *Contents* one of the model's *Attributes* to be displayed on the *Modelling Window,* its *Font format* selected and its *Alignment* set. The *As comment* field can also be set to display the attribute field inside a note icon. The *With attribute name* field can be set to display the name of the *Attribute* in front of its value.

## Object Appearance

Applies to objects selected in the *Designer Module*. The *Object appearance Dialog Box* allows the *Symbol* (where there are alternatives), *Fill color*, *Line color*, *Line style*, *Weight*, *Width* and *Height* to be selected. There is also an option to de-activate the symbol, in which case it will appear 'greyed-out' in the model. You can quickly display the *Object appearance Dialog Box* by double-clicking on an object in the *Explorer Module* or *Designer Module*.

Object appearance can also be changed by applying a template to the model. For more information on changing the object appearance properties see Chapter 10.

## Occurrences

Applies to selected objects and displays all *occurrences* of the object in other models in the database. A model can be directly opened by selecting it in the list and clicking on the Open model Button. Right-clicking on a model in the list will bring up a *Right-Click Menu* with options to Open the model, Go to its Occurrence in Explorer, or show its attributes or properties. Occurrences are also displayed in the *Objects Tab* of the *Properties Bar* in the *Designer Module*. See Chapter 15 for more on occurrences.

## Relationships

Applies to objects and shows all the relationships defined in the database between the selected object and all other objects. This includes relationships established by making connections between objects in the *Designer Module* and other defined relationships such as the implicit relationship established by creating functions hierarchies (see Chapter 13) or by nesting objects (see Chapter 9). Relationships are also displayed in the *Relationships Tab* of the *Properties Bar* in the *Designer Module*.

## Superior Models

Shows all the models containing objects with assignments to the selected model. A model can be directly opened by selecting it in the list and clicking on the Open Button. Right-clicking on a model name in the list will bring up a *Right-Click Menu* with options to Open the model, Go to its Superior model, Go to its Occurrence in Explorer, or show its attributes or properties. Superior models are also displayed in the *Superior models Tab* of the *Properties Bar* in the *Designer Module*.

## User Group Association

Available in the *Administration Module*, allows the *ARIS System Administrator* to assign the selected *User* to one or more *User Groups*.

## Variants

For models and objects, shows any *Master* of the selected model or object, or any *Variants* of the model or object. See Chapter 15 for more on variants.

### 14.2.3    Properties Bar

In addition to displaying all the properties of a selected ARIS item using the *Properties Dialog Box*, a limited set of properties for models, objects and connections can be displayed directly in the *Designer Module* by using the [✔ Properties] *Properties Bar* (Fig. 14.2). The bar is context-sensitive and will display different tabs depending on what item is selected in the *Modelling Window*:

- Attributes           (Model, Objects, Connections),
- Assignments          (Objects),
- Relationships        (Objects),
- Occurrences          (Objects),
- Superior Models      (Model).

**Fig. 14.2** Properties Bar

The display of properties in the tabs of the *Properties Bar* is very similar to the dialog boxes in the *Properties Dialog Box*:

- **Attributes** – shows the important *ARIS Attributes* for the selected object (or the current model if no object is selected) and their values (see Section 14.3.5). To see more attributes, click on the **More attributes ...** button at the bottom right-hand corner and select an attribute from the dialog box.

- **Assignments** – displays the name and type of any model *assigned* to that object. Assignments can be created or deleted by clicking on the buttons at the bottom of the tab (see Chapter 12).

- **Relationships** – shows the *ARIS Relationship* (typically the connections) between the selected object and any other object in the database (not just the objects in the current model).

- **Occurrences** – shows all models in which the selected object appears including the current model. If the object appears in a model more than once it will be shown in the list more than once. You can open the model and go to the selected object by clicking on the **Open model ...** button at the bottom right-hand corner. This display is similar to the *Object Occurrences Tab* in the *Navigation Bar*, but the display is from an object perspective rather than a model perspective.

- **Superior models** – if no items are selected in the current model, the *Superior models Tab* shows any other models containing objects with assignments to the current model.

## 14.3    ARIS Attributes

All the items in the ARIS Database (including the database itself) have attributes with values that are either populated automatically by ARIS or can be maintained by the user, as shown in Table 14.2.

**Table 14.2** ARIS Attributes

| Item | Attributes | Visibility |
|------|-----------|-----------|
| **Database** | Name, description, project information, single link attribute. | Attributes Window. |
| **Group** | Name, description, single link attribute. | Attributes Window. |
| **Model** | Range of attributes including name description, four link attributes and user-defined attributes. | Attributes Window, Assignments Tab[1], Inserted model attribute[1]. |
| **Object** | Full range of attributes including name description, times, costs, simulation, four link attribute and user-defined attributes. | Attributes Window, Assignments Tab[1], Attribute Placement[1]. |

*(Continued)*

**Table 14.3** (*Continued*)

| Item | Attributes | Visibility |
|------|-----------|------------|
| **Connection** | Name, description, user-defined attributes, simulation, no link attributes. | Attributes Window, Assignments Tab[1], Attribute Placement[1]. |

**Note 1**: Available in *Designer Module* only.

### 14.3.1    The Attributes Window

Attributes can be viewed and edited using the *Attributes Window* (see Fig. 14.3).
To display the window, select the item to be inspected in the *Explorer Module* or
the *Designer Module* and do any of the following:

- Select <u>E</u>dit > Attri<u>b</u>utes from the *Main Menu*,
- Right-Click and select <u>A</u>ttributes from the pop-up menu,
- Press <F8>,
- Click on the *Attributes Icon* in the *Toolbar*.

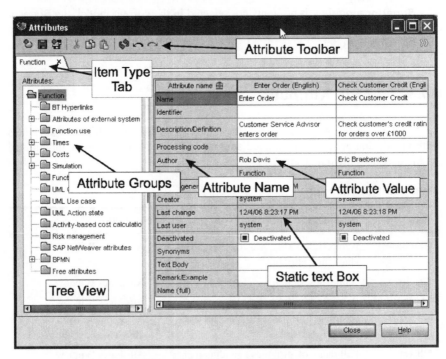

**Fig. 14.3** ARIS Attributes Window

The *Attributes Window* has two panes. The left-hand pane has an *Explorer Tree*
showing all the groups and sub-groups into which the attributes are arranged.
The right-hand pane has a tabular view of all the attributes in the selected group.

The ARIS Method and the current Method Filter determine the set of available attributes.

If the cell for a particular attribute is shaded, this is a *static text box*. This attribute is automatically maintained by ARIS and cannot be changed by the user. Each attribute is of a defined type (e.g. string, integer, etc.) or has a drop-down list or calendar input. The attribute will only accept inputs of a valid type and some attributes also check for valid entries.

In addition to the attributes defined by the ARIS Method, there are a number of *User attributes* of different types in the *Free attributes* group (see Section 14.5.2) which can be defined by users for their own purposes. The Method Filter defines the availability of these *User attributes* and their names. The *Attributes Window* has its own *Attributes Toolbar* as shown in Fig. 14.4.

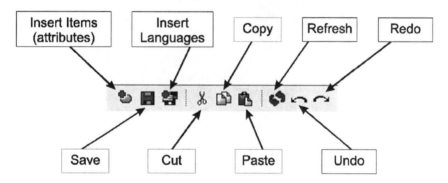

**Fig. 14.4** Attributes Toolbar

## 14.3.2    Attributes Column Display

If you select more than one item in the *Designer Module* or *Explorer Module* (excluding databases) and display the *Attributes Window*, the table in the *Attributes Window* will show a separate column of attributes for each item selected (see Fig. 14.3). This enables easy comparison and entry of attributes.

If you select items of different types (e.g. a group, a model and an object), a different tab will be created for each type of item. You can switch between the different views by selecting the tabs at the top left-hand corner of the window (see Fig. 14.3). You can have multiple tabs and multiple columns in each tab.

You can alter the width of individual columns in the table by dragging the right-hand border of the column title cell or selecting Right-Click > Optimal column width. You can re-size the width of several adjacent columns at the same time. First select all the columns you want to re-size (click in title cell of the first column and shift-click in the other columns) and drag the right-hand border of the title cell of any of the columns. All of the columns will re-size to equal widths (see Fig. 14.5). You can also alter the size of rows by dragging the bottom of the row border, but only one at a time. You can also select Right-Click > Optimal height.

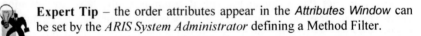

**(a) Before Re-sizing**

**(b) After Re-sizing**

**Fig. 14.5** Attribute Column Display Re-sizing

You can alter the order in which the columns are displayed by clicking in the title cell of a column and dragging it to a new position. You can also drag the *Attribute name* column to any position in the table.

You can't manually change the individual order in which the attributes in any selected group appear, but you can change the order in which they are sorted. Click in the title cell of the *Attribute name* column and you will see the sort order changes. There are three sort options as shown by the symbol in the title cell:

- **Method** – defined by the ARIS Method based on the most commonly used attributes,

- **Ascending** – alphabetic order (a to z),

- **Descending** – alphabetic order (z to a).

**Expert Tip** – the order attributes appear in the *Attributes Window* can be set by the *ARIS System Administrator* defining a Method Filter.

The *Attributes Window* appears as a completely separate window to the window displaying the currently selected ARIS module (e.g. the *Designer Module*). As a result you can leave the *Attributes Window* open and return to any of the other ARIS modules. If you now select another ARIS item (e.g. an object) and issue a command to display its attributes, it will be added to the appropriate tab in the currently open *Attributes Window*. In this way you can build up a whole range of attribute tabs and columns by individually selecting chosen items. You can select items from other databases and they will appear in separate tabs for that database and the item type. As well as selecting more items by returning to the ARIS window, you can also add additional attributes by clicking on the Insert items Button on the *Attributes Toolbar*. An *Explorer Tree* will be displayed in the *Insert items Dialog Box* for you to choose additional models or objects.

### 14.3.3    Editing Attributes

In the *Attributes Window* you can change the value of any attribute which is not a *static text box* in two ways:

*   **Overtype mode** – click in the attribute cell and type. The new entry will replace the existing entry.

*   **Edit mode** – double-click in the attribute cell. A cursor will appear and new text will be inserted at that point.

To move down attributes in a column, press <Enter> or the cursor down key after each entry. To move across columns, press the cursor right key or <Tab> key, after each entry. Using the cursor key will keep you in the original row, while the <Tab> key will move down to the next row once you have reached the far right-hand side of the column. Long text entries will wrap within the boundaries of the cell. If you wish to put in a hard line break, press <Shift+Enter>.

> **Warning** – although long text entries entered into attributes will wrap within the boundaries of the cell, when displayed using attribute placement (see Section 14.1), the text will appear all on one line unless you enter hard line breaks by pressing <Shift+Enter>.

To copy and paste entries across cells:

1.   Select the source cell,
2.   Right-Click > Copy (or <Ctrl+C>),
3.   Select the target cell,
4.   Right-Click > Paste (or <Ctrl+V>).

When cells are selected they appear grey with an orange border. You can't copy a single source cell to multiple target cells, but you can copy multiple source cells to a same-sized block of multiple cells elsewhere. The target cell or cells must not be a *static text box,* which is read only. Even more useful, you can paste a range of cells from Microsoft Excel straight into the table of attributes. This means you can prepare data (particularly simulation data) outside ARIS and paste it into the *Attributes Window*.

If you want to copy part of an attribute text value from one cell to another, use the *Edit Mode*, but use <Ctrl+C> and <Ctrl+V> to do the copy and paste. The right-click copy and paste commands are not available in this mode and if you use the commands from the *Attributes Toolbar*, the whole cell will be copied.

### 14.3.4    Saving Attribute Changes

Attributes values are saved to the database when you select the Save  Button on the *Attributes Toolbar* or press <Ctrl+S>. If you just close the *Attributes Window* you will be prompted to save the attributes.

You can access the attributes of an object from the *Explorer Module* or from within the *Designer Module*. If you accessed the attributes by selecting objects in the *Designer Module*, then saving the attributes has no connection with saving (or not saving) the model. It is important to realise that once you have saved any attribute changes these immediately apply to those objects in the database, irrespective of which models the objects may be used in. The attribute save operation cannot be undone, but changes to attribute values prior to saving can be undone and redone using the Undo Button <Ctrl+Z> and Redo Button <Ctrl+Y> on the *Attributes Toolbar*.

### 14.3.5    The Attributes Tab

In the *Designer Module,* it is possible to view the *Attributes* of the model and its objects using the *Attributes Tab* in the *Properties Bar*. To make the tab visible, select the *Properties Checkbox* at the top of the *Designer Window* or select the View > Properties checkbox on the *Main Menu*. Select the *Attribute Tab* and you will see a list of attributes as shown in Fig. 14.6.

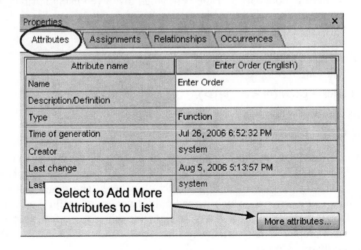

**Fig. 14.6** Properties Window – Attributes Tab

Unlike the *Attributes Window* that has an *Explorer Tree* in the left-hand pane and displays all attributes arranged in folders, the *Attribute Tab* displays just a subset of the more common attributes. If you wish to view or change an attribute which is not listed, click on the More attributes Button at the bottom of the tab. The *Insert attributes Dialog Box* (Fig. 14.7) shows the other attributes, allowed by the ARIS Method and the current Method Filter, listed in their folders. Select one or more attributes and press OK to add them to the *Attribute Tab* display.

**Hint** – to select a single attribute from the *Insert attributes Dialog Box*, double-click on it and it will inserted into the list in the *Attributes Tab* and the dialog box will be closed automatically.

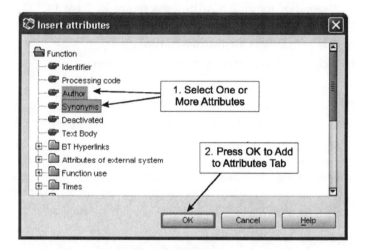

**Fig. 14.7** Insert Attributes Dialog Box

If you no longer want to see an attribute listed in the tab, select the attribute name in the left-hand column, Right-Click > Hide and chose whether to always hide the attribute or only hide it if its value is not maintained.

As with the *Attributes Window* (Section 14.3.1), you can click on the attribute name header of the left-hand column in the *Attribute Tab* and chose to sort the list in the order determined by the ARIS Method (the header has a small ARIS House in it) or in alphabetical order.

**Question** – I have entered a value into the attribute of an object using the *Attributes Dialog Box*, but the *Attributes Tab* in the *Designer Module Properties Window* does not show the value I have just entered.

**Answer** – The *Attributes Tab* may not always refresh its display immediately so select <u>V</u>iew > <u>R</u>efresh from the *Main Menu* or press F5 to refresh it.

**Warning** – *ARIS Attributes* are associated with the underlying *Object* definition in the *ARIS Repository*. If you make changes using the *Attributes Dialog Box* you will prompted to ask if you want to save your changes; these will then be saved to the *ARIS Database*. If you make changes using the *Attributes Tab* in the *Properties Window*, they won't be saved until you save your model.

### 14.3.6    Attributes Dialog Box

The *Attributes Dialog Box* can be displayed as one of the sub-dialog boxes in the *Properties Dialog Box* for all the ARIS items shown in Table 14.2. To view the *Attributes Dialog Box*, select an item and do one of the following:

- Select <u>E</u>dit > P<u>r</u>operties from the *Main Menu,*
- Right-Click and select P<u>r</u>operties from the pop-up menu,
- Press <ALT><ENTER>,
- Click on the *Properties Icon* in the *Toolbar,*
- Double-click on an object in the *Explorer Module* or *Designer Module.*

In the *Properties Dialog Box* now select the *Attributes Dialog Box* (Fig. 14.8). The appearance of the dialog box is similar to the *Attributes Tab* in the *Designer Module Properties Bar*. It shows a sub-set of the more common attributes and you can add additional attributes to the list by clicking on the More attributes... Button.

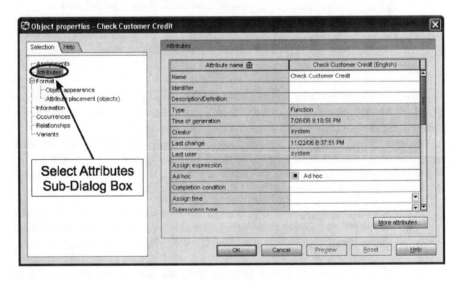

**Fig. 14.8** Attributes Dialog Box

# 14.4     Attribute Placement

The attributes of models, objects and connections can be viewed and set using the *Attributes Window* or the *Attributes Tab*. Normally the only attribute directly visible in a model is the *Name* attribute for a symbol. However, it is convenient to be able to display other attributes of models, objects and connections directly on a model. For instance to display the type of a connection between two objects (e.g. "*carries out*" for an *Organizational unit* connected to a *Function*). Attributes can be displayed on a model in three ways:

- Attribute placement (objects)  (Section 14.4.1),
- Attribute placement (connections)  (Section 14.4.2),
- Insert model attributes (Section 14.4.4).

Once placed, the position of an attribute display can be moved directly in the modelling window (see Section 14.4.3). It is also possible to add *Free text* to a model (see 14.4.5).

## 14.4.1     Object Attribute Placement

The visibility of object attributes is set using the *Object properties [Format / Attribute placement (objects)] Dialog Box* (Fig. 14.9).

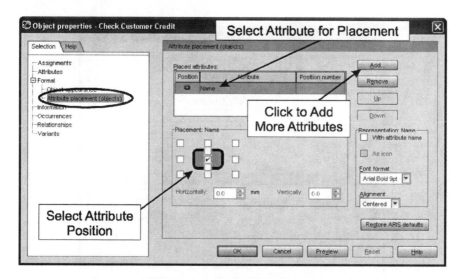

**Fig. 14.9** Object Attribute Placement

To set this, select one or more objects and do any of:

- Select the Edit attribute placements Button on the *Designer Toolbar*,

- Format > Edit attribute placements... from the *Main Menu or Right-Click Menu*,

- Format > Representation [*Format / Attribute placement (objects)*],

- Right-Click > Properties [*Format / Attribute placement (objects)*],

- Right-Click > Format > Representation [*Format / Attribute placement (objects)*].

The *Placed attributes* field at the top of the dialog box (Fig. 14.9) shows a list of all the objects attributes currently visible on the model. Normally only the *Name* attribute will be displayed. The *Placement* field below shows a representation of the object with a tick showing the position where the attribute is placed.

### Adding and Removing Attributes Placements

To add a new attribute placement, click on the Add... Button. The *Add attributes Dialog Box* will appear (Fig. 14.10) showing a list of available attributes as defined by the Method Filter. If you scroll up and down the list you will see some attributes have a small icon (a green symbol with a tick) against them. This indicates the attribute '*is maintained*' (e.g. it has a value in it, set by ARIS or the user). If you want to see just maintained attributes, click on the *Only show maintained attributes Checkbox*.

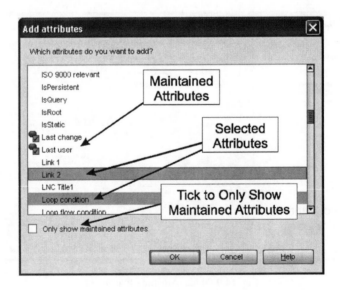

**Fig. 14.10** Add Attributes Dialog Box

You can select one or more attributes (use <CTRL-click> to select multiple attributes or <CTRL-A> to select them all) and press OK. You will now see the *Placed attributes* field now has more attributes listed. As you click on each attribute, the *Placement* field below changes to show the settings of the selected attribute. Initially they will be set to the default and placed at the centre of the object.

You can remove an attribute placement by clicking the R̲emove Button (you can't just remove the ticks from all the placement positions).

## Changing an Attribute Placement

To move the placement of the attribute you can select it in the *Placed attributes* field and tick one of the other boxes inside, or surrounding, the object representation in the *Placement* field.

Attributes containing *Free text* will be displayed on a single line unless you force a line break by entering <Ctrl+Enter>. If you place two or more attributes at the same standard position, ARIS will display them on separate lines, one beneath another. The *Position number* column in the *Placed attributes* field will show the order in which they will appear. You can alter the position by selecting the attribute and using the U̲P and D̲OWN buttons.

 **Hint** – to identify attributes with placements at the same position, look for attributes with entries in the *Position number* column in the *Placed attributes* field. The list is ordered to group attributes in the same position together and the *Position number* shows the order in which they will be displayed.

Table 14.3 shows other attribute placement settings.

**Table 14.3** Objects Properties / Attribute placement (objects)

| Command | Action |
|---|---|
| *With attribute name* | Displays the attribute name as well as its value. |
| *As icon* | Some special attributes have icons associated with them that can be displayed instead of their value (e.g. the *Existence* attribute). Checking this box will display the icon. |
| *Font format* | Selects the font for the attribute display. Note: the list of fonts is those pre-defined by the *ARIS System Administrator*. |
| *Alignment* | Sets alignment for attributes with multiple lines of text (*Left*, *Right*, and *Centred*). |
| *Restore ARIS d̲efaults* | Resets the symbol appearance properties to those set by the Method Filter and any applied Template. |

You can choose the *Font format* used to display the attribute by selecting from the *Font format* drop-down list in the *Representation* area of the dialog box. When people first use this, they expect to be confronted with a list of the normal Microsoft Windows font formats as you would, for instance, when selecting a font style in a word processor. ARIS doesn't work like this. The font styles available within a particular database must be defined by the *ARIS System Administrator*.

You can select whether the attribute text is left, right or centre justified using the *Alignment* drop-down box, and whether the attribute name should prefix its contents by ticking the *With attribute name Checkbox*. Some attributes (e.g. *Existence* in the *Analysis* attributes group) only have Boolean logic values (e.g. "0" or "1") to represent "on" or "off". Rather than display "0" or "1", some of the attributes (but not all, and not user-defined Boolean attributes) allow a "+" or "-" icon to be displayed by ticking the *As Icon* Checkbox.

You can quickly change the font of an already displayed attribute by selecting the object or connection in the *Designer Module* and Right-Click > *Format* > *Font format*. Any changes made will be applied to all the displayed attributes associated with the object or connection.

### 14.4.2    Connection Attribute Placement

The visibility of connection attributes is set using the *Object properties [Format / Attribute placement (connections)] Dialog Box* (Fig. 14.11).

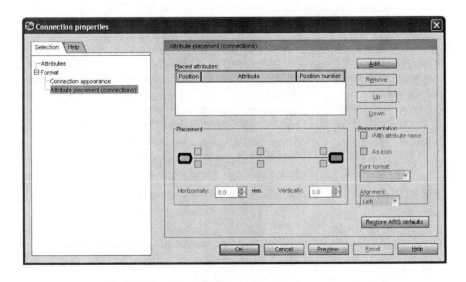

**Fig. 14.11** Connection Attribute Placement

To set this, select one or more connections and do any of:

- Select the Edit attribute placements Button on the *Designer Toolbar*,

- Format > Representation [*Format / Attribute placement (connections)*] from *Main Menu*,

- Right-Click > Properties [*Format / Attribute placement (connections)*],

- Right-Click > Format > Representation [*Format / Attribute placement (connections)*].

The *Placed attributes* field at the top of the dialog box (Fig. 14.11) works exactly the same as for the objects (see Section 14.4.1 above) except by default it is empty. Additional attributes can be added using the Add... button. Typically the *Type* attribute will be the only maintained attribute. The *Placement* field below shows a representation of the connection with a tick showing where the attribute is placed. The icons at the end of the line represent the connected object types so you can work out which end of the line it refers to. The procedure for adding, removing, changing and moving connection attributes is the same as for object attributes.

### 14.4.3    Moving Attribute Placements

Once you have made an attribute visible on the model using one of the *Properties [Format / Attribute placement] Dialog Boxes* you can move its position from within the *Modelling Window*.

Select the object or connection whose attribute you want to move (Fig. 14.12b). Each displayed attribute is now shown with a dotted box around it with a small cross (+) at the top left-hand corner. As you hover your mouse over the cross your cursor will also change to a cross. You can click on the cross and drag the attribute to whatever position you wish (Fig. 14.12c).

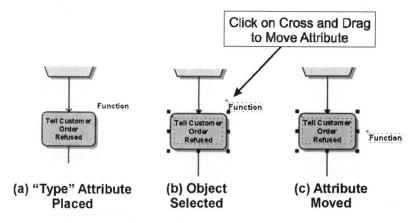

**Fig. 14.12** Moving Attribute Placements

If you now open the *[Format / Attribute placement] Dialog Box* you will see the *horizontally* and *vertically* fields now show the actual position where you moved the attribute to. These values represent the *x* and *y* coordinates of the attribute position in the *Modelling Window* in mm, centred on the object. If you set them to 0, 0, the attribute will be placed at the centre of the object (equivalent to ticking the centre box). You can offset the attribute display by entering positive or negative values into these boxes. You can use these to fine tune the attribute position.

### 14.4.4    Inserting Model Attributes

Models themselves have attributes. Those such as *Name, Author, Description, Last user, Last changed* are very useful for configuration control purposes. It is quite common practice in business and industry to display this sort of information on a drawing in a 'change control box'. Model attributes may be made visible on the model using the Insert > Model Attribute command or by selecting the Insert model attribute Button on the *Designer Toolbar*.

When you execute this command, at first nothing appears to happen. However, if you look closely you will see the cursor has changed to show a large letter "A". Move the cursor to the position where you want the attribute to appear and click the mouse. The *Model attribute properties Dialog Box* now appears to allow you to select the attribute you wish to display. You can preview the display with the Preview Button or just press OK to accept. The attribute value will now be displayed on the model at the chosen position.

The *Model attribute properties Dialog Box* has similar font settings to the object and connection placement boxes (see above) with one addition, the *As comment* field. Selecting this displays a yellow note graphic behind the text so it stands out from the background of the model (see Fig. 14.13).

You can move a displayed model attribute by selecting it and dragging it wherever you want it. If you move the objects in your model, or use automatic layout, any displayed model attributes may be displayed on top of objects or hidden beneath them. You can control this effect to some extent by arranging the display order or grouping the attribute display with an object (see Chapter 10).

You can change the settings of a displayed model attribute by selecting it and executing any of:

- Select the Properties Button on the *Designer Toolbar* and select [*Format / Model attributes*],

- Format > Representation [*Format / Model attributes*] from *Main Menu or Right-Click Menu*.

**Warning** – you cannot select an already displayed attribute and edit its properties by pressing the Insert model attribute Button; doing this will create a new model attribute display (it is possible to display the same model attribute multiple times). Instead use one of the properties commands (see above).

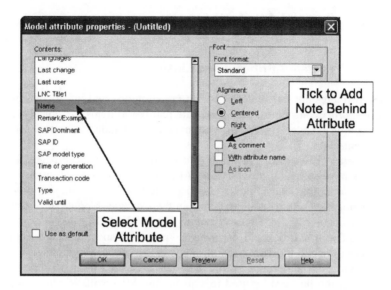

**Fig. 14.13** Insert Model Attributes

You can quickly change the font of an already displayed attribute by selecting it, executing Right-Click > Format > Font format and selecting a font from the *Select font Dialog Box*.

## 14.4.5    Inserting Free-form Text

Free-form text can be inserted into the model using the Insert free-form  text Button on the *Designer Toolbar*. Click the button and the cursor changes to a large letter "A". Click in the *Modelling Window* and enter the required text in the box. You can change the *Font format* of the text, and also display it as a comment (a yellow note box), by selecting the *Properties [Format / Free-form texts] Dialog Box* or Right-Click > Format > Font format... and select a font from the *Select font Dialog Box*.

> **Warning** – Free-form text objects are objects similar to other objects. If you copy and paste them you will be making an *occurrence copy*. If you change the text in one occurrence of the object, the other occurrence will also change. To create independent text entries, use Copy and Paste as > Definition copy.

Although Free-form text can be useful it is usually better to add text to the attributes of objects, of connections or of the model and makes these visible.

## 14.5      Special Attributes

### 14.5.1    System Attributes and Links

ARIS Attributes are intended for storing modelling-related information (e.g. descriptions, processing times, etc.) about the real-world items the objects represent. They are not intended for storing vast amounts of detailed information about the items themselves.

However, ARIS objects can be linked to documents or Web pages describing the items in detail using the four *Link* Attributes in the *System attributes* group. The link can point to any file with a Microsoft Windows '*association*' to an installed application. By selecting the item in the *Designer Module* or *Explorer Module*, the associated application can be run (Right-Click > R<u>u</u>n or <F7>) to display the linked file. The link could, for instance, point to a specification document or a spreadsheet containing data. It could point to a graphics program or a programming tool to show a screen-shot from a system used for a particular part of a process. In fact, the link can be used to start up any Microsoft Windows application with a relationship to your business model.

In this way, ARIS models can be used as a repository for all your key business knowledge by directly linking the location of that knowledge into key process, data and business models. By linking to a URL on your corporate Intranet, rather than a document on your local disk, you can ensure the link will be more readily available to anyone who views the model. The link will then automatically work if the model is subsequently published on the Web.

### *Creating a Link*

To create a link:

1.  Select an object and open the *Attributes Window,*
2.  Select one of the *Link* attribute fields in the *System attributes* group,
3.  Select the browse button,
4.  Use the *Select file Dialog Box* to select a file from your local hard disk or networked file server, or enter a file name or a URL directly into the attribute field,
5.  Optionally enter a name for the link in the *Title* field.

### *Making a Link Visible*

Having assigned a link to an ARIS object, the title and an icon representing the link can be made visible within models in the *Designer Module*:

1.  Select the object,
2.  Right-Click > P<u>r</u>operties [*Format / Attribute placement (objects)*],

3.   Press the Add Button,

4.   Select the *Link 1* attribute in the *Add attributes Dialog Box,*

5.   Press OK,

6.   Select *Link 1* in the *Placed attributes* list,

7.   Tick one of the boxes in the *Placement* area.

   The icon Microsoft Windows associates with the file whose path was entered in the *Link* attribute (e.g. the Microsoft Word Icon) will be shown alongside the object in the *Designer Module*. Next to the icon will be displayed the text entered in the *Title* attribute, as shown in Fig. 14.14a.

> **Hint** – if you make a *Link* attribute visible in the *Designer Module*, there is no need to also make the *Title* attribute visible; it will be displayed adjacent to the link icon by default (Fig. 14.14a). If you do make the *Title* attribute visible, its contents will be displayed twice (Fig. 14.14b). If you enter nothing in the *Title* attribute, the file path to the link will be displayed by default (Fig. 14.14c). If you don't want a title or the path displayed, enter a space in the *Title* attribute.

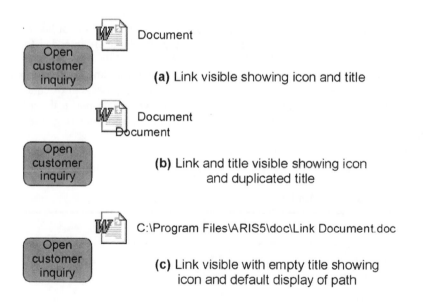

**Fig. 14.14** Link and Title Attribute Display

### Using a Link

Any item in the ARIS hierarchy (e.g. databases, models, objects – but not connections) can have a *Link* attribute defined. The application pointed to by the link can be initiated in several different ways. Select the item and do any of the following:

- <u>F</u>ile > R<u>u</u>n... from the *Main Menu*,
- Right-Click > R<u>u</u>n...,
- Press <F7>,
- Press the *Run Button*.

If only one link has been defined, the appropriate application will be launched and the contents of the file displayed. If several links have been defined (up to the maximum of four), a pop-up menu will appear asking you to select which link you would like to run.

Links are a powerful tool enabling ARIS to be the entry point to a vast amount of information, particularly when ARIS models are published on a corporate Intranet.

### 14.5.2   User Attributes

A quick browse through the attribute groups displayed in the *Attributes Window* will show there is a vast range of attributes available. Some are intended for general use (e.g. *Description/Definition* or *Remark/Example*) while others have specific uses in a particular context (e.g. *Avg. processing time* for simulation and animation). You may use any of the attributes for your own purposes, but of course this may clash with the use intended by ARIS and the value you put in the attribute may be used inappropriately by an ARIS software component (e.g. the ARIS Simulator).

To provide more flexibility for users, ARIS has a range of additional *User Attributes* of various types (Table 14.4) in the *Free attributes* group.

**Table 14.4** ARIS Free Attributes

| Attribute Type | Use |
| --- | --- |
| User Attribute Text | Free text. |
| User Attribute Boolean | "on" or "off" ("0" or "1"). |
| User Attribute Int | Integer numbers. |
| User Attribute Values | Drop-down lists of user-defined values. |
| User Attribute Float | Non-integer number. |
| User Attribute Date | Date format. |
| User Attribute Time | Time format. |

| User Attribute Point in Time | Time format. |
| User Attribute Duration | Time format. |
| User Attribute Link | Additional Link Attribute. |

The ARIS System Administrator sets the availability of these *User attributes* using a Method Filter and chooses their names (which can be changed) and the list of values for attributes with drop-down lists.

 **Warning** – while *User attributes* can be very useful they must be used with great care. On a shared server you must define a common set of *User attributes* suitable for all databases on the server. You should also be wary of importing filters that may re-define *User attributes*. Even when working 'stand-alone', you should be wary of using *User attributes* in case you may wish to move your database onto a server at some point in the future.

# Chapter 15    Definitions, Occurrences and Copies

In this chapter we discuss the difference between occurrence copies, definition copies and variant copies, and introduce some guidelines for what and when to copy.

## 15.1    Occurrences and Definitions

The ARIS Repository is based on the concept of creating object '*definitions*' and pointers to their '*occurrences*' in models. In many of the examples given so far we have described copying and pasting objects, either within the same model or between different models. However, because of the way objects and models are defined, there are in fact several types of copy we can use:

- Copy,
- Occurrence Copy,
- Definition Copy,
- Variant Copy,
- Master Copy,
- Shortcut.

The exact way in which copying works depends on whether you are copying models or objects, and when copying objects, whether you are using the *Explorer Module* or the *Designer Module*. These are summarised in Table 15.1.

**Table 15.1** Types of Copy

| Copy Type | Model | Objects in Explorer Module | Objects in Designer Module |
|-----------|-------|---------------------------|---------------------------|
| **Copy** | Creates a new model with occurrence copies of all objects and connections. | Creates a definition copy of the object – see below. | Creates an occurrence copy of the object – see below. |
| **Occurrence** | Not available | Not available | Places a new occurrence of the original object in a model. |

(*Continued*)

**Table 15.1** (*Continued*)

| Copy Type | Model | Objects in Explorer Module | Objects in Designer Module |
|-----------|-------|---------------------------|---------------------------|
| **Definition** | Creates a new model with definition copies of all objects and connections. | Creates a new object with the same attribute values (including name) as the source object. Just called *copy* in Explorer Module. | Creates a new object with the same attribute values (including name) as the source object. |
| **Variant** | Creates a definition copy of the source model. Creates a variant relationship between the source and target model, and between objects in the source model and their copies in the target model. | Creates a definition copy of the source object, but with a variant relationship between the source and target object. | Creates a definition copy of the source object, but with a variant relationship between the source and target object. |
| **Master** | Not available | Not available | Creates a definition copy of the source object, and makes it the master of the source object. |
| **Shortcut** | Creates a pointer to an existing model. | Creates a pointer to an existing object. | Not available |

## 15.2    Copying Objects

Objects can be copied in a number of ways as shown in Table 15.2. The availability of the commands and the exact nature of the copy depends on whether you are performing the copying in the *Explorer Module* or *Designer Module*. The easiest approach is to select an object, click the right-hand mouse button and drag the object to the location where you want to make the copy. When you release the mouse button, a pop-up menu will appear giving a choice of copy options.

### 15.2.1    Object Occurrence Copies

Each time we place a new object in a model using the *Designer Module*, ARIS creates a definition of the object in the ARIS database. It also creates a pointer to the '*occurrence*' of the object in the model. The definition of the object will be shown in one of the *Explorer Module* groups, usually the same group as the model.

**Table 15.2** Methods for Copying Objects

| Copy Method | Explorer Module | Designer Module |
|---|---|---|
| Main Menu, <u>C</u>opy and <u>P</u>aste | Definition Copy | Occurrence Copy |
| Right-Click > <u>C</u>opy and <u>P</u>aste | Definition Copy | Occurrence Copy |
| `<Ctrl+C>`, `<Ctrl+V>` | Definition Copy | Occurrence Copy |
| Select object, Right-Click, drag mouse and release. | Definition Copy, Variant Copy, Shortcut. | Occurrence Copy, Definition Copy, Variant Copy, Master Copy. |
| Right-Click > <u>C</u>opy and Right-Click > Pa<u>s</u>te as | Definition Copy, Variant Copy, Shortcut. | Definition Copy, Variant Copy, Shortcut. |

The occurrence of the object is represented in the model by its symbol. In the *Designer Module*, if we perform a straightforward <u>C</u>opy and <u>P</u>aste of the object using the *Main Menu* commands or Right-Click commands, or use the right-hand mouse key and drag the object to make a specific occurrence copy, we place another copy of the object's symbol in the model. The copied symbol represents another occurrence of the object. There is still only one object definition in the database, but it now has pointers to the two occurrences of the object in the model. Equally, we may place the occurrence copy in a different model, but no matter how many occurrence copies of an object there are, there is only one definition of the object shown in the *Explorer Module*. For that reason we cannot make an occurrence copy in the *Explorer Module*.

All the copied symbols in the model point to the same object. Both source and copied objects have the same GUIDs. The GUID (Global Unique Identifier) is, as its name suggests, unique no matter where in the world the object has been generated. You can view the GUID from the *Properties [Information] Dialog Box*, however it is a rather long text string. As an alternative, objects and models have an *Identifier* attribute. If identifiers are turned on (use the database *Properties [Identifiers] Dialog Box* in the *Administration Module*), the *identifier* field will, provided it has not been manually edited, show an alphanumeric string that is unique within the current database.

If we make the *Identifier* attribute visible (see Attribute Placement in Chapter 14) we will see they are the same (Fig. 15.1a) for the original object and the occurrence copy. If we select one of the object symbols, open the *Attributes Window* and change one of the attributes (e.g. the object's name), then save and close the *Attributes Window*, we will see the name changes in both the copied object and the original source object (Fig. 15.1b).

Similarly, any other properties the object has, for instance model assignments, will also be visible in the occurrence copy. So we can see both source and copied objects in Fig. 15.1 have an *Assignment Icon*. The relationships stored in the database for an object are the sum total of the relationships made to all occurrences of the object in whichever models they may be defined.

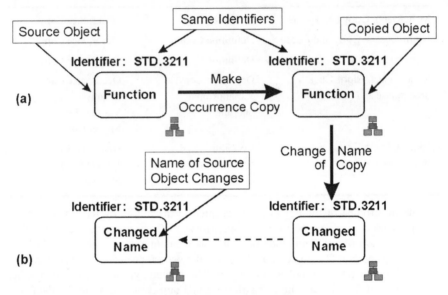

**Fig. 15.1** Object Occurrence Copy

**Table 15.3** Valid Use of Object Copies

| Object | Occurrence Copy Same Model | Occurrence Copy Another Model | Definition Copy Same Model | Definition Copy Another Model |
|---|---|---|---|---|
| **Events** | Never | For linking | Rarely | Rarely |
| **Rules** | Never | Never | Rarely | Rarely |
| **Functions** | Never | Never | When you need one similar. | When you need one similar. |
| **Resource Objects** | Frequently – library objects. | Frequently – library objects. | Rarely – only when you need one similar. | Rarely – only when you need one similar. |

Table 15.3 summarises the circumstances in which we use occurrence copies. We frequently make occurrence copies of resource objects (organisation, data, systems, etc.), for instance, when we want to show the same *Organizational unit* "*carries out*" a number of different functions. We only make occurrence copies of functions and events in special circumstances.

## 15.2.2      Object Definition Copies

A definition copy of an object creates a new object with the same values for its attributes (including its name) as the original source object. Although the name of the two objects will be the same, they will be totally unrelated and have different Global Unique Identifiers (GUIDs). Changing the name, or other attributes, of the copied object will have no effect on the source object (Fig. 15.2b). Moreover, once the copy has been made, it is not possible to determine from which object the copy was made. The appearance of the source object will be copied, but other properties, for instance, relationships and model assignments, will not be copied. Hence, the copied object in Fig. 15.2b does not have an *Assignment Icon*.

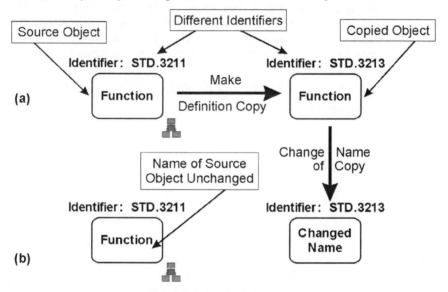

**Fig. 15.2** Object Definition Copy

The definition copy is the default copy method in the *Explorer Module* when using the standard C̲opy and P̲aste *Main Menu* or Right-Click Menu commands. To make a definition copy in the *Designer Module*, you must use the right-hand mouse key and drag method, because the default copy is an occurrence copy.

We frequently use definition copies when we want to create a second object with similar attributes to one we already have. Rather than create a new object and enter all the attributes again, we take a definition copy and change the name of the copied object. Table 15.3 summarises the valid uses of object definition copies.

**Hint** – ARIS does not require definition copies of objects to have different names (it uses the GUID to establish uniqueness), but we strongly recommend changing the name of the copied object to make database management easier. If you really can't think of a different name, append the copied objects with a sequence number (e.g. "plan project (1)" and "plan project (2)").

### 15.2.3    Object Variant Copies

A variant copy is a special form of a definition copy. It creates a new, unique object with the same attribute values as the source object. Normally, once a definition copy has been made it is not possible to identify the original source object. However, the variant copy creates a relationship between the source object (the *master*) and the copied object (the *variant*).

In all other respects there is no relation between the objects, but the variant relationship allows us to trace the parentage of the object. The appearance of the source object will be copied, but other properties, for instance, relationships and model assignments, will not be copied.

Both source and variant objects have unique GUIDs. Because, we have two completely unique objects related to one another by the variant relationship, we can move the objects independently to any ARIS database in the world, but still recognise they are related if they are later brought back into the same database.

To create a variant copy:

1.   Select one or more objects in the *Explorer Module* or *Designer Module*,

2.   Click the right-hand mouse key,

3.   Drag the object(s) to the required location,

4.   Release the mouse key,

5.   Select Create variants (*Explorer Module*) / Create variant here (*Designer Module*).

     Or

4.   Copy, followed by Paste as > Variant(s).

If used in the *Designer Module*, a new object or objects will be created with the appropriate variant relationship to the original object.

In the *Explorer Module*, the *Create variants Dialog Box* (Fig. 15.3) is displayed. This dialog box is actually intended to support the creation of variant copes of models (see Section 15.3.3) and is not very useful for creating variants of objects. Just click OK and a variant will be created in the chosen group.

### 15.2.4    Object Master Copy

Creating a master copy is the opposite of creating a variant copy. Once again it creates a definition copy, but this time it establishes the original object as the *variant* and the copied object as the *master*.

You can only create a master copy in the *Designer Module*:

1.   Select the object,

2.   Click the right-hand mouse key,

3.   Drag the object to the required location,

4.   Release the mouse key,

5.   Select Create master here.

If you repeat the operation on the source object, it will make another variant copy of the master copy you created the first time you did the operation.

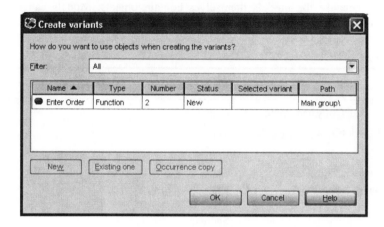

**Fig. 15.3** Create Variants Dialog Box (Object Copy)

## 15.2.5    Object Shortcuts

A shortcut is not really a copy in the same way that occurrence, definition or variant copies are. Shortcuts cannot be used in models; they are simply pointers to model or object definitions in the *Explorer Module* group structure. They can be placed in any group and are mostly used to gather together, in one group, references to related models or objects that exist in various other groups.

1.   Select an object,
2.   Click the right-hand mouse key,
3.   Drag the object to the required location,
4.   Release the mouse key,
5.   Select Create shortcuts here.
     Or
2.   Copy, followed by Paste as > Shortcuts.

Shortcuts can only be made in the *Explorer Module* and the name of the shortcut is of the form "Shortcut to objectname". If you change the name of the original object, the name of the shortcut will not change, but the link to the original object will remain.

## 15.3    Copying Models

Copying models is based on similar principles to copying objects, but is more involved because the models themselves contain objects. Models can only be copied in the *Explorer Module*, as summarised in Table 15.4.

**Table 15.4** Methods for Copying Models

| Copy Method | ARIS Explorer |
|---|---|
| Main Menu, <u>C</u>opy and <u>P</u>aste | Copy |
| Right-Click > <u>C</u>opy and <u>P</u>aste | Copy |
| <Ctrl+C>, <Ctrl+V> | Copy |
| Select object, Right-Click, drag mouse and release. | Copy, Definition Copy, Variant Copy, Shortcut. |
| Right-Click > <u>C</u>opy and Right-Click > Pa<u>s</u>te as. | Copy, Definition Copy, Variant Copy, Shortcut. |

### 15.3.1    Model Copy

There is no occurrence copy for models, but the standard copy is similar. It creates a new, unique, model and in it places occurrence copies of all the objects and connections from the source model (Fig. 15.4). Thus, the model exists as an entity in its own right (with its own GUID), but the objects and connections do not, they are just occurrences of the objects and connections in the source model. Any changes to the object attributes made in the copied model will affect the attributes of the original occurrences in the source model. Properties of the objects in the source model (e.g. model assignments) will be visible in the copied model. The name of the copied model will be the same as the source model, but with a sequence number appended to the end. Thus "High-level Process" becomes "High-Level Process(1)". However, the name of the source or copied model may be changed independently later. Because there is no actual relationship between the source and copied models, there is no way to tell which source model the copy was made from.

Once the copy has been made, the copied model can be used just like any other model. The copied model may be changed such that there is little resemblance to the original source model. In fact, you may delete all the objects and connections in the copied model and replace them with completely different ones.

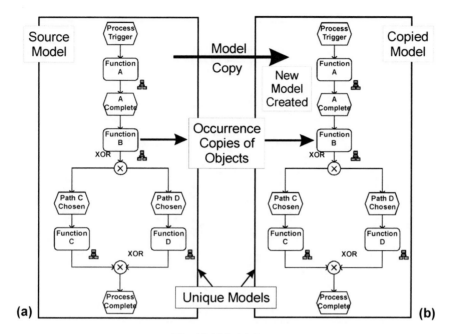

**Fig. 15.4** Model Copy

The relationships defined for any object are the sum total of the relationships defined in all models where the object has occurrences. Thus, if new relationships are made between the object occurrences in the copied model, they will add to those relationships defined in the source model. Therefore, you need to be careful when creating copies of models as you may add a lot of potentially conflicting relationships to the database. Definition copies or variant copies are usually safer.

### 15.3.2 Model Definition Copies

A definition copy creates a new, unique model and in it places definition copies of all the objects and connections from the source model (Fig. 15.5). The copied model is, therefore, an exact replica of the source model, but the model, its objects and connections all have unique GUIDs.

The copied model can be changed at will without having any effect on the original source model. Properties of source objects (e.g. model assignments) are not transferred to the copied model. Once again, the name of the copied model will be the same as the source model, but with a sequence number appended (e.g. "High-Level Process(1)"). There is no link between the models and no way to trace the source of a copied model.

A definition copy of a model is typically made when you want to re-use a previously defined process in a different context, and want no interference between the original and copied models.

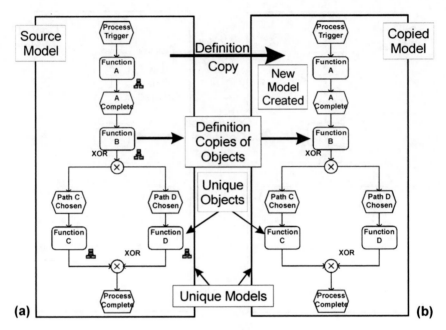

**Fig. 15.5** Model Definition Copy

### 15.3.3   Model Variant Copy

The variant copy of a model is basically a definition copy (Fig. 15.6). However, it does more than just make a copy of the model, it creates:

- A definition copy of the model,
- A variant relationship between the original model (the *master*) and the copy (the *variant*),
- Variant relationships between all the objects in the master model and the objects in the variant model.

So, the variant copy establishes a relationship between the source model (the *master*) and the copied model (the *variant*), and also a relationship between every object in the source model and the definition copy of the object in the copied model.

This means we have a replica of the model, but this time we can trace the master of the variant model and all its objects. Once created, we can use and modify the variant model, just like any other. However, because of the variant relationship at the object level, we can make a comparison between the master model and the variant model to find out what has changed. Variant copies can be made of models that are themselves variants of other models, hence establishing a variant chain.

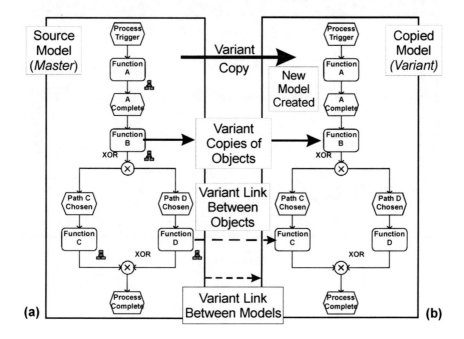

**Fig. 15.6** Model Variant Copy

### *Managing Objects in a Variant Copy*

When you make a variant copy of a model, you will be presented with the *Variants Dialog Box*. This is the same box we saw when making variant copies of objects in the *Explorer Module* (Fig. 15.3), but this time we can use all of its facilities.

To make a variant copy of a model:

1.  Select one or more models in the *Explorer Module*,

2.  Click the right-hand mouse key,

3.  Drag the model(s) to the required location,

4.  Release the mouse key,

5.  Select Create variants (*Explorer Module*).

    Or

5.  Copy, followed by Paste as > Variant(s).

The *Variants Dialog Box* (Fig. 15.7) will be displayed and will list all the objects in the source model.

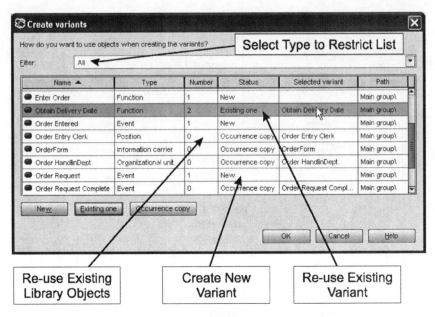

**Fig. 15.7** Variants Dialog Box (Model Copy)

For each object the list will show:

- **Name** – the name of the object,
- **Type** – the type of object (e.g. function or event),
- **Number** – the number of existing variants of the object (zero if the object has no variants),
- **Status** – indicates if a new variant copy will be created, an existing variant used or an occurrence copy made depending on the option selected (initially "new"),
- **Selected variant** – the name of a selected existing variant or occurrence copy to be used instead of creating a new variant copy (initially blank),
- **Path** – the group in the *Explorer Module* where the object copy will be saved.

The columns can be sorted in ascending or descending order by clicking on the column header. If you want to limit the list to just a specific type of object (e.g. functions), you can select an object type from the drop-down box in the *Filter* field at the top of the dialog box.

At first sight this dialog box looks rather complex, but it can be used to give very precise control over which objects are placed in the variant model copy. If you just want to create a straightforward model copy with all new variant object copies you can just click OK.

If you want more control over how the objects are created you can select one or more objects in the list and select one of the three buttons at the bottom of the screen:

- Ne<u>w</u>,

- <u>E</u>xisting one,

- <u>O</u>ccurrence copy.

The <u>N</u>ew option creates a new definition copy of the source object with a variant relationship. This is the default and it is not necessary to specifically select this option for objects for which you want a variant copy. This option is only useful if you have previously selected one of the other options and want to change your mind.

If the *Number* column in the list is not zero, this shows the object in the model already has some variants. If you want to use one of these variants instead of creating a new one, select the object in the list and click the <u>E</u>xisting one Button. If there is only one variant available, its name will be placed in the *Selected variant* field and the *Status* field will change to "*Existing*" to show that the existing variant will be used rather than a new variant created. If there is more than one existing variant, the *Existing Variants Dialog Box* (Fig. 15.8) will show a list of these from which you can select the one you want. Click *OK* and the dialog box will close and the *Selected variant* and *Status* fields will be updated.

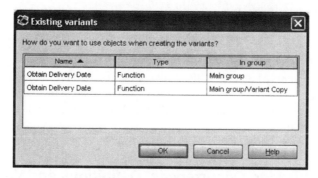

**Fig. 15.8** Existing Variants Dialog Box

The <u>O</u>ccurrence copy option allows you to place an occurrence copy of the object into the variant model rather than to create a variant copy. Select the object in the list and click the <u>O</u>ccurrence copy Button. The *Selected variant* field will be updated with the name of the occurrence copy and the *Status* fields will be changed to "*Occurrence copy*".

This last option is very useful when you want to create a variant copy of a model, but wish to have occurrence copies of some of the objects. For instance, you may want new functions, rules and events, but to keep the same resource objects (e.g. organisation, data and systems). It is also useful when you want to create a variant copy of a model that is linked to other models using common events.

As we know, it is vital that the linking events are occurrences of the same object, so when you create the variant copy, use the technique described above to make occurrence copies of the trigger and outcome events.

If you look back at Fig. 15.7, it shows an example of the *Variants Dialog Box* when creating a variant model copy using different object copy types. The outcome *event* **Order request Complete** has been selected to be an occurrence copy along with library objects **Order Entry Clerk** (*Position*), **Order Form** (*Information carrier*) and **Order Handling Dept** (*Organizational unit*). *Function*, **Enter Order**, to be a new variant copy and *function*, **Obtain Delivery Date**, to use an existing variant.

### 15.3.4    Model Shortcuts

Shortcuts for models are simply pointers to model definitions in the *Explorer Module* group structure. They can be placed in any group and are mostly used to gather together, in one group, references to related models that exist in various other groups.

1.  Select a model,
2.  Click the right-hand mouse key,
3.  Drag the model to the required location,
4.  Release the mouse key,
5.  Select Create shortcuts here.

Or

2.  Copy, followed by Paste as > Shortcuts.

Shortcuts can only be made in the *Explorer Module* and the name of the shortcut is of the form "Shortcut to modelname". If you change the name of the original model, the name of the shortcut will not change, but the link to the original model will remain.

## 15.4    Viewing Occurrences, Definitions and Variants

### 15.4.1    Viewing Object Occurrences

You can view the occurrences of objects in three ways:

•  *Properties [Occurrences] Dialog Box*,
•  *Model Properties Bar, Occurrences Tab*,
•  *Objects Properties Bar, Occurrences Tab*.

## Properties [Occurrences] Dialog Box,

For a selected object in the *Explorer Module* or *Designer Module*, the *Occurrences Dialog Box* (Fig. 15.9) displays all occurrences of the object in all the other models in the database.

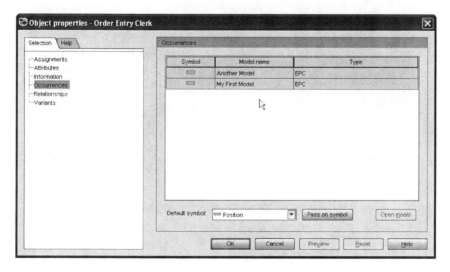

**Fig. 15.9** Occurrences Dialog Box

The model where another object occurs can be directly opened by selecting the occurrence in the list and clicking on the Open model Button. Right-clicking on an object occurrence in the list will bring up a *Right-Click Menu* with options to Open the model, show its attributes or properties or Go to > Occurrence in Explorer. The last option will open the *Explorer Module* and open the group structure so that the definition of the selected object occurrence is visible.

 **Expert Tip** – where an object can be displayed using several different types of symbol, you can make all the occurrences have the same symbol as the selected occurrence by clicking on the Pass on symbol Button.

## Navigation Bar, Occurrences Tab

In the *Designer Module*, the *Occurrences Tab* (Fig. 15.10) in the *Navigation Bar* provides a list of all the object occurrences in the model and visually shows their symbol types. When you select an occurrence in the list, the *Modelling Window* automatically scrolls so the object is visible. The selection can be used for viewing the attributes and properties of the objects as well as making copies and assignments.

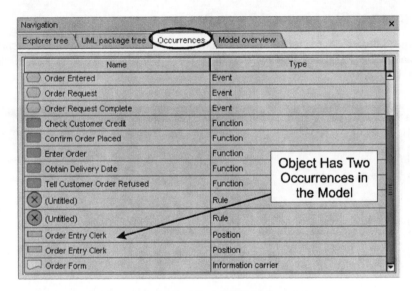

**Fig. 15.10** Navigation Bar, Occurrences Tab

## Properties Bar, Occurrences Tab

In the *Designer Module,* the *Occurrences Tab* (Fig. 15.11) in the *Properties Bar* shows a list of all the occurrences of the selected object in all the models in the database in the same way as the Properties [*Occurrences*] *Dialog Box.* If there is more than one occurrence in any one model, the list will have more than one entry. The *Occurrences Tab* differs from the *Occurrences Tab* in the *Navigation Bar* in that it displays all occurrences of a selected object, not just those in the current model.

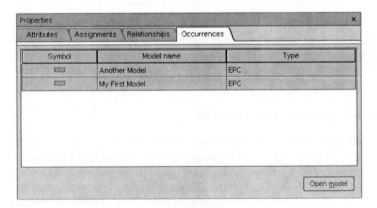

**Fig. 15.11** Properties Bar, Occurrences Tab

If you select one of the occurrence entries and click on the Open Model Button, the model containing the occurrence will be opened in a new *Modelling Window* tab and the object occurrence selected.

### 15.4.2    Viewing Object Definitions

The definition of an object is stored in the *Explorer Module* group structure. It can be seen by selecting the group where it is defined using the *Explorer Tree* in the left-hand pane and clicking on the *Objects Tab* in the right-hand pane (see Chapter 8). The object's details can be viewed from using the *Object properties Dialog Box* (*Right-Click > Properties*).

 **Hint** – to quickly find which group any particularly object is stored in, select an occurrence of an object in the *Explorer Module* or *Designer Module* and Right-Click > Go to > Occurrence in Explorer. ARIS will switch to the *Explorer Module* (or the *Explorer tree Tab* in the *Designer Module)* and the group structure will open at the group containing the object definition.

### 15.4.3    Viewing Object Variants

Object variants can be viewed with the *Properties [Variants] Dialog Box* (Fig. 15.12). Select an object in the *Explorer Module* or the *Designer Module* and Right-Click > Properties.

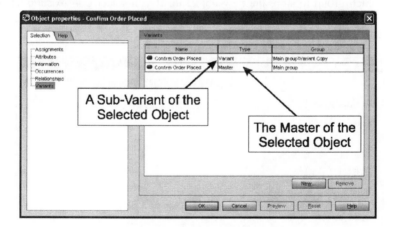

**Fig. 15.12** Variants Dialog Box

All the objects with a variant or master relationship to the selected object will be displayed in a list. The *Type* column shows whether it is a variant or master relationship. You can break the variant or master link by selecting a object in the list and clicking on the R<u>e</u>move button. This doesn't remove the object, but just removes the link between the selected object and the variant or master object.

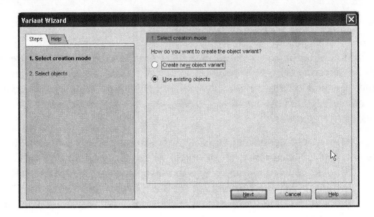

**Fig. 15.13** Variant Wizard

You can add a new variant link to the selected object by clicking on the Ne<u>w</u>... Button. This will display the *Variant Wizard* and the *Select creation mode Dialog Box* (Fig. 15.13) allows you to choose whether to create a new object and make it a variant of the selected object or whether to create a variant relationship between an existing object and a selected object.

If you select Create ne<u>w</u> object variant, the *Select group Dialog Box* asks you to select which group to store the new object in. If you select <u>U</u>se existing objects, the *Select objects Dialog Box* (Fig. 15.14) allows you to select one or more objects to assign as variants.

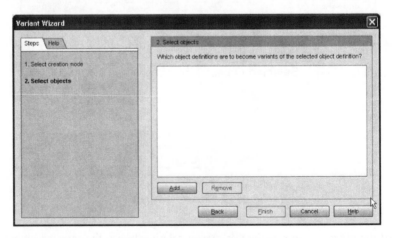

**Fig. 15.14** Select Objects Dialog Box

Initially the dialog box is blank, so click on Add... and the *Select object Dialog Box* (Fig. 15.15) will allow you to select one or more objects. These are then displayed in the main dialog box and you can R**e**move ones you don't want or **A**dd... more. Click on **F**inish and the new variant relationship will be created.

**Fig. 15.15** Select Object Dialog Box

## 15.4.4    Viewing Model Variants

Model variants can be viewed with the *Properties* [*Variants*] *Dialog Box* (Fig. 15.12). Select a model in the *Explorer Module* and Right-Click  > P**r**operties. The dialog box looks exactly the same as for object variants (Section 15.4.3) and has the same commands for adding and removing variant relationships.

# Chapter 16    Standardised Modelling with ARIS

> In the chapter we explain the benefits of standardising your approach to business process modelling. We describe some of the key aspects of modelling that need to be standardised and explain how such standards can be documented, promoted and supported in your organisation.

## 16.1    The Need for Standardisation

### 16.1.1    Benefits of Standardisation

It is vital to define standards when embarking upon Business Process Management in your organisation. *ARIS Business Architect* and *ARIS Business Designer* are powerful and functionally rich tools that need careful management and support. In Chapter 4 we talked about Business Process Architecture and in other chapters we have given you an idea how ARIS can be used to create both simple process models and complex hierarchies of interlinked models of different types. It should have become obvious that there are many different ways in which ARIS can be used to achieve the same basic aims.

We recommend you should keep to the ARIS Method as far as possible, but even when abiding by the method, there are many alternatives and options to consider. So in a professional BPM organisation, common modelling standards become essential in achieving BPM objectives, such as:

- Improving process quality,
- Using best practice,
- Promoting a professional and rigorous approach,
- Reducing design times and costs,
- Encouraging the use of a common process vocabulary,
- Encouraging design reuse,
- Reducing training costs,
- Promoting common understanding, thus reducing errors,
- Creating a common repository,
- Establishing agreed interfaces, thus avoiding duplication and error.

The primary goal in applying modelling standards must be to improve the quality and effectiveness of the processes. This way we can improve the service we give to our customers. By applying a degree of professionalism and rigour to the way we design and analyse our processes, we will improve their quality. We may achieve this on an individual project or product, but more significant benefits are realised by applying best practice across all of our BPM projects. Not only does this improve effectiveness and reduce costs through economies of scale, but it also presents a single corporate image to our customers.

### 16.1.2    Driving Reuse Through Standardisation

As businesses become mature in the use of common methods, an important goal becomes the reuse and standardisation of common processes and sub-processes. After all, the basic processes for marketing, selling, manufacturing, delivering and billing for a product will be much the same for each product; it is only the detail that differs. Quite often, even the detailed sub-processes can be categorised into a small number of standard variants with the appropriate one being picked for the specific product.

In practice, achieving reuse is more difficult than it sounds. However, it is almost impossible to achieve unless a common approach is used for design and documentation. Only by representing the processes, and the resources needed to implement them, in a common way can designers have a hope of working out how to re-use them. The key to successful reuse is the effective specification of the interfaces between processes and between the business departments implementing the processes.

### 16.1.3    A Common Process Repository

Our ultimate aim may be to create a single repository of processes for our business and to publish those processes to all employees who need to see them. It only makes sense to try and achieve this if we have a standard approach to how the processes are designed and documented, and a common understanding of what particular modelling representations mean.

### 16.1.4    Using ARIS to Drive Standardisation

By choosing to use a standard methodology, implemented in the *ARIS Design Platform* products, we are provided with a framework that limits the number of decisions we have to make about our intended approach. In addition, by implementing a single tool and method we can achieve cost reduction through the commercial benefits of only buying one product. We can also reduce training costs. Process modellers only need to be trained to use a single tool. They can then move from one department to another with the minimum amount of re-training. In addition, if you apply common standards for the use of the tool across those different departments, trained modellers moving into a new team will already be familiar with much of what goes on.

So we can see that using ARIS helps promote and enforce standards, but using ARIS 'properly' also needs standards. *ARIS Business Architect* and *ARIS Business Designer* are functionally rich tools with lots of different ways to achieve the same thing. They need 'reining back' to a core set of modelling methods that achieve your business goals. If ARIS is not used properly, many of the benefits are lost. For instance, if models are not produced so they correctly follow the ARIS method, and have appropriate attributes populated, the ability to run analysis or perform simulation at a later date may be lost. At the very least, additional work may be needed to correct the models or add additional data. Furthermore, if individual modellers are working alone, but later it is intended to combine the work into a single database, it is essential to have agreed standards.

## 16.2   What to Standardise

We have seen above that it is vital to set standards for using ARIS. It is important to ensure people are adequately trained to use both the tool and the standards, and to ensure the standards are in fact used. There is a whole range of things we can standardise in ARIS. Some of the most important are:

- Basic rules for process capture and modelling,
- The core set of models, objects and symbols,
- Modelling of who?, what?, when?, where? and how?
- Relationships and what they mean,
- How to represent common scenarios,
- Use of attributes,
- Model appearance,
- Approaches to model linking and structure,
- ARIS database structure, libraries and reuse.

### 16.2.1   Basic Rules for Process Capture and Modelling

We recommend establishing a clear procedure for how to go about process capture and design.

Make it clear to people undertaking those roles whether they are expected to use ARIS during process capture sessions or whether ARIS will be used afterwards to re-document workshop output. If the later is chosen, it is vital to make sure the right information is captured and documented so effective ARIS models can be created later. If you want ARIS to be used in process capture sessions (by far the most effective approach if the skills are available), make sure modellers are adequately trained and feel confident using ARIS when working in front of other people.

Define which models should be produced. Should modellers produce just *EPCs*, or should they create other models types such as *FADs, Organizational charts, Data models,* etc. Are they expected to use library objects or create their own? How will individual models be merged together into a master database? How will reuse be managed? These are as much project management issues as ARIS issues. They need to be thought out carefully for each team and each project. They should be defined in the project plan and rigorously enforced.

Because this is such an early and important stage in the process engineering lifecycle, mistakes made here, or opportunities missed, may have expensive consequences later on.

### 16.2.2    A Core Set of Models, Objects and Symbols

Decide on the core set of models, objects and symbols your organisation will use and create appropriate ARIS Method Filters to restrict modellers to an appropriate set based on their project roles. Under no circumstances should you let people model using the **Entire Method** filter, as this offers all the possible model types, objects and symbols available in ARIS. We guarantee if you don't restrict the method there will be considerable inconsistencies in how people model (i.e. half your modellers will use *Organizational unit* objects and the other half will use *Organizational unit type* objects). This will lead to significant problems as modelling progresses.

You should have a good idea of the models, objects and different symbols to use from following the examples and suggestions given in this book.

### 16.2.3    Modelling of Who?, What?, When?, Where?, Why? and How?

Having defined the core models, objects and symbols, make it clear to users when and how to use them. Write down generic modelling conventions for your organisation to use as a template for all upcoming projects. Use examples to explain what has to be modelled. An *Event-driven process chain* or a *Function allocation diagram* could be used to describe those elements:

*   **Who does it?** – *Organizational unit.*

*   **What do they do?** – *Functions* transform *Technical terms* contained in *Information carriers* into *Entity types* contained in *Information carriers.*

*   **Where do they do it?** – at the *Location.*

*   **How do they do it?** – using *Knowledge categories* and following *Documented knowledge.*

*   **Why do they do it?** – to produce a *Product/Service* and support *Objectives.*

*   **When do they do it?** – following a trigger *Event* and prior to an outcome *Event.*

Decide for your organisation and project exactly how you wish to use these objects and the minimum set of information to be modelled in each project. A good approach is to create an '*ARIS Reference Model*' containing examples of the approaches you wish people to use.

We find people are generally good at modelling organisations and systems, but tend to forget about the data.

### 16.2.4   Relationships and What They Mean

The ARIS Method defines the relationships between objects, but you need to consider exactly what they mean in the context of your organisation. For instance, consider the organisation relationships "*carries out*" and "*must be informed about*". What do these mean for your organisation? You have to decide which relationships you want to use and how you interpret them for future process analysis. You can show the meaning of this connection in the reference model.

### 16.2.5   How to Represent Common Scenarios

It is important to agree conventions for modelling certain types of process scenario so people can easily recognise them when they occur in models. In Chapter 7 we showed in detail how to model decisions and branches. For these scenarios there is usually only one way to correctly model them, however for other scenarios (e.g. loops, hand-over to other organisations, etc.) there are often alternative approaches for how to model, or decisions to be made about how much detail requires modelling.

For instance, when one organisation hands the process over to another organisation, is it just sufficient to show successive functions "*carried out*" by different *Organizational units*, or do you need to model the detail of how the 'hand-over' is actually done? Similarly, with loops: is it sufficient to return a process path to an earlier part of the process for those operations to be repeated, or do you want to recognise that the process will not be repeated in exactly the same way the second time around?

These decisions can only be made in the context of the stated aims for the organisation, the current project and knowledge of whether subsequent analysis or simulation is required. However, in general we would recommend you model what actually happens, rather than some idealised abstraction of it.

### 16.2.6   Use of Attributes

It is very important to agree standards defining which attributes will be used, what they will be used for, and those for which it is mandatory to enter values. Unless prompted, people will rarely fill in any attributes, except perhaps for the "*Description/Definition*" field. If you want them to complete more information for later analysis, it is important to make this clear. It is also important to use Method Filters to restrict the list of available attributes to just those few that are required, rather than confront users with hundreds, none of which they understand how to use. Where you want users to enter very specific information, consider using the drop-down list definitions available for some *"User Attributes"* (see Chapter 14). These will restrict entry to a set of pre-defined values.

### 16.2.7    Model Appearance

On the one hand, the appearance of a model makes no difference to its semantic context. Objects, relationships and attributes should represent all the meaning in the model. No semantic knowledge should be conveyed through the colour, size or style of objects and connections. On the other hand, the appearance of a model can have a significant impact on people's understanding and acceptance of its contents.

*ARIS Business Architect* and *ARIS Business Designer* allow users to create their own pre-defined modelling templates to change the look and feel of process models. This helps to standardise model visualisation, but also to get more acceptance for your business models. Set standards for the following appearance issues:

- Naming conventions for different object types (i.e. a function should be named by using a verb and a noun),
- Display of objects names (e.g. use of the <u>R</u>emove colour behind text option and Te<u>x</u>t Attributes in symbol settings),
- Use of alternative colours and line sizes,
- Standard Font Format and the use of alternative Font Formats,
- Use of Free-form text,
- The content and appearance of a model properties text box,
- Use of horizontal or vertical layout,
- Use of automatic layout.

For EPCs, we strongly recommend a vertical layout and the use of the automatic layout facility.

### 16.2.8    Approaches to Model Linking and Structure

We discussed in Chapter 13 how to link models together in a hierarchy and to create vertical model structure. We also looked at how to segment models and link them together in a horizontal structure. Both of these approaches can be used independently, or together, and it is important to decide on the exact approach you wish to use and on the levels of modelling hierarchies you need in your Business Process Architecture (see Chapter 4).

## 16.2.9     Libraries and Reuse

Achieving successful reuse of ARIS elements requires a high degree of standardisation and cooperation. This can be relatively straightforward to implement when people are working within a single project area and using a common database on a networked ARIS server. However, it is much more difficult when people are widely dispersed over many teams and using stand-alone databases. That's why you should enable an organisation-wide modelling server. You should promote the creation and re-use of library objects, which can be stored in dedicated group folders in ARIS, accessible based on user-rights.

If people are working using stand-alone databases you need to use *ARIS Business Architect* features like *Merge* and *Consolidate* to administer those kinds of projects.

# 16.3     Conventions Handbooks and other Standardisation Approaches

One of the most important parts of the Business Process Management is establishing of standards for process modelling and design, and for the use of ARIS. We need a set of approaches to:

- Define standards,
- Implement standards,
- Aid the use of standards,
- Verify the use of standards,
- Measure the effects of implementing standards.

Any one of these approaches by themselves is useless. There is no point in trying to enforce standards if you haven't given people adequate training and support in how to use them. Similarly, there is no point in providing massive help and support if you have no idea if the standards have any benefit.

Each of these approaches needs a mixture of formal documents, tools, templates, guidelines and so on. These are all brought together through a process standards framework. This should be a document (or Intranet web page) listing all the aspects of your work for which standards have been defined, and itemising those resources supporting the standards. Normally this document is called the '*ARIS Modelling Convention Handbook*'.

Typical resources and the approaches for standardisation are:

- Formal Standards Documents,
- Guidelines,
- Intranet Help and Support Site,
- Sample Databases and Models,

- Method Filters,
- ARIS Server,
- ARIS Web Server,
- Object and Model Libraries,
- Templates,
- Training,
- Report Scripts,
- Semantics Checks,
- Audits, Reviews and Quality Gates.

### 16.3.1    Formal Standards Documents

Formal standards documents should be kept to a bare minimum. People will be put off by large documents. Process modelling is a practical activity; wherever possible your standards should be incorporated into resources people can actively use. Where you must have documents, also publish them on the Intranet.

There are some typical elements an ARIS Modelling Conventions Handbook should contain:

- About the document:
  - Version history, change request management and distribution list,
  - Objectives of the document,
  - Definitions and abbreviations.
- Modelling conventions:
  - Business Process Architecture and hierarchies (modelling levels),
  - Model types (standard ARIS model types and user-defined model types),
  - Naming conventions for models and objects,
  - Attributes for models and objects (mandatory and optional).
- Visual conventions:
  - Modelling layout standards,
  - Modelling direction,
  - Templates to use,
  - Standard fonts,
  - Symbols placement,
  - Object naming,
- Administration conventions:
  - Database group structure,

-     User and user group management,
-     User access rights,
-     Language management for multi-language projects,
-     Object libraries,
-     ARIS Method filters.


## 16.3.2     Guidelines

To support the ARIS Modelling Conventions Handbook, we recommend you produce guidelines, or '*ARIS Guide sheets*' (Fig. 16.1) describing your standards and giving examples of how to use them. Keep them as succinct as possible. Limit them to a single sheet and produce a number of sheets on different topics.

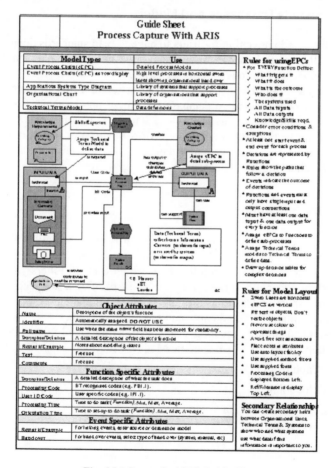

**Fig. 16.1** Example ARIS Guide Sheet

Publish the set on your Intranet site; provide them as handouts, laminated sheets, bookmarks or mouse pads.

### 16.3.3    Intranet Help and Support Site

A good Intranet site giving access to BPM standards, guides sheets, hints and tips is essential. It becomes the focal point for disseminating information and the recognised place where people can seek help. You can also provide a download area for the latest Method Filters, sample databases, report scripts and layout templates.

You may also wish to provide forms so people can request help or information, or report suspected software bugs. The Intranet site then becomes the interface between the ARIS users in your organisation and IDS Scheer.

### 16.3.4    Sample Databases and Models

It can be tedious and unexciting for users to have to read standards documents and guide sheets. It is much better to 'show them how' using example databases containing valid models of various process scenarios.

Where you have defined standards for group structure, font formats and overview models, provide a standard database with these pre-defined. Users can take copies of these databases and use them as a starting point for their own projects. When people are working on a networked *ARIS Business Server* and request the *ARIS Server Administrator* create a new database for them, always make sure they are provided with a template database.

### 16.3.5    Method Filters

Method Filters are the cornerstone of your standards implementation. By defining filters and ensuring they are used, you can enforce a great many aspects of your standards. You need to think carefully about which Method Filters you need and what they should contain. Filters may be role-specific, task-specific, project-specific or user-specific. Useful as they are, Method Filters require time and effort to define and maintain, so you do not want too many of them.

We recommend initially creating task-specific filters and adding others only when absolutely necessary. Task-specific Method Filters can be defined for:

- Process Capture and Design,
- Process Modelling,
- Process, Systems and Data Modelling,
- Business Modelling.

Determining which objects, relationships and attributes you need in these Method Filters is no easy task. Your first instinct might be to go straight to the *ARIS Filter Wizard* in the **Administration Module** and start defining what you need. From experience, we found this was not the ideal approach. The wizard is easy to use, but it is difficult to work out what needs to be defined

The best approach is to produce an '*ARIS Reference Database*' containing examples of all the different model types, object types, and relationships for each filter. In parallel, create a small document containing set of tables describing each model, object, symbol, relationship and attribute required.

Initially, this seems a more laborious task than directly using the *ARIS Filter Wizard*, but once completed you can create your filter directly from the Reference Database.

 **Expert Tip** – with *ARIS Business Architect* you can create a Method Filter automatically based on your reference database. Every model type, object, symbol, connection or attribute that is used and completed in the database will automatically be created in the filter.

After creating the Method Filter you can use an *ARIS Report* to detail the contents of the filter and you can then check it against the definition document. Finally, you should apply the filter to the ARIS Reference Database containing the example models and check whether all the models, objects and connections are visible.

### 16.3.6    Using an ARIS Server

By encouraging users to work on databases residing on a networked ARIS Server you can ensure that many of your standards are adhered to. You can enforce the use of standard Method Filters, Templates and Font Formats, and easily provide users with example databases and models. Later, you may also wish to add specialist Method Filters for:

- Simulation,
- Web Publishing,
- Other ARIS applications.

In addition, you will have visibility of the user's models so you can carry out official (or unofficial) audits. Working on a server is definitely the preferred approach for implementing standards.

### 16.3.7    Using an ARIS Web Server

Providing a corporate ARIS Web server and an ARIS Web publishing service is another way of getting visibility of users' models and enforcing standards. It effectively operates as a 'quality gate' where you can refuse to publish models if they don't adhere to the corporate standards. Initially you can take a soft approach by helping bring users' models up to standard. Later, when they should know better, you can take a firmer stance and reject non-conforming models.

### 16.3.8     Object and Model Libraries

Libraries of useful objects and models help enforce standards by encouraging people to make use of models or objects already conforming to the standards. This promulgates best practice because users see what good models should look like. It also enforces standards because, in order to use your models, users have to follow your basic approach.

 **Expert Tip** – offering a dedicated and well-structured object library to your modelling team enforces the re-use of already existing objects. You can structure your object library based on group hierarchies and handle access rights via user groups. Based on the group structure and the access rights management of your object library you can also install a 'release and approval cycle' for new objects in your library.

### 16.3.9     Templates

Producing a standard set of '*ARIS Templates*' will help encourage a standard 'look and feel' to models and also allows the appearance of models to be altered in a standard way for specific purposes (e.g. reports and documents, Web Publishing etc.).

### 16.3.10     Training

Training is a vital part of implementing standards. It goes without saying that we would expect users to have basic ARIS training, but it is essential to also provide training in the standards and methods you expect them to use with ARIS. This can either be provided as separate training or by customising standard ARIS training courses to focus on your corporate methods and standards. By only issuing '*ARIS Licence Keys*' to those people who have undertaken the prescribed training, you can at least ensure they have the skills and awareness to implement your standards.

### 16.3.11     Report Scripts

By providing both standard and custom '*ARIS Report Scripts*' you can enforce standards for the appearance of the output produced from models, and also of the modelling itself. For instance, if you provide users with model reports showing the relationships between functions and resource objects (e.g. the **Process Overview.**

*rsm* report), to use them, users will have to correctly model function allocations. People who just use ARIS as if it were a drawing tool, and don't model relationships correctly, will find they are denied the opportunity to produce printed reports. Custom reports are particularly useful in this respect. Because few users are likely to produce their own, most will have to use those provided for them, and hence will have to adhere to the modelling standards on which the reports are based.

### 16.3.12    Semantics Checks

The main weapon for ensuring modelling standards have been adhered to are '*ARIS Semantic Checks*'. In the simplest applications you can just use the structure rules to check for conformance to the basic ARIS Method. In more complex applications you can write elaborate custom scripts to check for all aspects of your standards.

 **Expert Tip** – *ARIS Business Architect* and *ARIS Business Designer* offer a completely new and powerful macro facility enabling you to automate trigger actions, such as running a semantic check, when certain modelling events occur. ARIS Report Scripts, semantic checks or dedicated macros can automatically be triggered by more than 35 different event types such as the saving or changing of a model.

However, it is important not to just use semantic checks as a stick with which to beat people. It is very demoralising to present someone with a large report detailing many errors. Only use the semantic check as the last stage in the verification of standards. You should ensure users are aware of the standards, where necessary have been trained in their use, and have the time and tools necessary to implement them. It is costly to find lots of errors and non-conformances at the end of the project and send the model back for re-work. Successful standards are those built into the tools, techniques and procedures used in day-to-day modelling work.

### 16.3.13    Audits, Reviews and Quality Gates

It is no use defining standards, promoting them and providing tools for using and verifying them if, at the end of day, you do not know if they add any value. It is essential that designs are reviewed and have to pass through quality checks ('quality gates') at key stages in the design lifecycle. By taking measurements of the errors found, their likely effect, and the time and cost taken to rectify them, you can start to demonstrate the effectiveness of your standards. It will also give you the raw material from which to build a business case for further investment into tools and techniques, and for improving business process design and re-engineering. Just like any design activity, process modelling must be managed, reviewed and audited.

# Chapter 17    Roles and Responsibilities
for BPM

In this chapter we provide a short overview of the roles and responsibilities
involved in a BPM project and introduce some key modelling principles.

## 17.1    The Roles and Responsibilities for BPM

### 17.1.1    Managing Business Process Management

Previous chapters provided detailed information about the ARIS concept, the *ARIS Design Platform* products with their powerful features and the need for a Business Process Architecture and modelling standards. It should now also be clear that the process of Business Process Management itself has to be managed.

To manage this process you need to be aware of the key phases of a BPM project and you have to establish an appropriate organisation with the necessary roles and responsibilities. If an organisation is serious about creating competitive advantages and attaining its corporate goals, it must be equipped with an *'optimal organisation geared to its strategic BPM goals'*. The best way to implement a BPM approach, and the related governance processes, in your organisation is to build a *'BPM Competence Centre'* and to set-up the roles to support the following BPM phases:

- **Process Strategy Phase** – to define the organisation's BPM strategy,
- **Process Design Phase** – how to standardise and roll-out BPM,
- **Process Implementation Phase** –the roll-out of BPM into the organisation,
- **Process Controlling Phase** – reviewing and optimising BPM standards.

The *'BPM Governance Process'* defines the accountability framework for creating a decision-making process that determines the services, architecture, standards, and policies for continuous management of business processes. It ensures that a management process is in place for setting goals and establishing policies, practices, procedures, organisational structure, roles and responsibilities to ensure enterprise goals will be achieved. A major role in this BPM governance process is played by the BPM Competence Centre and its related roles.

### 17.1.2     The BPM Sponsor

Before you start to establish a BPM Competence Centre you have to ensure the commitment of the top management to the concept of Business Process Management (BPM). That means that you have to identify a '*BPM Sponsor*' who is willing to initiate and drive this important topic from a top management perspective. They have to understand that setting up a BPM Competence Centre, and establishing the process of BPM in an organisation, can have a significant impact and requires organisational change. They should be aware that BPM is not a separate function or activity, but that it is inextricably linked with the business because:

> **"Process is not just something your business does**
> **– process is your business."**

The BPM Sponsor must also agree that people responsible for the operational business processes need the support of '*Business Process Experts*' from the BPM Competence Centre who understand about BPM methodologies and concepts. The BPM Sponsor is a member of the organisation's '*BPM Steering Committee*'.

### 17.1.3     The Head of Business Process Management

The '*Head of Business Process Management*' supervises and manages all process management activities at a group level or regional (local) level and manages a team of organisation-wide Business Process Experts organised together as the BPM Competence Centre. The Head of Business Process Management should be experienced in BPM and be well accepted by the business. They should have detailed knowledge of process design methods, coupled with strong negotiation and communication skills, so their authority will be accepted by the organisation's senior management.

### 17.1.4     The BPM Steering Committee

The BPM Steering Committee is responsible for setting, monitoring and directing the BPM strategy of the business. The steering committee is chaired by the group Head of Business Process Management and is attended by the BPM Sponsor. The steering committee is also attended by the regional Heads of Business Process Management (in a large organisations) and specific Business Process Experts as required.

### 17.1.5     Business Process Experts

The Business Process Experts work as internal process management consultants for organisation-wide business projects and are in charge of methodological excellence and the roll-out of BPM knowledge into all projects. They belong to the

BPM Competence Centre and are led by the group Head of Business Process Management.

## 17.1.6     The BPM Competence Centre

The BPM Competence Centre is led by the Head of Business Process Management and comprises of Business Process Experts from throughout the business.

The responsibilities of the BPM Competence Centre are BPM leadership, implementing a regulatory framework for BPM, offering project support, providing training and communication, and process governance. The major tasks for the BPM Competence Centre are:

- Definition of, and obtaining agreement for, the BPM Strategy,
- Managing and coordinating all BPM activities,
- Selecting and supporting the organisation's BPM tool,
- Managing the process standardisation group,
- Operating all process methods and software tools,
- Designing the organisation's Business Process Architecture,
- Providing BPM training and coaching,
- BPM project support to the whole organisation,
- Drafting and agreeing process-related key performance indicators (KPIs),
- Communication and internal marketing of BPM,
- Providing leadership to the regional Heads of Process Management and Business Process Experts.

## 17.1.7     The Process Owner

The 'Process Owner' owns a dedicated core process and is responsible for the operating performance and continuous process improvement of their processes.

They can be located at a group level or at a local / regional level. The Process Owners should have a good knowledge of the business and of the process areas under their supervision. They should also have knowledge of the Business Process Architecture and the IT systems in use. Furthermore, they should have expertise in process management and the use and management of process Key Performance Indicators (KPIs). Typical responsibilities and activities of the Process Owner are:

- Process performance (meeting KPIs),
- Process improvement,
- Customer satisfaction,
- Process interfaces and integration into the Business Process Architecture,

- Defining process KPIs in compliance with the organisation's process KPI structure,
- Record and publish process KPIs (e.g. time, cost and quality),
- Communication with process participants and Process Coordinators.

### 17.1.8    The Process Coordinator

The '*Process Coordinator*' is a special and extended role of a Process Owner. They own a dedicated business process area, or a core process at a group level, and are responsible for coordinating the interfaces to other process areas.

They should have a good knowledge of their business area and the Business Process Architecture. They work together with other Process Coordinators and members of the BPM organisation to establish transparent, measurable, comparable and well-standardised processes for their area. They lead and coordinate the activities of all Process Owners in their process area and try to find the most practicable routes to process standardisation.

### 17.1.9    The Process Modeller

An important role needed for a business process design project, and for a BPM organisation, is the '*Process Modeller*'. They are located in the local business organisation and are responsible for business process modelling and process verification in compliance with the defined BPM modelling standards. Typically they will also be responsible for promoting the BPM and modelling tool knowledge.

Some experienced Process Modellers may take on more responsibility in their teams by offering technical services such as Method Filter configuration, database administration, creating and maintaining modelling libraries or publishing models. They are often trained and supported by Business Process Experts.

## 17.2    Modelling Principles

We have now finished describing *ARIS Business Architect* and *ARIS Business Designer* and some of the principles for using ARIS in a BPM project. We would like to end by presenting our interpretation of a set of modelling principles resulting from the outcome of research projects and our own experiences on Business Process Modelling, which we believe will stand you in good stead as you start to use ARIS in your organisation:

- **Principle of correctness** – a correct model must have the correct semantics and syntax. The method must be complete and consistent and the model must comply with the method. Only then can the model be validated against the real world using ARIS Platform products and shared with other analysts.

  **"Stick to the ARIS Method (well mostly)."**

- **Principle of relevance** – items should only be modelled if they are relevant to the model's purpose. Modelling too much detail wastes time and money and confuses people.

  **"Don't model the universe!"**

- **Principle of cost versus benefit** – the amount of effort to gather the data and produce the model must be balanced against the expected benefit. Remember: 80% of the benefit comes from the first 20% of effort. Getting the last 20% will cost you another 80% in effort.

  **"Know when you have done enough."**

- **Principle of clarity** – the model must be understandable and usable. Business models are complex, so break the models down into understandable chunks that fit into an overall structure or process architecture.

  **"Keep it simple – clever models often confuse."**

- **Principle of comparability** – ARIS is a very rich tool. It can be used in lots of different ways to achieve the same end. The real benefit comes from communicating and sharing. To do this you must take a common approach to modelling with ARIS.

  **"Define standards and stick to them."**

- **Principle of systematic structure** – models produced in different views should be capable of integration. Again stick to the method, adopt common naming conventions, and produce libraries of common objects.

  **"Don't re-invent the wheel, re-use wherever you can."**

and to these we would like to add one more:

**"If it looks sensible it probably is sensible –
if it looks silly it definitely is silly!"**

# Appendix A     Function Keys and Shortcuts

## Function Keys

| Key | Operation |
| --- | --- |
| F1 | Display ARIS Help. Context-sensitive if an item has been selected. |
| F2 | Open the selected item and select its value for editing (e.g. the object name). |
| F3 | |
| F4 | |
| F5 | Refresh the current window. |
| F6 | In the *Designer Module*, toggles the connection mode on or off. |
| F7 | Run the application specified in the selected items *Link* attribute. If more than one *Link* attribute is defined, the user will be given a choice. |
| F8 | Display the *Attributes Window* for selected items. |
| F9 | |
| F10 | Select the menu bar and open the File menu. |
| Alt+F4 | Exit ARIS. |
| Ctrl+F1 | Display ARIS *Method Help*. Context-sensitive if an item has been selected. |
| Ctrl+F2 | In the *Designer Module*, opens the *Print Preview Dialog Box* . |
| Ctrl+F4 | Close current window. If necessary, prompts you to save changes. |
| Ctrl+Shift+F4 | Close all model windows. |
| Ctrl+F6 | In the *Designer Module*, toggles round open models. |
| Ctrl+Shift+F6 | In the *Designer Module*, toggles round open models in reverse order. |
| Shift+F6 | In the *Designer Module*, displays the *Properties Dialog Box*. |
| Shift+F10 | Display context-sensitive menu for selected item. Equivalent to a right-hand mouse click. |

## ARIS Designer Navigation and Selection Keys

| Key | Operation |
| --- | --- |
| Cursor up | Scroll model up. |
| Cursor down | Scroll model down. |
| Cursor left | Scroll model left. |
| Cursor right | Scroll model right. |
| Ctrl+Cursor | Nudge selected object by one pixel in direction of cursor. |
| Shift+Cursor | Nudge the selected item by one grid line in the cursor direction. |
| PgUp | Scroll up one page. |
| PgDn | Move down one page. |
| Ctrl+Home | Move to top left-hand corner of *Modelling Window*. |
| Ctrl+End | Move to bottom right-hand corner of *Modelling Window*. |
| Click | Select an item. |
| Ctrl+Click | Select multiple items. |
| Ctrl+A | Select all items. |
| Drag Object | Move the object to the nearest grid settings. |
| Ctrl+Drag Object | Create an occurrence copy. |
| Alt+Drag Object | Move the object to the nearest grid settings, overriding grid settings. |
| Alt+Drag Side | Change size of selected side of object, overriding grid settings. |
| Ctrl+Drag Side | Change size of both opposite sides of an object to nearest grid setting. |
| Ctrl+Alt+Drag Side | Change size of both opposite sides of an object, overriding grid settings. |
| – | Reduce the zoom factor by 10%. |
| + | Increase the zoom factor by 10%. |
| Esc | Remove selection. |
| Ctrl+C | Copy. |
| Ctrl+D | Create occurrence copy. |
| Ctrl+Shift+D | Create definition copy. |
| Ctrl+F | Display the *Find Dialog Box*. |
| Ctrl+P | Print. |

| Ctrl+S | Save. |
|--------|-------|
| Ctrl+V | Paste. |
| Ctrl+X | Cut. |
| Ctrl+Y | Undo last command. |
| Ctrl+Z | Redo last command. |
| Alt+Enter | Opens the *Properties Dialog Box* for the current model or for the selected objects. |

# Attributes Table Navigation and Selection Keys

| Key | Operation |
| --- | --- |
| Cursor up | Move up one cell. |
| Cursor down | Move down one cell. |
| Cursor left | Move left one cell or character. |
| Cursor right | Move right one cell or character. |
| Enter | Move down to cell in next row. |
| Home | Move to left-hand cell or start of cell. |
| End | Move to right-hand cell or end of cell. |
| PgUp | Move to the top cell. |
| PgDn | Move to the bottom cell. |
| Ctrl+Home | Move to top cell. |
| Ctrl+End | Move to bottom cell. |
| Click | Select cell. |
| Shift+Click | Select contiguous block of cells. |
| Shift+Cursor | Select contiguous block of cells. |
| Ctrl+Click | Select multiple items. |
| Esc | Closes *Attributes Window*. |
| F2 | Opens selected cell and place cursor at the end of the entry. |
| Double-Click | Opens selected cell and places cursor at mouse pointer position. |
| Alt+Cursor down | Open the drop-down list in a cell. |
| Shift+Return | Enter hard line-break. |
| Ctrl+C | Copy. |
| Ctrl+V | Paste. |
| Ctrl+X | Cut. |

# Glossary

| | |
|---|---|
| **ARIS** | Architecture of Integrated Information Systems. |
| **ARIS Method** | The implementation of the ARIS concept in the ARIS Platform by use of a special product like *ARIS Business Designer* or *ARIS Business Architect*. |
| **ARIS Platform** | The range of ARIS products including *ARIS Business Architect*, *ARIS Business Designer*, *ARIS Toolset*, etc. |
| **'as-is'** | The current processes operated by an organisation. |
| **Attribute** | ARIS modelling information stored for models, objects, relationships and databases. |
| **BPEL** | Business Process Execution Language. |
| **BPM** | Business Process Modelling. |
| **BPR** | Business Process Re-engineering. |
| **BSC** | Balanced Scorecard. |
| **Business Model** | The collection of all ARIS models and databases that represent the entirety of the business. |
| **Business Process** | The definition of the tasks, and the sequence of those tasks, necessary to deliver a business objective. |
| **Business Process Architecture** | A hierarchical structure of process description levels covering the whole organisation from a business process point of view. |
| **Business Process Management** | A systematic approach to managing and improving an organisation's business by the active, coordinated management of all aspects of the specification, design, implementation, operation, measurement, analysis and optimisation of business processes in order to effectively and efficiently deliver business objectives. |
| **Connection** | On an ARIS model diagram, the line connecting two objects denoting an ARIS relationship. |
| **CRM** | Customer-Relationship Management. |
| **Database** | A collection of related ARIS models representing a significant business area. |
| **Diagram** | The visual representation of an ARIS model. |
| **EAI** | Enterprise Application Integration. |
| **EPC** | Event-Driven Process Chain. |
| **ERP** | Enterprise Resource Planning. |

| | |
|---|---|
| **eTOM** | Extended Telecommunications Operations Model |
| **FAD** | Function Allocation Diagram. |
| **GUI** | Graphical User Interface. |
| **GUID** | ARIS Global Unique Identifier. |
| **HOBE** | ARIS House of Business Engineering. |
| **ICT** | Information Communication Technology. |
| **IT** | Information Technology. |
| **ITIL** | IT Infrastructure Library. |
| **Item** | A thing that can be manipulated in the group structure in the *ARIS Explorer Module* or *ARIS Designer Module*. |
| **KPI** | Key Performance Indicator. |
| **LAN** | Local Area Network. |
| **Method Filter** | A filter applied to ARIS databases that limits the range of models, objects, relationships and attributes that can be used and displayed. |
| **MDA** | Model-Driven Architecture. |
| **Model** | An ARIS diagram of a particular type (e.g. data model) visually representing the objects and relationships stored in the underlying ARIS repository. |
| **Object** | An ARIS representation of a real-world entity (e.g. task, organisation, system, data item). |
| **Occurrence** | The graphical representation in a model of an object definition. |
| **PC** | Personal Computer. |
| **Properties** | The totality of all information known about ARIS models, objects, relationships and databases. |
| **Relationship** | An ARIS representation of the interaction between real-world entities represented by ARIS objects. |
| **Server** | A file storage system on a PC or networked file server holding a set of ARIS databases. |
| **SCM** | Supply-Chain Management. |
| **SCOR** | Supply-Chain Operations Reference model |
| **SOA** | Service-Oriented Architecture. |
| **Structurally Relevant** | Objects that describe the flow and logic of a process model (e.g. events, functions and rules). |
| **Symbol** | Used to denote the occurrence of an ARIS object on a model diagram. |

| | |
|---|---|
| **Template** | Allows the graphic appearance of models and objects to be pre-defined and applied to many objects and models in one operation. |
| **'to-be'** | The future, target, processes to be operated by an organisation. |
| **TQM** | Total Quality Management. |
| **UML** | Unified Modelling Language. |
| **URL** | WWW Universal Resource Locator. |
| **VACD** | Value Added Chain Diagram. |
| **WAN** | Wide Area Network. |
| **WWW** | The World Wide Web (or Web). |

# Subject Index

Page numbers in **bold** refer to more significant discussions of topics with multiple references.
Page numbers in *italics* refer to figures illustrating the topic.
Entries starting with a lower case letter refer to ARIS relationships (e.g. "activates")

Lightning Source UK Ltd.
Milton Keynes UK
03 April 2010

152279UK00001B/27/P